HOW TO GET
THE BEST HOME LOAN

HOW TO GET
THE BEST HOME LOAN

W. Frazier Bell

John Wiley & Sons, Inc.

New York • Chichester • Brisbane • Toronto • Singapore

Library of Congress Cataloging-in-Publication Data

Bell, W. Frazier, 1950–
    How to get the best home loan / by W. Frazier Bell
       p.   cm.
    Includes bibliographical references and index.
    ISBN 0–471–55850–8 (cloth). – ISBN 0–471–55851–6 (paper)
    1. Mortgage loans. I. Title.
  HG2040.15.B45   1992
332.7$'$22–dc20   91–46576

Printed in the United States of America
10 9 8 7 6 5 4 3

This book is dedicated to my wife, Harriet, who has suffered through my many years in the real estate industry.

ABOUT THE AUTHOR

Mr. Bell has been involved in many facets of the real estate industry since 1973. A graduate of the University of Virginia, he has been a builder and a Real Estate Broker, and is currently a mortgage banker in Charlottesville, Virginia. He is a Direct Endorsement Underwriter for FHA loans, past president of the local mortgage bankers association, and teaches Real Estate Finance at Piedmont Virginia Community College. When he is not chasing mortgages, he is chasing trout in the nearby Blue Ridge Mountains.

CONTENTS

A FABLE

Once there was a man who lived in a cave. It was a nice cave—not the best, but it suited his needs. One day another man came along who decided he wanted this cave. In the normal manner of business at that time, he demonstrated this desire by beating the owner over the head with a club. Now, the owner liked his cave, but he knew he could find another one that he liked just as well without much trouble. So, it only took one bashing over the head to convince him to give the cave to the man with the club.

Without undue hardship he soon located another, better cave. It had added amenities such as a spring (indoor plumbing), a deep pit (trash compactor), and a beautiful view of the valley. Settling in, this man and his family enjoyed their new and improved environment for several years, as the neighborhood grew and new people moved into the area. One day a newcomer to the area saw the appeal of this particular abode and expressed an interest in perhaps trading something of value for it. The owner was perfectly content and resisted the advances of this potential homebuyer. After being bashed over the head five or six times, he decided that maybe the cave really was not worth that much, and he moved again.

Being a little more shrewd than most of his neighbors, he decided that if he wanted to keep a home long enough to appreciate its true value, he would have to find something other than the standard cave. So, he cut down some trees and built a crude but secure hut. The nice thing about this particular structure was that he could build it where he wanted to live and not be limited to living only where he could find a cave. He could also have all of the necessities of life close by. He found a nice spot on the bank of a stream where he could get water and bathe, gather firewood and game from the forest, and still have a beautiful view.

Other families saw the advantage to having a hut by the water, and the neighborhood began to sprout huts of various designs and sizes. Because he could see that additional features would make his home more comfortable, our homeowner added a wing for the children and another hut in which to house the assorted animals they kept.

Since there was plenty of room, and everyone could build exactly what they wanted, there was little need to bargain for someone else's hut. Our family grew. The father died, and the oldest son took possession of the hut. As each generation grew up and passed the property along, improvements and modifications were made to make the property more comfortable. A fireplace was built, boards were laid over the dirt floor, and cracks in the walls were chinked. More rooms and fireplaces were added. Unfortunately, these fireplaces tended to burn almost as readily as the firewood. Our little hut by the stream was reduced to ashes on numerous occasions, only to be rebuilt each time a little bit bigger and stronger, and with a functional utility to meet the ambiance of the times.

As the times changed, so did people's tastes. And, as will happen, our house had just burned down again. The couple had been eying one of the homes built in the new, two-story brick style, and they lost no time in having plans drafted and put into shape. Soon, there arose from the ashes a splendid example of good taste in architecture. Everything was of the latest design, including brick fireplaces to minimize the chance that this would only be a temporary shelter.

As time passed, more and more people built by the water, leaving fewer desirable locations. Because good sites were harder to find, they became more valuable. About this time our family found itself in a precarious financial situation, brought about by the eldest son's penchant for cockfighting (his bird soon became Sunday dinner). Having the premier location in the area and one of the most admired homes, our family soon had an offer—in those days considered quite generous—from people of more prosperous means who were looking to buy a home reflecting their higher station in life. Deciding that they really did not need such a grand home, and that they would be able to clear all debts and still have enough remaining to purchase a smaller, but comfortable home, our family sold the house for $2,000 plus five barrels of the finest tobacco. With this they would eventually establish a trading company and in later years have a home more opulent than the original. However, our story concerns the recently sold manor.

Our new owners took great pride in their new home and improved upon it at every opportunity. Surrounding land was bought, so that the property became one of the larger, more profitable estates in the region. This property was handed down from generation to generation; occasionally a few acres here and there were given to one of the children for them to build their own smaller, but compatible home near the great house.

During the early part of the twentieth century there came a time when the current heirs to the estate did not produce any children. In their later years they decided to sell the family home and retire on the resulting fortune of $70,000. The local bank gave the purchasers a loan of $20,000 at 3% to be paid off in 10 years. The new owners enjoyed the property until the stock market crash of 1929 forced them to sell the property for $30,000.

The new owners paid cash. They were shrewd, evinced by their ability to survive and flourish during the Depression. They acquired new properties until the estate contained well over 4,000 acres of prime land stretching all the way to the edge of the local town. By the 1950s, however, the good genes running in this family had begun to play out. Portions of the farm were sold to pay debts and maintain the style of living to which they had become accustomed. Other parcels were subdivided; and small, tasteless, ranch style homes were built, row upon row. These homes were bought by members of the new rising middle class for prices ranging from $10,000 to $12,000, depending on whether you wanted a carport and wall-to-wall carpet. The purchasers would put 10% or more down and finance the balance at 5% for 15 or 20 years. Their annual incomes were about $4,000 to $6,000.

The manor home was soon surrounded by large numbers of houses of every design known at that time. Paved roads, curbs, and storm sewers replaced the old country road that had run through the farm. By this time, the original property consisted of the manor home and various parcels of land scattered throughout the growing urban sprawl. The upkeep of the main house had become increasingly expensive, and it was showing a great deal of deferred maintenance. In the early 1960s the owner decided to sell it to a prosperous young doctor with a growing family. The house and three acres sold for the princely sum of $27,000. The physician added another $4,000 in renovations. The bank was happy to lend money to someone that it knew would be making large sums of money within the next few years. The doctor put down 10% and financed the remainder at 6% for 30 years.

The doctor's family grew up in the home, went to college, and then moved on to new areas and greater challenges. The parents found themselves living in a house with 12-foot ceilings, five bedrooms, a study, a family room, living room, dining room, large eat-in kitchen, three and a half bathrooms, a two-car garage, and a large dependency building. They sold the house and its three acres in 1980 for $200,000 and moved into a townhouse that they bought for $70,000, paying cash and taking the one-time exemption from the capital gains tax. The purchaser of the manor house borrowed $120,000 and financed it at 9% for thirty years. The purchaser's income was about $44,000 per year.

The scattered parcels of land retained by the previous owners were slowly developed over the years. In the mid-1960s one 25-acre parcel was developed into twenty-one lots that sold for $3,000 apiece. By 1980 these lots were worth $18,000 each, and new lots in the more prestigious area were selling for $50,000 each. By 1989 the $18,000 lots were worth from $35,000 to $50,000, the $50,000 lots were selling for $135,000 to $175,000, and the $70,000 townhouse was worth $130,000. New homes with three bedrooms, two bathrooms, a living-dining room (known as a "great room" to increase sales appeal), and an eat-in kitchen crammed into 1,200 finished square feet on an unfinished basement were selling for $100,000 to $200,000, depending on location.

To finance these homes, purchasers put down from 5% to 50% and borrowed the remainder from numerous different lending sources, with mortgages that were at a fixed interest rate for fifteen to thirty years, five- to ten-year balloon loans, at adjustable rates, or even loans that charged you more interest than you were paying (known by the innocuous name of "negative amortization"). Between 1980 and 1989, interest rates ranged from 8.5% to 17%. Purchasers' incomes ranged from $28,000 to $65,000, depending on the price and the interest rate.

Our original manor home, now on three acres, was worth $550,000. If you put down 20%, financed the remaining $440,000 at 10.5% for thirty years, you would need to earn about $15,000 to $16,000 per **month** to qualify for the loan. Some people have begun to live in caves again.

INTRODUCTION

Millions of people will buy or refinance a home each year. Buying the home, for the majority of people, is not an unpleasant task. It can, in fact, be fun. Asking a person you probably do not know, who works for a big company, to lend you a large sum of money, and then waiting while the company pokes around in your personal finances, is not much fun—especially when you are asked seemingly meaningless and sometimes humiliating questions, without the foggiest idea of what is going on.

I can tell you that the company is checking more than just your finances, and that the whole exercise is likely to cost you a good bit more than it would if you knew a few simple facts. To make matters worse, many loan officers are not as knowledgeable or experienced as they want you to believe, and chances are good that you will have to deal with one of these rookies. In any case, there are seemingly constant changes in the mortgage-lending industry's guidelines. Because of all these factors, obtaining a mortgage can be a very unsatisfactory and expensive experience.

In the case of mortgage lending I completely agree with the popular "Question Authority" bumper sticker. It is all too easy for the lender to intimidate the borrower because the lender has the power of knowledge. The borrower often meekly follows along, even while wondering, "Why is that? I don't understand. Boy, I sure hope that when I get through all this, they approve my loan." This book will change that. By knowing what the lender is doing, and why, you will find the process made immeasurably smoother. This knowledge can, in many cases, also save you hundreds or even thousands of dollars.

The borrower should keep in mind that nothing stays the same. Or, as the saying goes, "the only constant is change." And change has come exponentially to the mortgage lending industry since the late 1970s. When I was a Realtor, my job changed to the point where it entailed more information management than sales; getting the borrower through the loan process to closing began to take more and more of my skill and time. The once short, simple application became a nightmare of paperwork. Now, as a lender, I have found myself caught between the anxiety of the borrowers, and Realtors, and the demands of the underwriters who approve the loans. Much of this anxiety is caused by a lack of knowledge on the part of the borrowers and Realtors.

As a result, I began to find myself spending twice as much time taking the loan applications in order to explain each part of the process as I asked the required questions and had the borrowers sign all the required forms. Then I spent more time educating the Realtors so that they could become more professional and knowledgeable sources of information for both buyer and seller. In this book, I have combined all that I have taught, and been asked, along with a great deal more. The book will therefore be of use to both borrowers and Realtors.

By reading this book before applying for a loan, or even during the process, you will gain the knowledge necessary to get the right loan, at the right price, from the right lender. You will head off many potential problems and expensive mistakes. The book is organized such that each section is built on the previous one. It is important that you read it from the beginning to have a clear understanding of why lenders do the things they do, and why certain loans may be better for you in your particular situation than others. In some sections you will probably have the urge to skip ahead to the parts you think contain all you really need to know. If you do that, however, you will miss valuable information that could clarify whatever it is that you are trying to learn. Many things in mortgage lending do not stand alone, but arise from other things. At some point, a light bulb may metaphorically appear, accompanied by a statement like, "Hey! That's why they made me do that!" I hope the discovery will be a pleasant one. That is not always the case.

There are several rules that one would be wise to consider when dealing with a lender. The first one is that famous Golden Rule of Lending: "He who has the gold, makes the rules." Usually, the one with the gold will be the lender. But it is possible for the borrower, or the Realtor if one is involved, to hold enough power to help move or change things when the process gets slow or unreasonable. Just remember that the lender wants to make the loan. It has a product it wants to sell, and if it doesn't sell that product, it will go out of business. Mortgage lending is also a service industry, so the lender is dependent on the reputation and goodwill that it creates for itself to continue receiving business. If a lender does not provide professional and courteous service, the competition will take its market share very quickly.

The next rule is to "assume nothing." Do not assume that you know the lender is doing something wrong, or that you are doing everything correctly. Ask questions. Check on the progress of the loan. See if there is anything that you, borrower or Realtor, can do to help speed the process. A good lender will often tell you without being asked if something can be done in that regard. But as I have already noted, don't count on getting a good one.

The last, and by far the most important, rule is to know your lender. Before making final loan application and paying any money, take the time to find out about the company with which you will be dealing. Is it established and well known? Is it financially sound? What is its reputation in the community? Do not base your decision solely on the recommendation of a friend, or on the single fact that the lender has the lowest interest rates. The saying that "you get what you pay for" sometimes applies to mortgage borrowing.

Because buying a home is such a large investment and creates such a large debt, you would think that all buyers would take the necessary time to study the subject—especially when they will be spending thousands of dollars, in application and closing costs, just to get the loan. Because they don't always take the time, they often pay too much for what they get in return.

This book is dedicated to the idea that anyone who is buying or refinancing residential real estate should know the process for obtaining mortgage financing, and why it works the way it does. The book is not intended to make you an authority on all aspects of real estate finance; what it will do is clear up many of the unknown aspects that keep borrowers from being able to make intelligent, money-saving decisions.

You can avoid the problems and costs that ignorance creates. Let other people tell you about the problems they had to overcome when they applied for a loan; you can tell them how you avoided those problems, and saved a large amount of money by doing so.

1

MY FATHER SAID HE NEVER HAD TO GO THROUGH THIS!

My father said . . . ; my neighbor said . . . ; my Realtor said . . . ; my attorney said . . . . Most people think they know something about real estate financing. And they are not shy about telling you their experiences, every one of which will probably be different. And all of their stories may be true. Each person's slightly different situation can alter the type of loan the lender recommends and how it is processed. Most loans, however, are approved or denied, based on some very fundamental rules. Over the years, these rules have become the standards by which the industry functions, but they have not always been in effect. That is why your father, and anyone else who hasn't received a loan since the late 1970s, can't tell you what it's like today.

A good example is my first loan, which I got in the early 1970s. There were basically two lenders in town: a mortgage subsidiary of a bank and a savings and loan (S&L). The S&L was run by an old man who knew just about everyone. I walked into his office one day and said, "I'm buying a house, and I need a loan." He said, "Just let me know about two weeks before you need to close. Who is going to be your attorney?" He wouldn't give you the loan if he didn't like your attorney. That was the entire application and approval. He did not even ask me how much I needed to buy the house. That may be a little easier than even what your father had to do for his loan, but it illustrates the fact that lenders of that time really did make loans the old-fashioned way: They used their own money, or **portfolioed** the loan. Remember the term *portfolioed;* we will talk about it later.

Several years after I bought that house, I did what every normal American does: I bought a larger house and went deeper into debt. This time I went to the mortgage banker, the one that was a subsidiary of a bank that made mortgage loans. He also knew me. Unfortunately, he felt it was necessary to get a little information and keep me waiting for several weeks before I got loan approval. He made references to "verifying" my application. Didn't he trust me? No, he thought that I was just fine. It was Fannie Mae who didn't know me from Adam. This made it sound as if we were dealing with someone from James Dickey's *Deliverance*. Fannie Mae might be fat, ugly, mean. Wore one of those sack dresses with small flower prints all over it. Looked at you with a kind of sour squint. Now, why would someone like that be looking at my loan?

As most people today are painfully aware, Fannie is not some mountain blossom, but an acronym for the **Federal National Mortgage Association, or FNMA**. Being a child of the federal government, Fannie Mae herself gave birth to some more mountain folk, **Freddie Mac** and **Ginnie Mae,** known to the more refined as the **Federal Home Loan Mortgage Corp. (FHLMC)** and the **Government National Mortgage Association (GNMA).** Fannie and kin are the ultimate authorities of mortgage lending. In most instances, you do what they say.

If you give these stories a little thought, it may seem logical to go to the S&L. For a long time, most people did exactly that. Actually, to an extent, the same is true today. But things have changed drastically since the late 1970s. How did things change so much? Let's take a look.

WHY DO THEY DO THE THINGS THEY DO?

Once upon a time in the old days (until the late 1970s), savings and loans, or thrifts, were the predominant lenders of mortgage loans. Their charters actually require that the majority of their loans be home mortgages. That is why S&Ls came into existence. The most important thing to know about thrifts is the source of their money. They got it from savers. I am sure that at some time or another you have had a passbook savings account, one in which you put $10 or $20 a month at 5% interest. That was, of course, back when inflation was 2%–3% a year. The thrifts would lend that money out at 7% or 8%, thus making a profit. Obviously, people were constantly putting in and taking out their money, which you might think would wreak havoc when that money was supposed to be tied up in a 30-year fixed rate loan. We know that this didn't happen, so how exactly did they make those loans when the money was coming and going? They borrowed it from the government. Actually, they would normally have sufficient assets on a day-to-day basis to cover most of their loans, but when they were a little shy of cash, they would go to the Federal Home Loan Bank and borrow short-term. The rates would be low enough that those 7% and 8% loans were still moneymakers. The more deposits they took in, and the more income they earned, the more loans they could make. It was a very neat arrangement that provided money for homes and a profit for the thrift.

Are you ready for a quick lesson in math? If Johnny borrows money and pays 12%, and then lends that money out at 8%, how much money will Johnny make on the deal? (Anyone who doesn't think that Johnny is coming out on the short end, please give me a call. I would like to ask you for a loan.) In the mid-1970s what happened to Johnny is exactly what happened to the thrifts.

Inflation and interest rates went into double digits, which meant that the cost of money for everyone, from lenders to home-buyers to the federal government, became very high. The big problem for the thrifts was that they had already lent money out at low long-term rates on the assumption that they would always be able to obtain money cheaply enough to cover those loans, plus overhead and profit. But when you have to pay 12% to cover loans that are already on your books at 8%, you have a substantial deficit on millions of dollars of loans, which is not healthy for the bottom line. To add to the thrifts' problems, people were taking their money out of their savings accounts at the thrifts and putting it into high-yield investments. This phenomenon is called *disintermediation:* the movement of funds from one place to another that is caused by a wide disparity in interest rates.

All of a sudden, those friendly folks down at the local savings and loan were not only losing money, but also rapidly running out of money to lend. During this period, when I was a Realtor, I sold some houses and took my clients to the S&L to make their loan applications. To our surprise, it was not making loans. It was taking deposits, but no loan applications.

This was the same thrift where I had received my one minute loan application years before. We went to a local bank and got a short-term note that would be paid in full when the purchase could be refinanced, that is, when the thrift again had money to lend.

Where did that situation leave us? It left us with houses to sell, people who wanted to buy them, high interest rates, and, most importantly, very little money available to make the loans on those houses. How did we fix this mess? By using Fannie Mae, Freddie Mac, and all the other investors in the secondary market.

2

THE SECONDARY MARKET

The secondary market consists of Fannie Mae (Federal National Mortgage Association—FNMA), Freddie Mac (Federal Home Loan Mortgage Corporation—FHLMC), Ginnie Mae (Government National Mortgage Association—GNMA), and a wide assortment of other investors. I'm not going to bore you with the history of these folks. What is important is why they were created and what that means to the borrower, the poor slob they try to torture in various ingenious and subtle ways. To understand how real estate financing works, you the borrower must understand how all the little things in the secondary market affect your ability to get a mortgage. Looking at the specifics of getting a loan will make things much clearer.

As the name suggests, the secondary market is the second market for mortgage loans. The **primary market** is the lender itself, to which the borrower applies for the loan. After the loan is approved and closed, the lender, or **originator** of the loan in the primary market, will in most cases sell that loan to an entity, or **investor,** in the secondary market. If the originator does not sell the loan, it is portfolioed, or put on the shelf, as it is known in the trade. We will discuss portfolio lenders in detail later. Right now the question is, "Why do they sell the loan, and how does that affect me as the borrower?" The answers are, of course, money. The sale will not affect the borrower, except minimally, once the loan is closed. Notice that I said "minimally" and specified "once the loan is closed."

First, let's discuss the mechanics of the secondary market in general terms. As we have already noted, Fannie Mae, Freddie

Mac, and Ginnie Mae are members of this shadowy group. There are many other members, or investors, in the secondary market. Insurance companies invest large amounts of their premium income in mortgages. Pension funds, banks, and thrifts also buy loans. Banks buy loans directly, or they have a mortgage subsidiary to purchase loans from other lenders.

When lenders buy loans from other lenders, they do it through what is called the *wholesale division* of that purchasing lender. Actually, hundreds of lenders have very large and aggressive wholesale divisions looking to buy mortgage loans originated by other lenders. That is why many loans made by a lender today will end up with another lender after they close. Why would lenders want to make a loan and then get rid of it? Don't they want to make money? Isn't that why they charge those usurious interest rates? The answers are, to make money, yes, and yes. If you don't understand, you are not alone. But to understand why, you first have to know what drives the secondary market, or what makes it profitable.

As we all know, lenders originate loans to make money. Now, if we set aside any consideration of interest income, exactly how do lenders make money? Let us look at a loan from the initial application all the way through to its final sale to the secondary market to see where all the money goes.

FEES, POINTS, AND OTHER GARBAGE

When the application is submitted, the lender will typically collect money for appraisal and credit report fees because the lender will be billed for them whether or not the borrower closes on the loan. These fees will vary from area to area and lender to lender, depending on many things, such as size and location of the property, the borrower's employment (self-employed, commission income, and so on), what the various appraisers and credit bureaus charge, and whether the lender tries to add a little something to those fees for itself. The amounts added to the appraisal and credit fees will create some fee income for the lender beyond the normal charges. Some lenders will also try to collect "Processing Fees," "Application Fees," or "Rate Lock-In Fees." These are part of what are called **Garbage** or **Junk Fees.** Garbage fees are in addition to the normal points and costs of closing the loan. In some states the lender cannot collect more than the actual cost of the appraisal and credit report fees, but they can collect an application fee. So, the lender will collect an application fee that just happens to pay for the appraisal and credit report in addition to the additional fee income, often nonrefundable. We will get into this in more detail later.

Points are the fees that really get your attention. They are part of the standard cost of closing a loan, and normally there are two different types of points, the **origination fee** and the **discount points.** These are expressed as a percentage of the loan amount, that is, one point is 1% of the loan, two points is 2% of the loan, and so forth. **Points can be quoted in one-eighth of one percent (0.125%) increments**. So you can be given lender quotes like 2.375 points or 1.875 points—sort of like a blue-light special for $19.95.

The origination fee goes to the lender for originating the loan. Usually 1% of the loan amount, it is most often collected at time of closing. Sometimes the lender will collect it at application, refundable only if it cannot do the loan. Refinances are often handled in this manner; the borrower is not under the same sense of urgency, and is much more likely to jerk the loan than a purchaser. One of the great fears for originating lenders is that borrowers will pull their loan applications after the lender has put in time and effort, leaving the lender nothing to show for it. Another more common time for the lender to collect the origination fee is at the time the loan commitment is issued. Once the lender has done its work and has approved the loan, the borrower must start paying the piper in order to get it. Some lenders will even try to collect the fee before the loan is submitted for approval, although this timing is not nearly so common, and it is certainly not so acceptable to most borrowers. So, the origination fee is one of the primary income fees that the lender will collect, and it is normally 1% of the loan amount.

The other big fee is known as **the discount point(s)**. When a lender is asked for its interest rates, the quotation will include the rate and points, such as 10%, 1 + 2. The *one* is the origination fee, and the discount will usually be the bigger number, in this example *two*. Some lenders will quote the discount rate first, that is, 2 + 1; and others will just combine them, as in 3 points. When you are quoted points as one amount, make sure you ask the lender if that includes both the origination and discount points. You may think you have found the best deal, only to discover that you were only quoted the discount.

The important thing to remember about discount points is that **the lower you want your interest rate, the higher the discount points will be.** In other words, the discount points buy down the interest rate, as interest up-front. Or, they *discount* the interest rate. For example, say that 10.25% is 1 discount point, or 1% of the loan amount; then 10% might be 2 discount points, or 2%; 9.75%, 3 points; and so on. The number of discount points for a particular rate can differ significantly from lender to lender. This number is an important thing to look for if you are shopping for rates. People joke about getting a 3% interest rate. They can get it, but the discount points needed to buy that rate would support a small army.

Not that these points aren't expensive enough just to cover what is required to get the normal interest rate, but the lender can (and will) add onto them for its own profit. If the required discount points for 10% interest are 2, the lender might quote you 2.5 or 3. The extra is an **overage to the lender** that is taken as additional fee income, just like the garbage fees. If you don't fully understand discount points right now, don't worry. Just remember that they are a cost, and a potential source of fee income to the lender. You will get a short course on rate pricing later when we cover rates, points, and lock-ins.

So, the lender gets 1% to originate the loan and in all probability some type of overage on the discount, usually from 0.25% to 2% or more. On a $50,000 loan a 1% origination fee and a 0.25% overage on the discount equal $625. If the lender gets a 1% overage on the discount, then it gets $1,000. If one loan office averages 15 to 30 loan closings per month, that activity can bring in $10,000 to $30,000 in fee income. Even after expenses, we can be talking about a lot of money. And the average loan today is well over the $50,000 we used as an example. But we're not through yet.

Remember the *garbage* fees? Our friend the lender is still devising ways to add to income. Now, let me add that some of these garbage fees are legitimate and necessary. One of the more common fees is called the *tax service fee*. This one-time fee pays a specialized servicing company to ensure that the taxes and insurance on each loan are paid each year when they come due. Some lenders may charge for next-day delivery (e.g., Federal Express™) of documents in connection with the loan. This is often a small price to pay for expediting your loan. However, no one has ever accused mortgage lenders of not being profit-oriented. Some of these fees can strain the imagination.

The lender is offering a service for which it collects a fee of at least 1%, and usually more. Then, after you have applied for this loan, or service, the lender begins to hit you with things like application, processing, underwriting, commitment, document preparation, and closing fees. Any or all of these fees can range from $50 to $500. Added to the origination fees of those 15 to 30 loans per month, you can see that the temptation is often too great for the lender to resist. Wouldn't it be simpler just to add them into the discount points? Yes, and some do. But, look at it from a marketing perspective: Doesn't 10% with 1% discount sound like a much better deal than 1.5% or 2% discount points? It's easier for the lender to set the hook and then reel you in slowly. Always ask about the lender's fees, why they are charged and if they are nonrefundable; and compare them with other lenders' fees before making final loan application, and paying any money.

In the real estate market in which I worked was a lender that used to take a loan application, process it completely, and then—when it was ready to be submitted to the underwriter— call the buyers and tell them that they would have to pay the 1% origination fee before submission as a commitment fee. Nonrefundable. Even if the loan was denied. As if this weren't bad enough, the lender made a practice of never disclosing this requirement to the borrower at application. How many people would complete the application if they knew it would cost them 1% just to find out if they can get the loan? The lender was using an unethical method (not disclosing the collection of the fee at time of application) to collect a normal fee. To understand the lender's perspective on this maneuver, let's look at their rationale.

The Cost of Doing Business

The borrower makes application and pays for the appraisal and credit report (for which the lender will be billed). Then the lender begins to process the loan. A file is set up, all of the verifications are mailed out, telephone calls are made, documents are received and checked for accuracy, all disclosure requirements must be checked, and, when all the necessary information is received, the loan is sent to the underwriter for approval or rejection. All of this work requires a large number of hours from personnel who expect to be paid as well as the expense of forms, office space, mail, and telephone—not to mention the cost of underwriters and the central office. If the borrower decides not to buy the house, or for whatever reason does not close the loan, what has the lender got to show for it? Probably no more than the cash to pay the appraisal and credit report bills. If the lender added some additional fee income into the costs, their loss would be less.

Even if the patient dies, the doctor gets paid. Why not the lender? I am not suggesting that anyone should have to die in the transaction, although that thought has certainly crossed the minds of many disgruntled participants. The reason very few lenders collect fees before closing is that most loans will close, and the lender will collect its fee, and more. Thus, the real reason is that competition won't allow it. Our local lender who tried to collect the origination fee at submission without prior disclosure came under intense criticism. Realtors stopped sending business to this lender, who had to stop collecting its commitment fee because none of the other lenders in the area did. It's whatever the market will bear.

If a lender has an extremely low rate, or a special loan that everyone wants, then it may be able to add a premium to the cost. Back when 30-year fixed rates were 13%, the mortgage company where I worked had an adjustable rate mortgage that started at 9.75% with 1 + 2.75 points. People were eager to get it. A rate of 3.75% in points didn't slow them down one bit. Today that may be different.

For an average loan amount of $70,000 with a 1% origination fee, a 1.5% discount (with 0.5% being an overage to the lender), and $150 in garbage fees, what is the gross income per month to a lender that closes 20 loans? That would be an average of $1,400,000 in loans per month. That value times 1.5% in fee income (1% + 0.5%), not counting the minimum required discount, equals $21,000, plus $3,000 in garbage fees equals $24,000. Take a mortgage lender with five offices and you can see why there is competition for loans.

Selling And Servicing Your Loan   It's Not That We Don't Like You, But ...

Why do lenders sell loans and how do they make money from them? So far, we have seen that the fee income by time of closing can be significant. After that, the lender is stuck with a thick folder of papers, a note that says the borrower owes it money, and a mortgage that says the property secures that debt. The lender also has its money tied up in a loan that may or may not earn it money, depending on whether the interest rate charged is torpedoed by rising rates over a sustained period of time. Remember what happened to the thrifts that got caught with a portfolio of low-interest loans in a rising market in the early 1980s? So do the lenders of today. Consequently, these lenders have adopted a method not only to solve their immediate problem, but also to make still more money off of the loan. As a result, borrowers are subjected to a big business approach to mortgage lending.

The lender to whom you make your payments is said to **service the loan.** That is, it takes care of the day-to-day, month-to-month, year-to-year management of the loan. Collecting the payments, crediting the interest and principal, making sure the taxes and insurance are paid, monitoring delinquent accounts, adjusting payments and sending new payment notices on adjustable rate loans and changes in escrow payments, and passing on the principal and interest payments after deducting their servicing fee—all of these are what lenders dream of in their sleep. The questions arise: Where are the principal and interest passed, and What servicing fee? This is where the lender and the secondary market come together.

When a lender quotes an interest rate of, let's say, 10%, that rate is a gross interest rate that includes a **servicing fee** built into it. The actual interest rate yield required by the investors in the secondary market will be less. For example, the required rate may be 9.75% and the lender adds in 0.25% for a **servicing fee.** This fee pays the servicing lender for all the things I just noted. Based on 0.25% of the principal balance and collected out of each month's payment, it doesn't seem to be a lot of money. And by itself it isn't. But remember all of those other loans that the lender is closing, and you can see that after a while the servicing income can become substantial. It is also reliable, as long as borrowers don't pay off their loans too quickly. As a matter of fact, lenders recognize that most 30-year loans will be paid off early, and they adjust for that possibility. Most 30-year rates are set on the premise that loans will be paid off in an average of 12 years, while 15-year loans are assumed to be prepaid in 8 years.

Servicing fees are not all the same. They range from as little as 0.25% to 0.625%, and in some instances even higher.

Obviously, the higher the fee added to the secondary market's required yield, the higher the final interest rate charged to the borrower, and that rate may not be competitive in the market. But the market does not normally set what the fee will be; it is often set by the secondary market investors. They are the ones who buy the loans. What the originating lender can do is add on to the minimum required servicing fee set by the investor, to create a little more income for the lender—and a little more interest for the borrower. The lender must weigh the additional fee against the competition it faces in the marketplace.

The lender that has completed and closed the loan has a big hole in its pocketbook. Several $100,000 loans can use up your cash very quickly. Not only that, but also the money tied up in the loan cannot be used again until the loan is paid off. As I noted, the average loan will last from 8 to 12 years. The lender must keep generating sufficient cash, or it will be out of the loan-making business. It has closed the loan and taken all the fee income that can be squeezed out, so the lender gets rid of it. The loan is sold to someone else, the Secondary Market.

Although the originating lender sells the loan, the borrower may continue to make payments to this lender. In this case, it has retained the right to service the loan for the purchasing investor, and to receive the servicing fee income. Often the originating lender will sell not only the loan, but also the servicing. That is, the borrower will make payments to the purchasing investor, and that investor will get the servicing income. The originator will receive a premium price for this **servicing released loan,** which means more profit for the originator. This is why it is not unusual for a borrower to end up making payments to another lender. The originating lender then has that money free again to make more loans that can be sold.

Because of the confusion brought on by the sale of servicing, the federal government now requires that all loan applicants be given a disclosure called, appropriately enough, the *Mortgage Servicing Transfer Disclosure* (see the Appendix for a copy of this form).

The significance of the secondary market is that it creates a place where lenders can sell, and buy, mortgage loans on a regional, national, and even international basis. This market helps to move money from areas where there is excess cash to areas where there is little. It also helps to relieve lenders of the burden of carrying portfolios of loans with potentially volatile interest rates, frees up the lender's cash, and, most importantly, provides a vast and reliable source of money for mortgage loans. (Remember my purchasers who could not get a loan at the S&L because there was no money?) Another benefit, for the borrower, is that the more investors there are competing for the pool of loans, the more they will aggressively price their purchases, which can mean lower rates for the borrower. Conversely, if loans are flooding the market, the secondary market investors can be more selective and less aggressive. Supply and Demand. Let us consider how the secondary market affects the borrower's ability to qualify for the loan.

THE SECONDARY MARKET UNDERWRITING GUIDELINES
Give me your first-born male child and a pound of flesh

When a lender sells loans to an investor in the secondary market, those loans must meet certain minimum standards, or guidelines. If they don't, then the investor won't buy them. As a result, the lender is stuck with unsalable loans, which makes the lender very unhappy. To remedy this situation, the lender will process each loan according to the guidelines specified by the investor to which they will be selling the loan in the secondary market.

All secondary market guidelines are based, in one form or another, on those established by Fannie Mae and Freddie Mac, the Kingpins of the Secondary Market. (With Federal Housing Administration—FHA—and Veterans Administration—VA—loans there are some differences, but the underlying concepts are the same.) These guidelines evolve, based on the constantly changing mortgage industry. These changes, in themselves, can cause mortgage lenders to feel as though they were becoming mentally unglued. But, the basic tenets have remained essentially unchanged.

Fannie Mae and Freddie Mac each publish volumes of guidelines covering everything from qualifying to closing to selling the loans. These form the core of what are known as **conforming guidelines,** or those guidelines that conform to conventional Fannie Mae and Freddie Mac rules. Other investors in the secondary market will adapt one or both, or parts of both sets of guidelines. If the guidelines are outside of the standards set by Fannie and Freddie, then they are called **nonconforming** guidelines.

A good example of a conforming vs. nonconforming guideline is the permissible loan amount. Fannie and Freddie set the maximum loan amounts that they will buy; these are adjusted periodically based on increases, or decreases, in the cost of housing. If the maximum conforming loan that they will buy on a single-family property is $202,300 (as of December 31, 1991), any loan amount over that limit is considered nonconforming, and they will not buy it. (Remember, these amounts can change yearly. In 1990 the maximum conforming loan was $187,450; on January 1, 1991, that changed to $191,250.) This nonconforming, or "jumbo" loan, as it is called because it exceeds the conforming limits, will then be marketed to other investors who specialize in "jumbos." These investors' guidelines will often be similar to the standard secondary market guidelines with the exception of loan amount.

The foundation of all loan guidelines, and hence all loan decisions, are based on four areas of the loan that the lender must consider:

1. Cash
2. Credit
3. Income (read "income and employment")
4. Appraised value of the property

Meet the test of each, and you qualify. Flunk one, and you may be rejected. A loan application may be strong enough in one area to compensate for a deficiency in another. This possibility will vary by lender, depending on the rigidity of the guidelines of the investors to whom they sell their loans. Regardless of the individual lender's quirks, all criteria are based on the Fannie Mae–Freddie Mac guidelines. Let's look at these guidelines and how they relate to the borrower's ability to repay the loan.

Cash   Where Did It Come from, and Prove It's Yours

The borrower must have enough cash to buy the house and close the loan. I don't think anyone would argue with that logic. The lender wants to know several things about this cash. To get this information, the lender will send an industry-wide standard form called a **Verification of Deposit** or **VOD** (see Appendix) to the bank, credit union, stockbroker, and so on to be filled out by that depository and then returned to the lender. This VOD will tell the lender several things about the borrowers and their money:

1. The kinds of accounts you have—savings, checking ...
2. The account number
3. The current balance
4. The average balance over the past two months
5. The opening date of the account
6. Any outstanding loans that the borrower has with the bank

The first three are simple to understand; it's the last three that can get you into trouble without your even knowing it. For example, say that you have two accounts, checking and savings. In the checking account you have a current balance of $2,000 and an average balance for the past two months of $1,500. No problem. An increase of $500 is not abnormal. But, let's say that the savings account was opened 30 days ago and $2,000 is the average since the account was opened. Why is this a problem? Lenders take a very dim view of new money. They want to know where the money was before you put it into that account. If you don't tell them, and prove it's your money, they won't make you the loan. (Remember the Golden Rule of Lending?) Why?

First, these seemingly paranoid lenders want to make sure that you did not borrow the money to purchase the property, incurring a debt that you have not told them of. If you borrow money, it must be borrowed on a secured basis. That is, you can get it by borrowing against a car, stock, other real estate—but it cannot be borrowed in an unsecured manner such as a personal note. In addition, the debt you create will be counted against you in the qualifying process.

Second, they want to make sure that the money in the bank really is your money and does not belong to someone else. And you have to prove it in writing. One of the cardinal rules of the industry is, "If it's in writing, it's true. If it's not in writing, it does not exist." How do you prove that the money really is yours? It depends on where the money did come from. If you transferred it from another account, just give the lender a copy of the last statement from that account. If you sold some stock, get a copy of the statement of sale and proceeds. Sell a house? Get a copy of the closing statement (H.U.D. 1) to show the net proceeds to you. Borrow it? A copy of the note from the lender showing that it is secured. Had it hidden under your mattress for the past five years because you didn't want your spouse to find it and spend it? Don't laugh; this is more common than people might think.

I have had borrowers who actually did save their money in their mattress, and others who put it in tin cans that they buried in the backyard. They were all honest, hard-working people who just did not trust banks. Proving that the money is yours can be tough. One Realtor had the borrower make photocopies of the money. Never mind that making copies of U.S. currency is absolutely illegal, which, incidentally, is not acceptable to the lender. The best that you can do is open a bank account where the lender can verify the money, and hope that you do not get an underwriter who is having a bad day.

Lease-purchase is a way of taking possession of the property and then accumulating the cash necessary for the down payment. It has become more common, especially in areas where properties are not selling quickly. It works like this: The potential purchaser offers to lease the property from the seller for a given period of time. The leaseholder has the option to purchase the property at a previously agreed upon price at any time during the rental period. Part of the rent paid to the seller is to be considered as cash toward the down payment. Both the seller and the purchaser benefit. The seller gets rent to cover the mortgage, and the eventual sale of the property, instead of having to continue paying the mortgage while waiting for the house to sell. The purchaser, who does not have enough cash to receive a loan, gets to move into the house and set aside the down payment as part of the rent. This is a very good way for buyers and sellers to get together in a slow market, or when the buyer has little cash but is otherwise qualified. There is just one potential problem that you need to consider.

If part of the rent is to be used as cash to purchase the property, only that portion above the normal market rent can be used. Let us suppose that a monthly rent of $800 has been set. You would like $200 of that to go toward the purchase. If the market rent is $600, there is no problem. If the market rent is $700, then only $100 can be used. How do you find the market rent for the property? You can talk to agents who specialize in renting similar properties, or you can get an appraiser to tell you. The lender will use an appraiser to determine the fair market rent when you make loan application.

To ensure that the portion of the rent set aside for the purchase meets the guidelines, the lender will have the appraiser do a Comparable Rent Schedule, by comparing the rent of the subject property to the rent of other similar properties. Basically, you will have to pay that amount you want to use toward the purchase above what you would normally have paid as rent. So, in our example, if the market rent is $800, you would have to pay $1,000 in order to get $200 per month credited toward the purchase.

The Gift

What if your Uncle Joe gave you some money? This gift may or may not be a problem. First, we have to define the source of this gift. Relatives are the best, and usual, source. Close friends aren't bad if you can show a demonstrated long and close relationship. Realtors and sellers are a no-no (except for certain closing costs that the seller and/or Realtor can pay. We will get to that shortly). Anyone with a financial interest in the transaction is not acceptable as a source for any of the money required for the down payment and certain closing costs. Assuming that Uncle Joe really is your uncle, and he really did give you the money, what's next?

He will need to give the lender a **gift letter** (see Appendix) that states why he is giving you the money, how much he is giving you, and, most importantly, that no repayment is expected or implied. All the money may not be intended for the purchase. Part of it may be to pay off debts or to buy furniture. That's fine. He just needs to say that in the letter. And (Uncle Joe will love this) Fannie Mae and most investors will require that he show that he has **the resources to give you the gift.** A copy of his most recent bank statement of the account from which he plans to take the money, or a VOD of that account, would be required—at the very least, a letter from his bank stating that he has sufficient funds to cover the gift. Then, the lender will want a copy of the gift check before it is deposited and a VOD of the account after it is deposited.

Uncle Joe says that he wouldn't be caught dead giving them that information. Then Fannie Mae says that she doesn't care—if he won't give the information, she won't buy the loan. She has hundreds of thousands of other borrowers who want to do loans, why worry about one? And you will have to accept this attitude. This type of confrontation drives loan officers to distraction.

They are stuck in the middle between an intransigent Uncle Joe, who just wants to help his relative buy a house, and Fannie Mae, the monolithic corporation that lives by the rules. One would hope there must be a good reason for all this fuss. And, in most instances, there is.

When you get the money, **the lender wants to make sure that it is not a loan, but a true gift.** If it were a loan, then the debt might keep you from qualifying, aside from the fact that the loan would probably be unsecured. If the transaction were stated as a gift when in fact it was a loan, and you ultimately defaulted on the mortgage because of excess debt, you would be in big trouble not only the with lender and the investor, but also because you would have committed fraud to obtain the loan. Obviously, if no one ever finds out, then you have no problem. But, by reprocessing the loan after it closes lenders can find out. They will do this to a certain percentage of the loans that are bought by the secondary market not only to ensure that borrowers are not giving false information, but also to ensure that the lender is giving reliable documentation. (All investors require the lender to have a quality control program.) It is a sign of the times when lenders who are fighting for their share of the market will make loans by altering the documentation to make a loan fit the guidelines. Imagine the secondary market investors' surprise when they find a debt that wasn't supposed to be there, and your written word stating that there is no such debt. It is not a good idea to lie on a loan application. Big Brother is watching.

Because the lender wants to make sure that the gift donor has the ability to give you the money, the lender requires the documentation we discussed earlier. While the system may not be perfect, showing that the donor has the money will at least make it more plausible that he will in fact give you the gift. Verifications are a picture of the borrower and the property at a given time. Lenders understand that things can change, but they also know that most borrowers recognize they must have the cash to close, and will be less likely to spend it before closing.

While some investors (including FHA and VA, which we will discuss later) may not specifically require that the gift money be verified as being in the donor's account, they will want copies of the gift check and the deposit slip showing that the borrower deposited it. These are followed up with a VOD to show that the gift has been deposited.

Now that we have been through all this, you are probably wondering, "Is a gift worth the trouble?" The answer is, absolutely. The process just sounds complicated. A good lender will walk you through it without a hitch. And, the more money you have available, the easier it will be to get the loan and buy more house. As a matter of fact, more loans are made with gifts than you might imagine.

Playing Games—Trying to Beat the Rules

Whenever people are using someone else's money, they quickly figure out ways to get around the rules. People discovered that if you get the money two or three months before you apply for the loan, then the VOD will show an average balance in line with the current balance, and suddenly you no longer need gift letters— or angry uncles. This action is called *seasoning the money* and it can work, in some instances. Anticipating this ploy, some lenders, and some types of loans, require that borrowers submit copies of their bank statements back as far as three to six months. Or, if there is an unusually large amount of money that would not normally be associated with the borrower's income, then the borrower may be asked to show how it was accumulated. It's part of the game, a bit like roulette. You pay your money and you take your chance. The longer you have held the money, the better the chance you will win the game.

While we are on the subject of your money, you should always give the lender the number of your check for the earnest money on a purchase contract. When the lender verifies the cash in the account from which the check was written, it will ask if the check has cleared. If it has, the lender will know to add it into the balance shown on the VOD. Otherwise, the borrower may not get credit for that cash. Especially if the deposit is for over $1,000, many lenders require that it be verified if it is to be counted. Often, this money is needed to qualify. Before closing, a copy of the canceled check is sometimes required.

Is It Enough?

Once it is established that the borrower has money in the bank and that it was not stolen, the question arises of just how much money is actually needed. On Fannie and Freddie (conventional) loans, **the borrower must have enough verified cash** to do the following:

1. Pay the down payment on the loan.
2. Pay all required closing costs associated with the purchase of the property and the loan closing.
3. Cover the equivalent of two months' house payments above and beyond the down payment and closing costs. This requirement is unrelated to how much the borrower has for the down payment. This is called the *reserve,* and it is required because everyone will need money for miscellaneous expenses when they move into a new house, like moving costs, drapes, utility deposits, food, and the first month's house payment.
4. When the cash down payment is less than 20% of the total purchase, 5% of the cash must come from the borrower's own resources. That is, the borrower cannot get that 5% in a gift. If the cash down is 20% or more, then the 5% rule does not apply (at least, not at the time this was written). There will be some exceptions to this rule, depending on the secondary market investor and the loan type.

And remember, all of this must be verified in writing before the lender will approve the loan. Government loans have slightly different requirements, which we will cover when we discuss FHA and VA. Fannie Mae has also come out with a new (1991) loan for low- to moderate-income borrowers, called the 3–2 loan that does not require reserves or 5% from the borrower's resources. We will cover it when we discuss loan types.

Let the Seller Pay It

Sometimes, or more often than sometimes, the borrower does not have enough money to pay the down payment plus the closing costs and show two months' worth of payments. And the buyer can't get a gift. If it is so close that it's just a matter of not having enough to cover all the closing costs, there is another source. Let the seller pay it. As in everything else, there are certain rules, but in this case Fannie and Freddie and almost all investors have identical, unequivocal guidelines. These, like everything else in mortgage lending, are subject to change at any time. What these rules say is that there are certain costs that the seller, or Realtor, or lender, can pay. And there are certain costs that only the borrower can pay. The rules also specify how much can be paid.

Let's separate the payable from the nonpayable. The only things that cannot be paid by anyone except the borrower are the **prepaid items.** We will cover these in detail when we get into closing costs, but prepaids include:

1.   Prepaid interest (the house payment for the month in which you close)
2.   Homeowner's insurance (first year's premium and escrows)
3.   Real estate tax escrows
4.   Mortgage insurance escrows (if the loan requires them)

Everything else is fair game—with one exception. Depending on the Loan-to-Value (LTV) ratio, or how much cash the borrower puts down, **only a certain percentage of the value of the property can be paid as closing costs by someone other than the borrower.** On conventional loans, the maximums are:

1.   95% LTV (or less than 10% down) = maximum of 3% of value
2.   90% LTV (10% or more down) = maximum of 6% of value
3.   75% LTV = some loans will allow up to 9% of the value

Value is the lesser of the sales price or the appraised value. When we get to FHA and VA, you will find that these percentages are quite different.

It is not unusual in many markets to ask the sellers to pay some points, and with the increasing cost of housing it is becoming more acceptable to ask them to pay some of the other costs as well. Depending on what the sellers' bottom line is, they may be more than willing to pay in order to make the deal work.

For example, the sellers are asking $100,000, but will take $97,000. If you offer them full price and ask them to pay $3,000 in closing costs, they will get what they wanted, and the house sells. If the house sells and everybody is happy, then it is a win-win situation. All you have to do is convince the sellers that they are winning by paying $3,000 of the borrower's closing costs. Here a good Realtor and lender are invaluable. They can provide the information and the negotiating expertise that make the difference between dead contracts and live ones.

Employer paid costs, usually associated with relocation, are not normally subject to the 3%/6% rule. The only time there may be a problem is when the employer advances the employee/borrower the equity in her present home and makes it subject to repayment. This creates a debt. Also, if the employer agrees to take over the payments on the house, the employer must state that the borrower will not be liable in the future.

Some lenders will offer **a higher interest rate with no points,** origination or discount. This reduces the closing costs, as long as the borrower is willing to take the higher rate. And, in some instances, the lender will also pay part of the closing costs in addition to no points. The company can do this because of the large premium that the secondary market will pay for this above-market interest rate. This is a type of *buy-up* loan.

The last question on the verification of deposit form asks if the borrower has any outstanding loans with that depository. In most instances, borrowers will tell the lender about all of their debts, but some borrowers actually believe that if the lender doesn't know about them, it won't find out about them. Not only will the bank tell the lender about these debts, but it will also tell the credit bureau, and the debts will show up on the credit report—which leads nicely into our next area of qualification.

Credit   Using the Other Man's Money

The borrower must have sufficiently good credit to justify making the loan. All current and recent credit, within the past 6 to 24 months, must be verified in writing. All lenders use several means to find out whether borrowers are in over their heads at that particular time. Many borrowers simply don't recognize many of their debts as such. A symptom of the times is the use of plastic as if it were money in the bank. Credit card obligations and other revolving credit are definitely considered as debt, even if they are paid off every month without incurring any interest charge. If borrowers use credit regularly, then they will be making a regular payment of some type.

The Credit Report—A Reality Check

The Standard Mortgage Credit Report is the only credit report accepted by all investors in the industry. It reports all credit of record for the past seven years. The lender is most concerned with credit within the past one to two years, but the seven-year history will give a good idea of the borrower's credit habits. It will show the following:

1. The borrower's name, address, employer for the past two years, age, marital status, gross income, and social security number.

2. Names of all available credit references with opening date of the account, highest credit amount, current amount, required payment, term of the credit, current credit rating, when information was given, period of time that the rating covers, number of late payments (if any), how late (30, 60, 90+ days late), dates they were late, any credit inquiries within the last 90 days (to catch any potential new, unlisted credit) and any credit shown on public records (judgments, bankruptcies).

With this information the lender can get an impression of the borrowers' credit habits. Do they consistently borrow to their maximum limit? Do they have several credit cards that are used frequently? Do they make their payments on time? No one is perfect. At one time or another everybody has made a late payment, by mistake or intentionally. What is most important is when, how many, how often, and on what debts late payments occurred. If you have one or two late payments in the past 12 months on a bankcard, and nothing else was late, that fact will generally not disqualify you for a loan. If you had late payments on the bankcard, the car payment, and other debts, that is, you have established a history of making late payments in the recent past, then your loan application may not make it past the credit report before it is denied, unless you have **an acceptable explanation.**

Why were the payments late? If it was by habit, or because the borrowers have shown that they cannot handle the amount of credit given, then it's evident that the borrowers are not in a position to take on additional debt. Some type of **economic catastrophe,** such as loss of employment, medical expenses, or other unexpected expenses can help to offset the poor credit. Even lenders can have a little compassion. It is up to the borrower to document why the payments were late and to prove that it is not a common practice. It is the lender's responsibility to tell the borrowers exactly what will be needed to accomplish this task and to guide them through it. Unfortunately too many lenders do not take this responsibility seriously, and it is the borrower who may suffer. You cannot assume that the lender will hold the borrower's hand through this process: only the good ones will make the extra effort. The borrowers, and the Realtor (if one is involved), should always take the initiative to ask what they can do to ensure that the loan goes smoothly.

The most important credit history that the lender will consider is the borrower's **previous mortgage and/or rent payment habits** for at least the past two years. (Be prepared to give the lender the names and addresses of your landlords and/or mortgage lenders for the past two years.) If you had one late payment in the past 12 months, the lender will usually forgive one transgression. If you had two late payments, you had better have a good reason or the loan will very likely be denied. If you had one that was received over 30 days from the due date, or over two late payments, I would not advise giving your landlord notice. Keep in mind that a mortgage payment is generally due on the first of the month, with a 15-day grace period. The lender gives the borrower the grace period to allow for delays in receiving income or for the possibility that the payment will be held up in the mail. (The letter carrier has always been one of my favorite scapegoats.) Having it does not mean that you can wait until the last day of the grace period to send your payment. If the payment arrives after the cutoff time on the last day of the grace period, usually 2:00 P.M., it is considered late.

I dealt with one couple who exemplified what not to do in making mortgage payments. They owned a home on which they had been making payments for over three years. They were transferred, and contracted to buy a new home, applying for a mortgage with Yours Truly. The mortgage payment verification showed that out of their past 12 payments, eleven were received 16 to 30 days late. Always giving the borrower the benefit of the doubt, I asked them to explain. It was very simple, really. They believed in using "other people's" money (their words). So they waited until the last minute to give it to them. This is not a good answer. The loan was denied, even though they could easily have made their payments on time each month. Lenders do not want to make loans to people who habitually make late payments. These particular borrowers told me that the lender was getting a late fee, so the lender was making more money out of the loan anyway. This is not usually true.

The lender may want to sell the loan to an investor in the secondary market, which expects to receive its interest and principal payment on a certain date every month, come hell or high water. If the originating lender retains the servicing rights to the loan, it is responsible for getting the payments to the investor on time, and will take money from its own account to make sure that these payments are made, even if they have not been received from the borrower. In combination with using its own money and then having to send notices and keep track of the delinquency, the servicing lender will use up the late fee. On top of that, lenders who originate and service loans do not want a high rate of defaults (a loan is technically in default the minute the payment is past due) and foreclosures. When the lender deals with an investor in the secondary market, one of the most important things that the investor considers, before buying the originating lender's loans, is the ratio of loans in default and foreclosure on the lender's books. If the ratio is higher than the average, the investor might infer that the lender does not use due care in underwriting and servicing its loans. They may decline to buy loans from that lender, or not pay competitive prices. This means that the lender either has one less source to which it can sell loans, or may not be able to give as low an interest rate. Either of these, obviously, can affect the interest rate that borrowers are able to get for their mortgage. Interest rates aren't as simple as you thought, are they?

When a borrower has a late payment of any kind on record, it is a secondary market requirement as part of the loan application process that he give a **written explanation** for it. Many people have late payments that they never knew existed. They find out only when they apply for a mortgage that a payment to Visa™ three years ago was reported late. The standard answer is that they do not know why it was late, but it must have been delayed in the mail.

One borrower for whom I did a loan exemplifies just how seriously the lender considers getting a written explanation. This man had a net worth of over $3 million and he was putting down over 30% cash. His credit report was four legal pages long with very little in outstanding debt. It was perfect, except for one little late payment. This account was with a major national retail chain, and it showed that a 30-day late payment had been made five years ago. Most late payments like this are removed after two or three years, but, for some reason, it was still there. I had to ask him to give me a written explanation for why this payment had been late. Needless to say, he had a hard time understanding why it was necessary. And I had a hard time adequately explaining why, except that I could not get the loan approved without it. The reason is that Fannie Mae says so, or it will not buy the loan. The borrower wrote that, because it was so long ago, he had no way of remembering, but he suspected it was because of the mail. And, yes, he did get the loan.

In this example, the debt was so old that it should have been removed from his credit report, but for some reason was not. It is possible for either the lender or borrower to mention this to the credit bureau, and it will often remove the discrepancy, thus saving time and borrower frustration. And, if you are wondering why I didn't think about that at the time I did the loan, the reason was that I had only been in the business about one year and didn't know any better. As I said, never assume that the lender is completely knowledgeable.

Regardless of what the reason for the late payment may be and how embarrassing it is to the borrower, it does help to tell the truth, even when it is painful. All information given to a lender is confidential, and sometimes a hopeless case can turn out differently from what it would seem.

Even a Lender Has a Heart—When Bad Credit Can Be Forgiven

A woman applied to refinance her residence. She also had a rental property on which she had a mortgage. Her mortgage verifications on both properties showed 22 late payments in the past 24 months. An inexperienced lender would assume that her application had no chance whatsoever. In this case, a few additional questions made all the difference.

When asked to explain, she told a story that truly made the underwriter cry. Her husband and three children had been in a car wreck in which the husband was killed and the children were seriously injured. The children were in the hospital for a long time, and then required extensive rehabilitation. They literally had to learn to walk and talk again. The borrower's medical insurance had run out long before all the hospital and therapy bills were paid. Knowing that she could not make all her payments every month, she made arrangements with her creditors to pay medical bills one month and mortgages the next. Her lender at that time accepted this plan as long as none of the payments was more than 30 days late, and a letter to this effect was put in her file. By the time she came to me for refinancing, she had paid off all the medical bills and had begun to make her mortgage payments on time. We made the loan to her.

This was an extraordinary occurrence over which the borrower had little or no control, and it was unlikely to happen again. Besides, the borrower did all the right things to help maintain her credit. She contacted her creditors before her problem got out of hand and worked out a plan to ensure the payments were made. No reputable lenders want to foreclose on a mortgage. They will go to great lengths to help the borrower if the borrower works with them.

While too much credit may be detrimental, little or no credit will not cause the lender to deny a loan, except for certain specialized mortgages. If a borrower has always paid cash, the lender will verify utility payments and any other payments for goods and services. Copies of checks for payment will often help. Borrowing only to establish credit is not necessary. After all, little or no debt may show frugality and the ability to save. The lender only wants to make sure that the borrower can make the mortgage payment and all other monthly obligations. If you are in the no-debt category, you are indeed in a minority. Americans are creating and maintaining credit debt in record amounts. The lender must ensure that this debt will not put the mortgage loan at high risk of default.

Different Ways of Being in Debt

Some of the more prevalent types of credit include the following:

1. Credit cards
2. Bank notes
3. Car loans
4. Education loans
5. Other mortgage loans
6. Alimony and child support payments

Each debt likely has different terms and characteristics that the lender will have to consider in determining the borrower's actual monthly obligations.

Proving That You Are in Debt

Credit cards and revolving credit are established in several ways.
First, the lender will qualify the borrower by using a standard
5% of the current outstanding balance as the monthly payment.
When the lender receives the credit report, it will use the reported payment to qualify the borrower. However, the credit report will not always show the payment or the actual current
balance. Credit bureaus often give the balance 30 to 60 days ago.
But (wouldn't you know) the borrower has just paid that $2,000
balance down to $500, or paid it off completely. The payment
the lender sees on the report throws the borrower into a ratio that
exceeds the qualifying ratios, while the balance of zero would
meet the guidelines. The astute lender will tell the borrowers
to bring in a copy of the canceled check, if they have it, to
show that the card was paid off, and it will also have the borrower request a statement from the creditor showing the current
balance.

You must be able to show conclusively, in writing, that the
debt has been reduced or eliminated. This can be done quickly
if the creditor is local. The lender just picks up the statement.
If the creditor is out of town, the lender can mail a request or
have the credit bureau update the report. (This usually incurs
an additional charge by the bureau.) Or, in this world of tech-
nical wizardry, the lender can send the request and receive the
information by facsimile machine. Most lenders accept the fax
copy as verification, but some require that the original verification statement be received before the loan can close.

Car loans and other bank loans are normal in today's society, but the increasing cost of automobiles has begun to put
a strain on the borrower's ability to buy a home. My answer to
that is, "Get your priorities in order. Buy the house first, then
the BMW™." It is not unusual to see a car payment that is as
large as a house payment. And this is on a depreciating asset.

When Is a Debt Not a Debt?

When the borrower has a loan that amortizes out in a given
amount of time, like a 4-year car loan, that monthly payment is
considered in the long term debts for purposes of qualifying until it has *10 months or less left to be paid.* (On FHA and VA loans
it is 6 months.) Now, for every rule, there is an exception. If the
loan has 10 months or even 5 or 6 months remaining but is for a

Mercedes at $800 per month, then the lender is less likely to ignore that debt. The borrower's application would have to be very strong not to count it. Also, a borrower with a payment of $250 who is right on the edge of qualifying without counting that payment may not be approved if the lender feels she cannot handle the debt load until the $250 is paid off. (The greatest risk of default and foreclosure will be in the first one or two years of the loan.) Debts of short duration will also be counted on loans of over 90% loan-to-value.

There is a way to avoid being denied because of a high-payment, short-term debt—convince a rich relative to give you the money to pay off the loan. There are several variations on this theme.

You can wait to see if the underwriter likes you. If the loan is approved with the debt, fine. If not, then you must assure the loan originator that you will be able to pay this off with a gift, if necessary, so that this information can be passed on to the underwriter. That the loan is paid off will then become a condition of loan closing. There must be a gift letter, and the receipt of the funds must be verified. (You didn't think they would let you get away without that, did you?) Or, you can pay the loan down to a low enough remaining balance, like 2 to 4 months, that even an underwriter would probably let it slide. If you do this, the loan must be paid down before the debt is verified the first time. Most secondary market investors will not accept a condition of paying down a loan. By the time it is verified, you are stuck with an all-or-nothing proposition. (Again, play the game. Do not try to argue your way through it. You are dealing with people who play God every day.)

Short-Term Notes

Bank notes, or **personal notes,** are the bane of those who live by an irregular payday. Commissioned sales people, such as Realtors, see money like an untuned car, in starts and spurts. To live during the periods when they can't quite seem to get their motors running, they will take out a "90-day note." They get $5,000 at 12% and then scramble to make the sales to pay it back. Then, when it is paid off and they can give a sigh of relief, they realize that the bank just got their last buck. So, the cycle starts again. Much to the delight of banks, this phenomenon is not confined to sales people, but also includes doctors, lawyers, and some people with expensive tastes.

Some loans don't have a regular monthly payment. The lender can't just count the whole debt as a single payment in qualifying a loan application. How does one come up with a reasonable method of setting a qualifying payment? If you have a bank note that is not on a monthly payment schedule, the lender will always adjust the payments to reflect an equivalent monthly schedule. If a payment is made quarterly, the lender will divide it by three and use that figure for qualifying. If the payment is interest only, the requirement for qualifying may vary from lender to lender. Usually, the lender will break the interest payment into monthly payments and use that debt according to this criteria:

1. The debt is not due within a short period of time, and/or ...

2. The creditors state that they will renew the loan when it comes due, and/or ...

3. The borrowers could pay off the loan out of remaining assets after they have purchased the house.

Some lenders are quite imaginative and take the loan and interest rate, assume an amortization period from 3 to 10 years, and use that to qualify the borrower.

Education Loans

Education, or student, loans have more options than a car on order from Detroit. For instance, most are deferred until the borrower is out of school from one month to one year, or further if the borrower goes to graduate school, or teaches, or requests a further deferral. Then payments are set up monthly, quarterly, semiannually, or yearly. And, if the payment is deferred, often neither the borrower nor the creditor knows what the payment will be when it starts.

A good example would be a borrower who recently graduated from school and has several student loans. One of them may be set up to begin payments and can be readily verified. That one's easy. Another may be deferred for another one to three years. This one is not so easy, depending on how the lender views the loan. Usually, if the loan is deferred for three to five years, it does not have to be counted as a current debt. If it is deferred for one or two years, then it is a current debt.

To make matters worse, the borrower too often forgets that he has a student loan, or thinks that it is not a debt because he is not paying on it. Everyone will go blithely along until the credit report arrives. Suddenly, the loan on which the borrower just barely qualified, and that the Realtor had been assured would be approved, is rejected because of new debts. The Realtor rationalizes that the lender should not count what is not being paid in order to save the sale, the borrower is angry because the lender never asked him if he had any education loans (mind-reading is a prerequisite to be a lender), and the sellers are angry because they had been told by the Realtor that the lender had assured her that the borrowers qualified.

The Borrower with More Than One Mortgaged Property—
Multi-Mortgage Mania

There are also guidelines for **borrowers who have other existing mortgages.** When a borrower has another property on which there is a recorded lien (mortgage), that payment is included in the total debt. However, that property usually will be rented. The secondary market allows you to take **75% of the gross rents** and subtract that from the mortgage payment (PITI) on the rental property. If the number is positive, you can add it to income for qualifying. If it is negative, then that amount is added to the total debts.

An example would be a property with a mortgage payment of $700 and a lease payment of $800. Most borrowers will say that they have a positive cash flow of $100 per month. But that is not what they report on Schedule E of their federal income tax returns. Secondary market lenders recognize that there are expenses and vacancies, so they use the conservative figure of 25% of the gross rent to cover these costs. If you can show by your past two years' tax returns that this figure is high, then the lender may decide to give you the actual cost. Using the 75% factor, the borrower would have a net of $600 (75% of $800), or a minus $100 that would be added to the debts for qualifying.

One more rule on other properties: Fannie and Freddie will buy any loan made on a principal residence, regardless of how many other properties the borrower may own with liens on them. But, if the borrower is seeking a loan on a nonowner occupied (NOO) property, the limit is a total of four properties that have financing, including the primary residence. One-to-four-unit dwellings are considered in this rule. Any properties with five or more units are considered commercial and are not counted. If a property has no recorded financing on it, then it is not counted. If the borrower owns the property with another person, the lender will consider the borrower to have 100% of the debt, not just 50%, because they are jointly and severally responsible for that debt. If one borrower disappears, the other will be obligated for the full loan. Borrowers will argue that they are not responsible for the payment, or only for their corresponding percentage of ownership in the property. You need to read the fine print on those mortgage documents that you sign at closing. You are committed body and soul, you don't get to choose.

If it sounds as if lenders don't want too much business from any one person, you are correct. In the past, the secondary market held many loans from individual people who invested in real estate. When times got tough and some of the the properties stood vacant, the borrower might take the rent from one to pay the mortgage on another. Then the person would borrow to make payments, until the whole thing began to collapse like a house of cards. So to make sure that they don't get stung again and taken for some incredible losses, Fannie and Freddie made the new rule. Most other secondary market investors follow it. Some allow even less. There are Portfolio Loans that do not follow this rule. Check with local lenders to see if they offer it.

D-i-v-o-r-c-e

In our society, divorce has become all too frequent. One of the standard questions that a lender must ask a borrower, male or female, is, "Are you obligated to pay alimony, child support, or separate maintenance?" A surprising number will answer "Yes." This obligation is a debt. The lender will require that the borrower provide **a complete, executed copy of the separation agreement and the divorce agreement** before the loan can be approved.

The lender is not interested in why the separation and/or divorce occurred, but in what the borrower's obligation is, and for how long. To determine these, the entire document must be provided. I have had many a borrower who tried to get by with giving me just the page outlining the payments, and then argued with me that the rest is irrelevant. Fannie and Freddie (and everyone else) won't buy the loan without the full documentation. If you fit the description, be prepared to provide the paperwork.

Notice that I said "executed" copies. That means copies of documents that have been agreed upon and signed. Occasionally, a borrower will try to buy a house before the separation is down on paper. This is another instance where the lender gets to play God. The borrower must have an executed agreement detailing if there will be any obligation to pay, and if so, what the terms will be, before the loan can be approved. On the other hand, some people will have lived apart for years without any formal written agreement. They will have to draw up a separation agreement and sign it before a lender will make the loan.

One borrower who applied for a loan tried to browbeat me into accepting just a statement from his attorney. When I demonstrated that I could not be intimidated, I then found out why he was so reluctant. His support payment was over $5,000 per month! The amazing thing is that he made so much money that he still qualified for a loan of over $120,000.

There will always be the occasional borrower who tries to sneak by the lender without telling about prior divorce and alimony obligation. Sometimes it will work, but what usually happens is that the divorce shows up on the credit report. Besides showing any joint credit that may have been in existence over the last 7 to 10 years, the credit bureau will check public records for the same period. Chances are, you're going to get caught.

For even more excitement, wait until the credit report shows judgments or bankruptcies that were not disclosed at application. These things won't necessarily prevent a borrower from getting a loan, but they are not desirable. Let's take them one at a time.

Judgments—Pay Me Now Or Later, But You Will Pay

Why do people get judgments? Usually they are filed against a borrower for two different reasons. The first is that the person didn't pay the debt, and the second is that the person didn't think the debt should have to be paid. The latter is usually a dispute over some type of goods the person received, or did not receive, and refused to pay for. I've seen judgments where the goods had been returned, and the creditor never gave credit for the return. The borrower then moved away and was never found so that notice could be served that a judgment had been filed. The person later discovers this unpleasant fact when trying to convince a lender to let them borrow a large sum of money. If you have had any adverse credit in the past two years, it will show up. More than likely, anything in the past seven years will be shown. Applying for a mortgage is one of the best ways to find out exactly what is on your credit.

Judgments have been for as little as $20. The borrower refused to pay, out of principle. He's right and the other guy is wrong. The mortgage lender may be sympathetic, but the secondary market is not. All judgments must be paid off before closing the loan, no exceptions.

Before you conclude that all you have to do to get the loan is make sure that pay off all your judgments, understand that these things are part of your credit history. One judgment for an understandable reason, such as a dispute, may not cause denial. But, if you have consistently poor credit, or the judgments were recently filed for bad credit, or the judgments were filed for nonpayment of rent, then you have a problem. Slow payment of rent is considered with the same prejudice as slow mortgage payments. Only a couple of late payments in the past 12 months can be the kiss of death.

Any recent poor payment history can lead the lender to conclude that you are currently not a good credit risk—even if you had the ability to have made the payments. If you know you have judgments that will show up on your credit report, even if they are paid, tell the mortgage lender about them right at loan application. That way, there will be more time to solve any potential problem, or to save the cost of application if it is apparent that they will cause the loan to be denied.

Bankruptcy—Spin the Wheel Again

Many people (too many) have used to bankruptcy to solve their credit problems. In a nutshell, bankruptcy is a way for a borrower who has more debts than income and assets either to rearrange his or her credit so that the debts can be paid, or, in extreme cases, to allow all or most of the debts to be written off so that the borrower can start a new credit life. Some people who declare bankruptcy do so because they have been advised by someone who may not be considering factors that can come into play several years down the road.

Let's say that our borrower has a good job and the family has a good credit history. Naturally, every bank and credit lender would love to have people paying them 18%. So, they send them unsolicited applications for credit, or they just send the credit card with an invitation to use it. Our borrower yields to the temptation of that snappy new sports car, and the rest of the family buys all new furniture because the original stuff looked "used." In general, they were only trying to keep up with the proverbial Joneses. Suddenly, where they once could pay bills and have money left to go out occasionally, they are now having to borrow from the bank to meet their obligations. This doesn't sound good, does it? Like faltering governments that try to renegotiate their debts, so should our borrowers—right after they destroy all their credit cards and cancel all their credit accounts. Cold turkey. Most creditors will work with a hard-pressed borrower because this way they may be able to get their money. If they don't, there is an option available to the borrower, through which the creditors may get zero.

When all else fails and the borrower can no longer make his or her debt payments, bankruptcy may be the only alternative. The best approach is Chapter 13 bankruptcy, if at all possible. This gives the borrower time to renegotiate his debt, in order to repay it and have money on which to live. The creditors may not get all their money back, or it may take much longer, but at least the borrower is attempting to meet these obligations. For people who are incorporated, Chapter 11 works the same way. Chapter 7 bankruptcy allows the borrower to void all debts and start over with a clean slate.

If the borrower exhibited poor judgment in using credit, future lenders will look at them very carefully to see that the same mistakes are not repeated. Sometimes, though, bankruptcy may be the only solution. If people lose their job, or have major medical expenses that are not covered by insurance, the debt may be so overwhelming that nothing short of a clean break will allow the borrowers to live within their means.

Bankruptcy would seem to be a way to keep a borrower from ever getting a mortgage again. This conclusion is not true. What it does keep the borrower from doing is getting a mortgage within the next 2 to 10 years from the date that the bankruptcy is **discharged,** that is, from the time the court says that the borrower is no longer in bankruptcy. Each investor, each lender, and even each loan type may require a different time period. Most accept **2 years after discharge.**

What Fannie and Freddie say is that they will consider buying a loan when the borrower makes loan application after having been **discharged for a minimum of 2 years.** They will consider a shorter period of time if the situation warrants it. For example, if the borrowers are **forced into bankruptcy by something beyond their control,** such as medical bills, a lender may make the loan in less than the 2-year period. Both FHA and VA follow essentially the same rules. But some investors do not want to consider anyone who has declared bankruptcy for any reason until it no longer shows on the credit report. And that is 7 to 10 years.

If the borrower has declared bankruptcy in the past, he or she needs to disclose that to the lender before writing any contracts of purchase. If the lender feels that it can make the loan, the borrower will have to provide the following:

1. A full executed copy of the Bankruptcy petition
2. A copy of the discharge papers
3. A complete written explanation as to why it became necessary to declare bankruptcy

People who have gone through bankruptcy are given the chance literally to start over. This means that they should learn from their mistakes or misfortune and maintain a good credit history in their second life.

Foreclosure, Or Deed in Lieu of Foreclosure

Another credit problem, although it is not so prevalent as bankruptcy, is foreclosure or giving a deed in lieu of foreclosure. If you have been foreclosed on, you can usually count on not getting any normal mortgage for the next 2 to 10 years, except in certain economic circumstances. (FHA and VA can be more lenient.)

When borrowers give a deed in lieu of foreclosure, they simply turn over the deed, and ownership, of the property to the note holder without going through the foreclosure process. This saves everyone involved a large amount of time and expense. It is used primarily in instances where the borrowers, through no fault of their own, can no longer afford to make the loan payments and cannot sell or rent the property to cover the loan. The situation in the Texas-Oklahoma oil patch during the 1980s' recession that put large numbers of people out of work is a classic example. Homeowners were without jobs and sufficient income to meet the mortgage payments. They couldn't rent their property because the market was glutted with houses to rent, and there certainly weren't many people looking to buy. Under the circumstances, most lenders agreed to take the deed in lieu of foreclosing on the property. If the situation is adequately explained and documented, many lenders will consider making a loan to the borrower within a two-year period. Borrowers who have gone through this may subsequently find that the lender reports it as a foreclosure to the credit agencies when it was not.

Good Credit—Once You Have It, Keep It

In maintaining good credit, remember these:

1. Do not borrow unless you need to.
2. Make sure that you can pay back what you borrow.
3. Plastic money is expensive.
4. Make your payments on time, especially your rent or mortgage payments.
5. If you can't make a payment on time, see the creditor to work out a plan that will keep your credit in good standing.
6. Credit can be destroyed easier than it can be built.
7. The only interest that is still deductible is mortgage interest (unless Congress changes its mind).

What Is Long-Term Credit?

You also need to know when debt is considered long-term and must be counted against you when qualifying for the loan, and when is it of such short duration that it does not need to be counted. We discussed this distinction earlier. Here are the rules:

1. Any **revolving debt,** such as credit cards, will be counted if there is an outstanding balance. The lender will use 5% of that balance as the qualifying payment unless the credit report shows a different payment or the borrower provides a statement of the account, showing a lower payment and/or balance, that is more recent than the credit report figures. Borrowers who have a bunch of credit cards will be considered as a higher risk because they could increase their debt rapidly.
2. On **installment loans** with a regular payment, such as car loans, the payment will not be counted in qualifying if the loan has 10 months or less left to pay (FHA & VA are 6 months). If the monthly payment

is excessive and will adversely affect the ability of the borrower to make the mortgage payments in the first year, then the payment will be considered. If the borrower's income cannot easily support it, then it will be counted, although consideration will be given to its short-term nature.

3. If a **borrower has co-signed a debt** with another person, that debt will be considered as the borrower's debt, even if it can be shown that the other person is making the payments. That the borrower is not making the payments will be considered as a compensating factor as long as the other person maintains a good credit history. Our borrower could ultimately be responsible for the debt. If the loan has had late payments, these will appear on the borrower's credit report, even though the friend is the one who is at fault.

4. If the **borrower puts down less than 10%** on the mortgage, all monthly debts are used to qualify, regardless of how long until they are paid off; but consideration is given for any short-term payments (FHA & VA are six months regardless of LTV).

5. Your **total house payment (principal, interest, taxes, insurance, and mortgage insurance and homeowner's dues if required) and monthly debt payments** should not exceed about **36%** of your gross monthly income. This can be stretched out to 38 or 40% in some cases, but don't count on it. If you put down less than 10%, most lenders will use 33% (FHA and VA are 41%).

Income   (It's Never Enough)

We now know there are certain minimum requirements for cash and credit to qualify for a mortgage. Nevertheless, the best credit and tons of cash will not get you the loan if you don't have enough income to pay the mortgage. I have had my share of borrowers who just knew they made enough income to afford house payments, only to be rudely awakened by our lending guidelines. I have also had borrowers that other lenders said did not qualify to whom I had made loans, and vice versa. Again, the decision can vary from lender to lender, investor to investor, and loan type to loan type. Certain minimum guidelines set by the secondary market form the basis for all lenders' decisions. If you satisfy these rules, then you qualify for the majority of conventional loans.

Past And Present Employment—How Many Jobs Have You Had in the Past Two Years? Prove It

A mortgage loan application will always include **a two year history of the borrower's employment,** obtained in writing by a **Verification of Employment (VOE**–see Appendix). It must cover a full 24-month period from the date of the application. If you have been in your job for two or more years, the process will be easy. But, if you have changed jobs within the past two years, every employer during that period will be sent a VOE to be filled in and returned to the lender. On occasion I have sent five or more VOEs out on one borrower.

The Verification of Employment has two sections, one for the current employer and one for previous employers. On the current employment section the employer is asked these questions:

1. Present position of employee
2. Date that employee began employment
3. Probability of continued employment
4. If the employee receives overtime or bonus income, and if so, whether its continuance is likely
5. What the employee's current base pay is and how often the employee is paid (for example, monthly)
6. The employee's earnings for the year-to-date (YTD) and for the past year
7. Overtime and bonus income YTD and for the past year
8. Commissions YTD and past year
9. A remarks section where the employer can say what a nice person you are, or nothing at all

The question regarding present position shows the lender that the borrower is employed in the job the stated on the application and that there is some relationship to other positions that the borrower has held within the past two years. The lender is looking for evidence of continuity of skills. Someone who was a computer salesman and becomes a computer operator demonstrates this, while a person who went from being a Realtor to being a computer salesman would not.

Under the section on date of employment the lender is interested in knowing how long the borrower has been in her present position. If it is a full two years (24 months) from the date of application, that job is normally all that be verified. If it is less than two years, then the lender will verify any previous employment back to the full 24 months. If there is any **gap in the borrower's employment,** normally anything over two weeks, then the borrower must explain this period of unemployment in writing. There is nothing wrong with having a gap in your employment. It is not that unusual. Many people changing jobs and/or moving will take time between jobs. Others may take time that they had not intended to take, in the form of unemployment. As long as the explanation shows that the borrower was willing to work, that the gaps are not normal, and they have a low probability of recurring, the borrower should not worry.

It is not unusual for someone to have changed jobs. Many people applying for a mortgage have taken a new job and are transferring into the area. Changing jobs for advancement or an increase in income is normal. That **the borrower has changed jobs without any additional benefit** may raise questions.

If the change occurred because the person was fired for incompetence, or has changed jobs frequently because of incompatability with management, then there may be a problem. These reasons suggest **employment instability.** To strengthen the case the lender may want to document more than two years of employment and income.

Amazingly, some people cannot remember where they were for the past two years. Borrowers have been known to give information at loan application, only to find out that they left out a job or had the dates of employment wrong by 6 months or more. How productive do you think someone was if he or she couldn't remember the job one year later? The biggest problem with questions resulting from queries concerning employment history is that the loan process is slowed down and approval is delayed. The lender may have all the verifications and information to approve the loan, only to be held up by a last-minute VOE that should have been sent at application.

For the question of the borrower's **probability of continued employment,** the usual answer is "good" or "excellent." Depending on the mood of the employer, there have been some other very interesting answers. More than one employer has put "subject to the economy." I have seen "on probation" or "on a 6-months trial basis." These don't indicate the employer has a lot of confidence that the employee will be around for very long. In the worst I have seen the employer informed us that the borrower was being laid off at the end of the week. This was bad enough, but when I asked the borrower about it, I found out that he had not yet been told. I did the employer's dirty work. The moral is "Never apply for a loan unless you are certain you have good job stability."

When the VOE is being filled in by **a previous employer,** the company only needs to give a few answers. The lender wants to know what the employee's last position was with the employer, what the person's income was at that time, the dates of employment, and reason for leaving. The problem with previous employers is getting them to return the VOE in a reasonable amount of time.

Another problem can be getting a VOE back at all. This situation is usually the result of a disgruntled former employer or someone within the company who did not like the borrower. The lender is not interested in disagreements unless they involve incompetence or job instability, which might suggest that the borrower may not be capable of holding a long-term position.

Current income should be in line with the borrower's type of employment and past years' income. A ditch digger would not be making $50,000 per year, but an accountant would be expected to earn that much or more. A borrower can be expected to get **raises and promotions.** When income goes from $20,000 to $50,000 it may need to be explained. Even a $5,000 increase may be questioned, depending on the lender. When the borrower's income goes from $50,000 to $20,000, the lenders will certainly want more information. As long as the changes are reasonable and can be explained satisfactorily, there should be no problem. When there is any doubt, the borrower or the borrower's employer may be required to give substantial evidence to back up the unusual change in income. Employers have been known to lie to help an employee get a loan. As a matter of fact, **if you work for a relative,** such as a parent, you will have to provide tax returns to substantiate income. Historically, too many relatives have lied to help get loans.

Overtime And Bonuses—Unless the Economy Slows Down

If overtime and bonus income need to be used in qualifying, the lender wants to be certain that it will continue to be earned if it has been received in the past. If there is this assurance, then the lender will ask the employer how much has been earned year-to-date and in the past year. Most lenders will require that two full years' be verified. Because this income can fluctuate, the lender will in most cases **average it.** If you made $2,340 last year in overtime and have made $700 for the first six months of this year, then the lender would divide the total of $3,040 by 18 months for an average of $169 per month.

The best way to use overtime and bonuses is not to use them. Qualifying for the loan on base income alone puts you in a much stronger position, not only because the lender will know there is additional income that was not used, but also because overtime and bonuses have a habit of disappearing just when you need them the most.

Commission Income

As more of us strive for financial success, commission income has become a means to attain higher earnings. In theory, the harder you work, the more you earn. In reality, the results often do not work out that way.

Because you have good days and bad days, the lender will look at commission income in the same way as overtime. Normally, you should have been in that job for **a minimum of two years** (some institutions will allow 1 to one and a half years). Your income will then be averaged over the number of months that it represents. (Doing so smooths out all the peaks and valleys that occur. After 10 years as a Realtor I can attest to the fact that it truly is a roller coaster ride).

If you are on **a draw against commissions,** the draw can be used if it is not subject to repayment. Some lenders will require that you have been in the job for six months to a year, to demonstrate staying power, before the draw can be counted. Ideally, your commissions for that period will meet or exceed the draw. The best idea is to wait until you have established a reliable earning pattern. This is what lenders really want.

Other Income—Stocks, Bonds, Alimony, Grandfather's Money, and the Self-employed

Now that we have covered the mundane aspects of income and employment, let's look at some the unusual and exotic ways of earning money.

Interest and dividend income.   Interest and dividend income is one of the more common sources of "additional income." Usually borrowers will have cash and/or assets on which they are earning some return. To use this income to qualify, they will have to show **1099 forms** (the equivalent of W-2 forms for interest and dividend income) from their past two years' tax returns (some lenders may allow the past two years year-end statements in lieu of 1099s) and their most recent statements showing balances and year-to-date income. If it fluctuates, it will be averaged. If it comes from bonds or other securities earning a constant continuing income then that income is used.

The key is whether the income and the underlying assets will continue to be available in the future. When the borrowers show they have held the assets for two or more years without reducing them substantially or the assets have increased, it is more likely that the borrowers will continue to hold them. If a borrower has just deposited a large sum (the origin of which can be verified) into an interest-bearing account, the lender must determine whether this income will be reliable in the future. A new five-year bond or three-year certificate of deposit would tend to have more staying power than a money market account. Dividends are normally counted as reliable income because most people buy stock for income or long-term growth.

The problems in using this income to qualify are usually with the borrowers themselves. I have seen them go through the entire loan application process using the interest and dividend income to qualify. Then when they are asked what they intend to use for the down payment and closing costs, I discover they are going to liquidate their investments to buy the house—Which, of course, means that they no longer have the interest and dividends to use as income with which to qualify.

Trust income.   Trusts make a very reliable source of income in most cases. A verification from the administrator of the trust and/or the past two years' tax returns will show the trust's ability to provide continued income.

One borrower that I remember was attending a university and living on his trust income. Unfortunately, he forgot that the trust was not just paying out interest. It was paying interest and part of the principal. At the end of two years, just as he finished school, the trust would be completely depleted. If it had paid out in a three-to five-year period, or continued to provide income into the foreseeable future, then most lenders would not have balked.

Luckily for our student, he had made the point of telling me that the existing loan on the property was assumable at 12.5%, a rate he was not interested in paying. When he found out that he could not qualify for the loan, which was currently a 9% rate, 12.5% started to look pretty good. It looked even better when I told him he could assume that particular loan and then refinance it at a lower rate without having to qualify for the payment. As a result, he was able to buy the property without qualifying and get the lower, current rate of 9%. Unfortunately, those loans (FHA) are no longer offered as assumable without qualifying.

Tax-free income.   Tax-free income has gained popularity as the government keeps tinkering with our deductions. Income from tax-free bonds and certain nontaxable military payments is not only usable income, but also represents more than the face value. Because lenders use gross income to qualify the borrower, the qualifying ratios, or percentages of the gross income that can be used for house payment and debts, take into account that the usable portion of a person's income will be significantly less after withholding. (VA loans are handled differently because of their method of qualifying.) When tax-free income is used, most lenders (not FHA) can "gross up" this income to compensate for the withholding adjustments built into the ratios. *Grossing Up* means that the lender can add onto the tax-free income what the normal withholding tax would have been. While most secondary market investors will accept this computation, do not assume that all lenders will use it, especially if you need the grossed up amount to qualify. Some lenders may only count it as a compensating factor.

Alimony and child support income.   Alimony and child support are probably the most widely available sources of alternate income. For many divorced women, and a few men, alimony and child support mean the difference between purchasing a home or renting.

The law states that a lender may not ask if the borrower is receiving alimony or child support; further, if the borrower does volunteer this information, the borrower can refuse to let it be used to qualify. Obviously, if the borrower can qualify without it, so much the better. Why? Because most divorces end on a less than amicable note. The lender wants reassurance that the income is reliable.

Copies of the borrower's bank statements from the last 6 to 12 months, showing the payments being deposited, is the usual method of verification. The biggest problem with this is that the former spouse seldom deposits the check either by itself or in its entirety.

As an example, say the lender is looking for monthly deposits of $500 around the first of each month. What the lender finds are deposits of amounts like $623.45 (alimony plus the proceeds of yard sale) or $254.13 (what was left after paying the dentist bill) or $0.00 (the alimony was taken as cash). Along with a letter of explanation from the borrower, most lenders will accept these variations as long as there is evidence that this income, plus or minus, appears each month.

There is an easier way to verify receipt of the alimony income. If the former spouse is under court order to pay alimony directly to the court, most lenders will accept a copy of that order as verification.

If the divorce was amicable (I've seen two), then the alimony recipient can ask the former spouse for copies of the last 12 canceled alimony checks. Sometimes the former spouse will even provide a copy of the federal income tax return to demonstrate this adjustment to personal income.

The idea is to **show that alimony and child support are reliable sources of usable income.** Once we know that it is being received, we need to ensure that it will continue for at least three to five years. If the child is 16 years old and the support continues until the age of 18, then the support is only a compensating factor and not usable as qualifying income. A difficulty arises when, as in most cases, the agreement specifies that the support will continue until age 21 if the child goes to college. At 16 no one can say whether the child will continue. Normally the lender decides that it will end at 18, and uses it as a compensating factor.

Just as the borrower who pays alimony or child support has to provide **copies of the executed agreements,** the borrower who is receiving it also has to give copies to the lender, if the income is being used to qualify. There are instances of divorce settlements for which the former spouse is not required to make any payments but does as a result of a feeling of obligation. (I've seen one.) If the borrower can show evidence of this, plus a written letter from the former spouse, some lenders will allow it as income. Most, however, will only use it as a slight compensating factor, since nothing forces the continuance of that income.

Note income.   People themselves will often act as small lenders, taking back a note for property that they sold, for money that they have lent to others, or for goods and services. The income is usable as long as it meets the standard Fannie Mae–Freddie Mac rules. For example, there must be a written agreement. You have to show evidence that it is being received (bank statements, tax returns). It has to continue for at least three to five years, depending on the lender and the secondary market investor. A secured note is much easier for the lender to accept than an unsecured one. Notes give you two advantages: They create income for qualifying, and they are listed as assets on your financial statement.

Gift Income.   For the well-heeled, gift income is a good way to distribute assets. By law, you can give up to a certain amount as a gift each year. If the donor has given this income in the past and states in writing an intention to continue it in the future, many lenders will accept this gift. Do not assume that every lender will use it. Some are less trusting than others. I have known underwriters who required copies of the donor's tax returns for the past two years to prove their ability to give the gift. Others may require verification of assets, or whatever the source of this largess may be.

Rental income.   Rental income is something that everyone wishes he or she could claim. You have an appreciating asset (we hope). It creates income. And it can show a paper loss, which means less taxes. Lenders look at rental income several ways.

The normal rental income is from an investment, or nonowner occupied, property. Taking 75% of the gross rents and subtracting that from the PITI payment on the property leaves 25% for vacancy and expenses. If the difference is positive, it is added to your income for qualifying. If it is negative, it is used in the long-term debt total, not the full PITI payment. Here is an example:

$$Gross\ Monthly\ Rent = \$800 \times 75\% = \$600$$

$$PITI\ payment = \$700$$

$$\$700\ PITI - \$600\ net\ rent = -\$100.$$

$$The\ negative\ \$100\ would\ be\ debt.$$

If you are **living in a duplex, or other multi-family dwelling** that is the subject property to be financed, or if the subject property is nonowner occupied, then an **operating income statement** must be completed by the appraiser. Unless you are very familiar with the form and have access to a *Marshall Swift Handbook,* get a lender to help you with this statement. It will normally show a loss. Using the 75% factor will give you a good conservative figure for preliminary purposes.

The lender will require **copies of leases.** For purposes of qualifying for a loan the standard is that the lease be for a period of at least a year with 3 or more months remaining. This will vary by lender. If you don't have a lease and operate on a month-to-month basis, many lenders will require that you execute at the very minimum a one-year lease with a 30 days' notice by either party. If the term remaining is less than two to three months, a new lease or a tenants' affidavit, stating that they plan to renew the lease, is acceptable. Other lenders will accept tax returns that show the property has been rented in the past plus a tenants' affidavit that they plan on living there for the foreseeable future.

If the tax returns show less than 25% vacancy and expense, the lender may allow the lower figure. Depreciation is always added back into the income when you are looking at Schedule E—Supplemental Income and Loss (from Rents, royalties, partnerships, estates, trusts, REMIC, etc.) on your tax returns. Adding back the depreciation will almost always create a positive cash flow on the Schedule E.

So, for rent income, you have the 75% factor, the operating income statement, the *Marshall Swift Handbook,* one-year lease, tenants' affidavit, and tax returns with Schedule E. Depending on whether the property is owner- or nonowner-occupied, the lender will require any or all of the above items in order to use the income for qualifying, or limiting the debt. If you are using rent to qualify, it should be safe to use the 75% factor.

The Self-Employed Borrower.   I have saved the best for last, the Self-Employed Borrower—the entrepreneur who has risked all to make large sums of money on which little or no taxes are due owing to large business expense write-offs. What a great life! That is, until you have to go to a mortgage lender.

Remember, income must be verified. How do you verify a self-employed borrower's income? By getting copies of his or her FULL tax returns, with original signatures, for the past two years. Plus a year-to-date Profit and Loss (P&L) statement, and a year-to-date Balance Sheet, if the borrower is incorporated or a partnership. The Balance Sheet and P&L statement must be done by an accountant or bookkeeper and signed by the preparer. A few lenders will not allow year-to-date income to be used if it is not from an audited P&L. Let's look at the details.

A borrower who is self-employed should have been in that position for at least two years. A shorter period may be acceptable in some situations if the borrower was doing essentially the same thing previously. A one- to one-and-a-half-year period may be acceptable, if you can demonstrate that your income is stable and increasing and can be reasonably expected to continue. If you bought an existing business that has been profitable, the lender may look at you after one year if you show that you are capable of continuing to make a profit.

Now, when I say make a profit, I mean enough money to live on, not just break even. The interesting thing about being self-employed is that it is not hard to lose money for tax purposes. Nevertheless, the bottom line is that the lender will look at your net income, after adjustments for paper loss add-backs such as depreciation. Do not expect the lender to fall for the routine about really making more than the tax returns show.

There are several different ways one can be self-employed. You can be a sole proprietor, a partner, an independent contractor, or incorporated, which has several different categories in itself.

Sole proprietor.   The **sole proprietor** is a self-employed person who simply earns his living by practicing a trade without benefit of being a partnership or corporation. At the end of the year, a sole proprietor files a normal tax return with at least a Schedule C, and usually several additional schedules.

Under the basic guidelines, the lender will look at your **tax returns, for the last two years with all schedules, signed by you, and a year-to-date P&L statement** prepared by a third party such as a bookkeeper or accountant. You don't normally need a balance sheet, because all the business assets are personal assets. The lender will take the net income for both years and YTD, add back all paper losses, add the totals, and divide by the number of months represented. The result will be the monthly income used to qualify.

Most people will show a profit. And the add backs can make a considerable difference. Because tax laws change frequently, some things may or may not be usable. Right now, we can talk about the basic ones.

Depreciation is number one. It truly is a paper loss and is added back into the net income. This can account for many thousands of dollars per year.

Depletion is another add-back. Without oil or gas wells, you probably won't need to worry about it.

The write-off for **use of part of your home for your business is usually** added back to the extent the room is used. The house payment is already considered a debt, so there is no need to hit you twice.

Unusual, one-time, nonrecurring expenses can often be added back or prorated over a longer period. An example would be the purchase of a $9,000 copier which you elected to write off under Office Expense. Because it is unlikely that you would spend $9,000 on a copier every year, most lenders will prorate it for three to five years, so that on a 5-year schedule, $7,200 would be added back. Of course, the best way to write it off is by depreciating it, instead of the one-time deduction.

On the first page of your federal 1040 form, you can add back most of the items listed under Adjustments to Income. **IRAs and Keoghs** are income that is not taxed. **Alimony** will be counted as a debt, so it can be added to income. **Penalty for early withdrawal** of savings can be added back as long as it is not recurring. As we discussed earlier, income or losses from schedule E can be adjusted usually to show a profit. A **capital loss** can be added back if you do not claim it on a regular basis, just as a **capital gain** is not counted unless it is claimed on a regular basis. People who buy and sell real estate and/or stocks continually would claim some type of capital gain or loss.

On the subject of tax returns, it is important the borrower understand that the lender can find several things that the borrower may not be eager to have known—things such as alimony payments, partnership in a money-losing business venture, or rents from properties that the borrower did not acknowledge owning. I had one couple who wrote off over $9,000 in one year for a show dog that they owned. Tax returns can often show debts or other obligations the borrower would never have considered revealing to the lender.

Another type of sole proprietorship is the **independent contractor.** Realtors are among the most common in this category. They work as an independent contractor for the company, with some of the costs of doing business paid by the company. In return, the agents split their commissions on all sales with the company. The agents are given W-9 forms by the company for tax purposes (instead of a W-2), and they use Schedule C to write off their own expenses.

Sometimes, the borrower cannot to come up with year-to-date figures for expenses. In such cases, some lenders will average expenses claimed on the Schedule C for the past two years and then subtract that adjusted average from the gross income (almost all borrowers know how much they have taken in). This procedure is appropriate as long as the expenses are not abnormally high or low for either of the years.

Let us consider an example for which the gross income of our sole proprietor for the first ten months of 1991 is $100,000. Expenses (adjusted for depreciation and so on) in 1989 were $22,000 and in 1990 were $31,000. Summing, $22,000 + $31,000 = $53,000 and dividing by 24 months = $2,209 average expense for one month. So, $2,209 × 10 months = $22,093 average expense for ten months. Thus, 1991 YTD net income = $77,907.

Partnerships.   Being a partner in a partnership is midway between being a sole proprietor and being incorporated. The difference is you are in business with other people and together you file a partnership return. In turn, you will have a Form 1065 to fill out on your returns to claim your portion of the income or loss.

For the lender, the key is whether the borrower **owns 25% or more of the partnership.** If it is less than that, only personal tax returns may be required if the borrower is using income from the partnership to qualify, or if there is debt associated with the partnership that must be disclosed. But, if the borrower owns 25% or more, then the borrower's **personal returns for the past two years, two years complete partnership returns, and YTD P&L and balance sheet.** Many a loan has been stymied when the other partners refused to allow the borrower to provide these documents.

Corporations.   The incorporated borrower can be **sole stockholder or own 25% or more** of the corporation. In either case the lender will require **full personal tax returns for two years, full corporate returns for two years, a YTD P&L, and a balance sheet.** If she owns less than 25%, then a simple VOE will verify her income. The lender needs to know if the borrower is the corporation, or works for it.

The lender needs to see if the company can indeed afford to pay the borrower the income she claims. In addition, it wants to see how viable the company is, if there are any debts that the borrower may ultimately be liable for, and if the company is being used as a cash cow, to be milked of all its income and assets, leaving a shell. The documents will show the lender if the borrower's employment and income are reliable and recurring.

In summary, the self-employed, partnership, or corporation borrower will need to provide the following:

1. Past two years, full federal tax returns with all schedules, and original signatures.

2. Year-to-date profit & loss statement (within the current quarter) prepared and signed by a third party (accountant or bookkeeper). Some lenders may require that it be audited in order to use the YTD income. This is required for sole proprietors, partnerships, and corporations.

3. Past two years, full federal partnership returns, signed.

4. Past two years, full federal corporate returns, signed.

5. Balance sheet (within the current quarter) prepared and signed by a third party. This is required for partnerships and corporations. The two years' and YTD net income are averaged for the number of months that are represented. This is the income used to qualify the borrower.

I have provided a basic *Self-Employed Income Analysis* form in the Appendix for anyone who would like to figure out what their usable income for qualifying might be.

*The Low Documentation Loan—The More Cash Down,
the More They Trust You*

There has been a way to avoid all the paper work above called the *Low Doc* or *No Income Verified Loan*. Depending on the lender and the loan, if the borrower put down between 20% and 30% cash, the income was not verified. The standard had been 30%, but various lenders have had programs whose minimum cash down varied. These loans have not been sold in the normal secondary market. Their requirements have sometimes been misleading. If you find any of these loans available, check them out carefully before committing to one.

If you noticed, I said "has been a way . . . ." Fannie and Freddie no longer will buy "No Income Verified" loans (as of spring 1991). As you might surmise, too many people, both borrowers and lenders, have abused this loan causing a higher than normal rate of defaults. Fannie does still offer the *Time Saver Documentation* loan, which only requires the most recent year's tax returns and allows substitution of documents, such as three months bank statements instead of a VOD. Freddie will also allow substitution of documentation, but does not accept just one year's tax return (as of 1991). Some investors out there may still be buying the No Income Verified loan. How long they will continue to offer them and what the price will be to the borrower is anyone's guess. Check with your local lenders to see if they offer this loan.

The Second Job and Other Part-Time Income

As people stretch to make ends meet, a second job may become a necessity. Lenders recognize this income as long as they are assured it will continue. Getting a second job for the extra income just to qualify is not going to help in the short run. Fannie and Freddie will use income from a second job only if you have held a second job for **at least two years, continuously.** It can be the same job or successive jobs. (VA will normally have the same time requirement as a conventional loan, while FHA may allow shorter periods.) The reasoning for this guideline is that the lender does not want the borrower to get a part-time job just to qualify and then later quit. If the person has been in a second job for at least two years, chances of continuation are great.

There are many other potential sources of exotic income, and the use of them for qualifying comes down to a very simple rule: It must be **reliable, recurring, verifiable, and extend into the future for at least three to five years.** Different lenders will interpret the rules to fit their secondary investor's guidelines by expanding or contracting the necessary documentation and time periods.

3

MAKING THE PAYMENTS
Avoiding Deficit Spending

The lender looks at your income and determines what is usable in order to be assured that that income is sufficient to make the mortgage payment, carry all current debt, and have money left for normal living expenses. Any excess income makes the borrower that much more qualified for the loan, and can make the lender more flexible. Here, again, you are faced with the basic guidelines established by Fannie and Freddie.

The two areas in which the borrower must qualify are **Income to Total Housing Expense,** and **Income to Total Housing Expense Plus Monthly Debt Payments.** The standard for mortgage loan payments is called the **Total Housing Expense,** and this includes the following:

1. **Principal and interest** payment (PI)
2. **One twelfth of the annual real estate taxes** (T)
3. **One twelfth of the annual homeowner's insurance premium** (I)
4. **Mortgage insurance** escrow, if the loan is over 80% LTV (MI)
5. One twelfth of any **homeowners association or maintenance fee,** if one is charged (HOA)

WHAT THE HOUSE PAYMENT REALLY PAYS (PITI)

The **principal and interest payment** is the payment necessary to amortize, or pay off, the loan amount (principal) and the interest over the specified term, such as 30 years. You can figure this payment by buying a financial calculator or a book of amortization tables, calling your local lender or Realtor, or using the table in the back of this book.

With the **homeowner's insurance**, the lender is only concerned that the dwelling itself is covered by the hazard portion of the insurance policy in the amount of the loan. (Some states now have laws that prohibit the lender from forcing the borrower to insure the dwelling for the loan amount if the value of the dwelling without the land is less than the loan amount.) All homeowners should get full coverage for things like theft and liability; buying enough coverage only to satisfy the lender would be a bad decision.

The hazard part of the homeowner's insurance protects not only the owner but also the lender in case the house, that is, the security for the loan, is damaged or destroyed. For that reason, most lenders require that the insurance policy be paid up in full for the first year at the time the loan closes; then the lender escrows one twelfth of that premium in the monthly payment. When the policy renewal date comes around the next year, there will be enough money in escrow to pay it again for another full year. By doing this, the lender is protected against the possibility that the owner will forget to pay the premium and end up owing the lender on a pile of ashes, instead of a house, if it burns down. It is possible to find a lender that does not require the insurance to be escrowed, but the borrower will be required to have a down payment of 20% or more.

Real estate taxes will be escrowed by just about all lenders because unpaid and past due taxes take a prior lien to any mortgage. If the owner does not pay them, then the local government has the power to sell the property in order to collect the delinquent taxes. If the owner owes $3,000 in taxes and $100,000 on the mortgage, the government is only concerned about the $3,000. When the property is sold for taxes, and someone pays $3,000 for a $200,000 property, the taxes are paid and the lender is left holding the bag. (Tax sales are one of the ways that those syndicated, get-rich-quick real estate seminars recommend as a path to the easy life. In reality, this type of thing does not happen so frequently as they might suggest. The lender will buy the property to protect its interests long before it lets the security disappear.) Tax escrow is a safeguard against the possibility that the mortgage lien position could be jeopardized. And let me add that the borrower will not necessarily be off the hook if there is no longer a house to secure the loan. The lender can, and will, file a deficiency judgment against the borrower for any amount still owed on the original mortgage. Try to borrow money with a large, mortgage-sized judgment against you.

Almost assuredly, the insurance and tax escrows will make your payment rise each year. It is ironic that most homeowners want this increase to happen. If the house goes up in value (which you hope it does), you will need to increase your insurance coverage, and the locality where you live will raise the assessed value, and your taxes. The good news, if that is how you want to see it, is that the one twelfth of these increases added to your monthly PI payment should not make much difference in the new total payment.

If you put down less than 20%, and get a mortgage for over 80% LTV, you will be required to have **mortgage insurance.** This insurance covers the lender against the possibility of default and foreclosure on loans of over 80% LTV. If you put down 20% on almost all loans, you don't have to worry about it.

If you live in a development that has a **mandatory homeowner's association fee or some other type of assessment**, this fee will be considered as part of your housing expense. The lender will not escrow for it, but it will be counted in the qualifying process because it is a mandatory expense. Most association dues or assessments are for maintenance of roads and common areas. Others, mostly in town house and condominium developments, will also cover outside maintenance, trash collection, and cable television subscription. These developments are generally called **Planned Unit Developments, or PUDs.** These costs are not optional, and they can be very expensive. Make sure you understand exactly what they are and what they cost before committing to buy. Some states now require that the purchaser be notified within a few weeks of signing a contract to purchase that there are covenants and restrictions, and that they contain homeowner fees.

4

L-T-V (LOAN-TO-VALUE) MEANS R-E-S-P-E-C-T

Now we know that the house payment can include principal, interest, taxes, insurance, mortgage insurance, and homeowner's association fees (PITIMIHOA). Based on standard secondary market guidelines, this total mortgage payment should not exceed 28% of your total gross monthly income (GMI). As we discussed earlier, the ratio for housing plus debt is 36%. These ratios can expand or contract, depending on several factors.

You want to show the lender that you are a good risk. The more positive factors you can demonstrate, the easier it is to qualify and the more the qualifying ratios can expand. Or, the more negative factors, the harder it is to qualify and the less flexible the ratios will be. A deciding factor is the amount of cash that you put down and the resultant loan-to-value (LTV) ratio.

While you can figure out the actual LTV by dividing the loan amount by the purchase price—for example, a $90,000 loan divided by a $100,000 sales price equals 90% LTV with 10% down—the lender uses a different point of view. Using a $100,000 sales price and a $92,000 loan, most people would calculate a 92% LTV, and they would be right, and wrong. Lenders will acknowledge that this situation represents 92% of the value and 8% equity (cash down) in the property, but for qualifying purposes they look at loans in multiples of 5%. Take that 92% loan. In the lender's eyes, it is considered a 95% loan, just as an 87% loan would be considered as a 90% loan and a 80.01% loan would be 85% LTV for qualifying. Lenders round up to the next nearest 5%. Any loan with less than a 20% down payment will be considered a high-risk loan, requiring mortgage insurance. The idea is that the less cash that you put down, the greater the risk. So, if you want a high-risk loan, you have to show that you, as the borrower, can minimize that risk.

If you put down the bare minimum (5% cash) allowed for conventional loans, some lenders will use the more conservative ratios of **25%** for housing expense and **33%** for housing expense and monthly debt. They will rarely go over maxima of 28% and 36%, respectively. And remember, on loans with less than 10% down, all monthly debts are counted, not just those with over 10 months remaining. The more cash you put down, the more secure the lender feels.

On average, for any home loan on which a borrower defaulted and on which the lender foreclosed, the lender has received about 80% of the property's value. When you put down less than that magic 20%, the lender starts to squirm.

No lender wants to face the possibility of having to foreclose on a $100,000 house with a $90,000 loan and ending up with $80,000 with which to pay off the loan and expenses. That is bad economics. Borrowers argue that they are good credit risks and that the house will appreciate quickly anyway. Therefore, the lender will be covered in a short time by normal inflation. That is true—as long as the property does appreciate, which is certainly not a given. Besides, what will protect the lender from a recession, or a depression, or devaluation (say a copper smelter is built next door), or the borrower being fired, or gambling away the house payment, or declaring bankruptcy? Even if you can prove very persuasively that you are a well-qualified borrower at the time, the lender wants to cover the possibility that you may turn into a pumpkin after the loan is closed.

One way that lenders insure themselves against high-risk loans is to require that the loan have **mortgage insurance.** Remember the mortgage insurance escrow that I said could be included in your monthly payment? If you have sufficient cash to put down 20%, then that will save you the cost of mortgage insurance and allow the lending company to be more liberal in their qualifying.

However, what if you only have enough cash for 10% down? You have several choices. You can put down your 10% and get the mortgage insurance. You can "hit up" the proverbial rich relative for the other 10% as a gift. Or you can get an 80% loan, put down the 10% cash, and get a second deed of trust mortgage for the other 10%—if you qualify.

SECOND MORTGAGES
Spreading the debt

If the lender and the type of loan will allow it—and you qualify—
then you can get a first mortgage plus a second mortgage and not
have to pay mortgage insurance on the first mortgage. Certain
loans will still require some mortgage insurance coverage because of the total risk involved. While the first mortgage lender
is in a low risk position in case of foreclosure, it will scrutinize the borrower more closely because of the higher possibility
that default could occur. Don't assume that, because the first
mortgage is 80% LTV or less, the lender is not as concerned.
People who put less of their own cash into a property will always have a higher probability of defaulting. Not only is their
payment higher, but they will also have less to lose monetarily
if they are foreclosed upon.

Most lenders will allow the borrower to get a second mortgage that, in combination with the first, will equal up to 90%
total loan-to-value (TLTV). Others will only go to 85% TLTV.

The first mortgage will be first in line, or in the first position. In any situation where the loans are to be paid off (sale of
the house, foreclosure, sale for nonpayment of taxes, and so on)
the first will always be paid off before any other mortgage. The
second mortgage, being in the second position, will be paid off
second, that is, if there is any money left to pay it.

Secondary market investors have begun to recognize that
second mortgages are putting them more at risk, so Fannie Mae
and Freddie Mac have set guidelines for the maximum TLTV:

I. *Single family dwellings, maximum TLTV*

    A. 90% TLTV on owner-occupied and second homes,
with the first not to exceed 75% LTV

    B. 70% TLTV on nonowner occupied-homes, with
the first to be a fixed rate loan only

II. *Two-unit dwellings, maximum TLTV*

    A. 90% TLTV on owner-occupied homes, with the
first not to exceed 75% LTV

    B. 70% TLTV on nonowner occupied-homes, with
the first to be a fixed rate loan only

III. *Three- to four-unit dwellings, maximum TLTV*
   A. 80% TLTV on owner-occupied homes, with the first not to exceed 75% LTV
   B. 70% TLTV on nonowner-occupied homes, with the first to be a fixed rate only

As you can see, lenders don't mind a second mortgage; just don't ask them to give you a high LTV on the first. These ratios are used only when you are applying for the first mortgage. After you have the first mortgage, there is currently no prohibition to getting as high a second mortgage as possible. Some lenders allow an 80% LTV first mortgage with a 90% TLTV, especially if you have mortgage insurance on the first mortgage. This case is called an "80–10–10" loan (80% first mortgage, 10% second, 10% down). If you need it, check with your lenders; they may have a loan that will allow it. In any instance, this type of financing will have limited availability.

Second mortgages are higher-risk loans, and as such, will normally carry a higher interest rate and a quicker payoff period. Typically, they will be 1–5% higher in interest rate and will amortize out, or have a payoff period, in 3 to 15 years. It is rare to find a second mortgage that goes beyond 15 years, except in some combination loans when you get the first and second mortgages together from the same lender, or unless the TLTV is low. What does a second mortgage have to do with qualifying? The amortization period is short and the payment is higher, adding to the housing expense. The payment on the second mortgage must also be added to the house payment in qualifying you. It is part of your Total Housing Expense.

THE QUICKER YOU PAY, THE LESS YOU PAY

If you compare a payment for a 30-year and a 15-year loan, you will notice that the 15-year payment is much higher than the 30-year one (see the comparison in the appendix). For example, on a $50,000 loan at 10%, the monthly payment for a 30-year loan is $438.79, for a 15-year, $537.30.

This difference is due to the fact that the 15-year payment includes **a higher amount of principal** each month, meaning that the loan is paid off quicker, in 15 years. (When we discuss loan types, I will show you a little trick that shortens the amortization on loans.)

Let us consider as an example the purchase of a $100,000 property with $10,000 down (10%), an $80,000 first mortgage (80% LTV) at 10% for 30 years, and a $10,000 second mortgage (10%) at 11.5% for 15 years. The loan payments would look like this:

1st	$ 702.06	P&I (principal and interest)
2nd	116.82	P&I
Total	$ 818.88	P&I

The $818.88 figure will be used, along with escrows and any HOA fees, to qualify. Now we can add yet another possible expense to the list making up the total house payment:

1. Principal and interest payment (PI)
2. One twelfth of homeowner's insurance (I)
3. One twelfth of annual real estate taxes (T)
4. Mortgage insurance escrow, if required (MI)
5. Homeowner's association fees, if required (HOA)
6. Other financing, such as a second mortgage, third mortgage, and so on

THE EQUITY LINE OF CREDIT

The equity line of credit, which has become extremely popular since the mid-1980s, is also a second mortgage, unless there is no other mortgage on the property. Then it will be a first. Unlike a mortgage, however, it is a **revolving line of credit** that allows the homeowner to borrow against it repeatedly. Pay it down, and then borrow again just like a credit card, which it is, with one very important distinction. This credit is secured by your home, and if you don't make the payments the lender can foreclose and you lose your house. This consequence is more severe than the poor credit rating and judgment that the typical bank card can impose. Using equity line of credit as a second mortgage to purchase a home is a viable idea as long as you can make the higher payments. Most equity lines require monthly payments of 1.5% to 2% of the remaining principal balance. Using a line of credit for other expenses requires more thought. Education expenses, debt consolidation (if you cancel the credit being consolidated), and home improvements are some of the more logical debts. Cruises around-the-world and stereo sound systems are not. As in all things tax-deductible, congress is considering ways to delimit the expenses paid out of a line of credit that can remain tax-deductible.

IN THE END, YOU STILL HAVE TO QUALIFY

Now that you know your usable income, house payment, long-term debt (within a safe approximation), and the ratios discussed earlier, let's summarize the criteria for qualifying for a conventional mortgage:

I. *Loans over 90% LTV*

   A. **25%** to maximum **28%** of gross monthly income (GMI) for total housing expense (principal, interest, taxes, home owner's insurance, mortgage insurance, homeowner's association/ condo/road fees if applicable) = PITI/MI/HOA.

   B. **33%** to maximum **36%** of GMI for total housing expense plus all monthly debt payments (including short-term debt) = PITI/MI/HOA/DEBT

   C. There is little flexibility on 95% LTV loans because of the high risk.

II. *90% LTV and less*

   A. **28%** of GMI for housing expense. (With little or no debt and/or with other factors and sufficient cash down, this can go as high as 31%+.)

   B. **36%** of GMI for housing expense plus all long-term monthly debts with more than 10 months left to pay off. (This ratio is not so flexible, but it can go higher, depending again on compensating factors.)

There will always be lenders and loans that do not fit the basic secondary market guidelines. For example, I know of one investor who will do ratios of 40%/40%, instead of the 28%/36%. But this loan is very restrictive as to which borrowers and properties it will take. In addition, the loan is very expensive. Always ask your lender what the company will allow. Also, FHA and VA criteria are different from conventional qualifying, as you will discover when you read the section on them. Try to qualify under the most conservative scenario, then start adding other factors if they are needed. The cleaner and simpler the loan, the easier it is to approve.

Now that we have gone through the borrower's life with a fine-tooth comb, everything else should be easy. After all, the borrower makes enough money, has great credit, and has the money to buy the house. There should be no need to bug her anymore, right? As much as everyone, the lender included, would like to agree, it just ain't so.

MORTGAGE INSURANCE
For those long on income and short on cash

Mortgage insurance can influence not only the borrower's house payment but also his ability to qualify. Earlier we briefly discussed the fact that any loan with less than 20% down will require mortgage insurance. Now we need to understand exactly how it affects our loan, and our ability to get it.

Many borrowers confuse mortgage insurance with mortgage life insurance, which pays off the mortgage if the borrower dies. While the lender doesn't want the borrower to die, it is more concerned about the fate of the loan. Historically, when a borrower has gone to foreclosure and the house has been sold, the lender received only about 80% of the value of the property. Also, the first years of a mortgage are the years of greatest risk. These facts mean several things to the borrower:

1. The less cash you put down, the more expensive the mortgage insurance.
2. If the type of loan is a higher risk, such as an ARM or any loan with increasing payments, the mortgage insurance is more expensive.
3. The insurance is more expensive in the first year.

Mortgage insurance protects the lender against loss if there is a default and foreclosure on the mortgage. Normally mortgage insurance covers the top 25% of the loan, thereby reducing the lender's exposure to 75% of the value.

For example, consider a $100,000 purchase made with 5% down. That creates a very high risk for the lender. In a foreclosure situation it could lose $15,000 or more. The company is not interested in making a high LTV loan without some protection, so it requires that the borrower purchase mortgage insurance to lower the risk.

There are about 20 mortgage insurance companies that lenders use. Most lenders have companies that they prefer to deal with because they have developed a good working relationship. Most of these companies' rates fall within a close competitive range, but they can change periodically. Before submitting the loan to the underwriter for approval, the lender will choose the mortgage insurance company that they feel will give the best service. The borrower is not involved in this part of the process other than to pay the premium.

As a loan originator, I use one company in particular; it does not have the lowest rates, but it does give the best service by far. And service is important, because even if the lender approves the loan it still must be approved by the mortgage insurance company. The last thing a lender wants is to spend time arguing the merits of a loan with an underwriter. Another reason a lender will use a specific mortgage insurance company is that it is strong financially. A weak company that ultimately goes out of business won't do the lender any good if one of its insured loans goes belly up.

One More Underwriter

The mortgage insurance company gets a copy of the loan package that is sent to the lender's underwriter. Even though the lender approves the loan, it still will be contingent on getting mortgage insurance approval. If that is not forthcoming, the loan will not close.

The lender for which I work had a borrower who applied for a 90% loan that was approved by my underwriter. Subsequently, the mortgage insurance underwriter rejected the loan. I then went for the shotgun approach, submitting the loan package to all of the mortgage insurance companies with which I dealt. They all turned this borrower down. At 90% LTV, I had a dead loan. Fortunately, the borrower's parents gave him the additional 10% down, negating the mortgage insurance requirement.

This loan was unusual, because mortgage insurance companies often have slightly less stringent guidelines than lenders. In fact, some of their criteria purposely do not fit the Fannie and Freddie guidelines so as to accommodate some of the other less-restrictive loans bought by other investors. Having more flexible guidelines is also another way for mortgage insurance companies to be more competitive. But, for Fannie and Freddie lenders the point is moot. The loan must meet the more restrictive guidelines.

The Less Your Down Payment, the More It Costs

The purchase of mortgage insurance will allow less cash down and a higher loan amount, but it will cost you. How much? That depends on the cash down, the loan term, the type of loan, the particular mortgage insurance company, and the type of premium that is paid. I will use a standard premium plan to explain how it works.

Standard coverage works just like regular homeowner's or life insurance in that there is an annual premium for the coverage. However, with mortgage insurance the first year's premium is much higher than the renewal premiums. On a 95% LTV 30-year fixed rate loan, a typical first-year premium would be right around 1% of the loan amount. That's right, $950 on a $95,000 loan. Think about those $180,000 loans. It's expensive, and you have to pay it at closing as part of your closing costs. (Closing Costs are covered in detail in Chapter 10.) The renewal premium will be around 0.39% to 0.49% of the loan amount each year through the tenth year. After the tenth year the premium is cut in half, and if you keep it the full 30 years, the thirtieth year does not have a premium. By then, I guess they feel pretty secure.

The 0.39% premium equals $370.50 per year ($95,000 × 0.39%) and is escrowed into your monthly payment. One twelfth is $30.88 per month. This is added to the PITI payment and the **PITI/MI** payment is used to qualify.

If you put more cash down, the premiums are less. The rates of one mortgage insurance company look like this for a 30-year fixed rate:

	Loan-to-Value		
	95%	90%	85%
Up-front premium	1.00%	0.40%	0.30%
Renewal premium	0.49	0.34	0.29
(Per 100 of loan amount)			

For a 15-year rate, premiums are cheaper:

	95%	90%	85%
Up-front premium	0.90%	0.40%	0.25%
Renewal premium	0.25	0.20	0.20
(Per 100 of loan amount)			

These numbers only show what the relative cost can be. Premiums change with time and companies (See mortgage insurance comparison chart in the Appendix).

To stay competitive and to offer a premium similar to FHA (see Chapter 5), mortgage insurance companies now offer a **one-time, financed premium** that not only is cheaper, but also adds nothing to your closing costs. Let us consider a 30-year fixed rate loan on a $100,000 purchase with $8,000 down. The premium is added into the loan amount like this:

$92,000 × 2.50% (premium) = $2,300.00

$92,000 + $2,300 = $94,300 loan with premium financed.

The payment is then based on $94,300. The premium used is only for illustration, and is not reliable. A similar 15-year fixed rate premium would be about 1.20%.

Note that, if the premium is financed, the total loan amount on fixed rate loans, say for a 95% LTV situation, can never exceed 95%. Likewise, on a 90% LTV, the loan amount with the premium financed cannot exceed 90%. At one time you could exceed the LTV on a fixed rate loan by the amount of the premium, but not on adjustable rate mortgages (ARMs) and buydowns. Fannie Mae and Freddie Mac made the changes to have standard LTV levels. Now all loans are the same. Just as in the case of renewal premiums, the more cash you put down, the lower the premium. This type of mortgage insurance works best when you are putting down 7% to 13%, and you are very tight on cash to close.

Let's compare the costs of up-front plus renewal premiums for mortgage insurance with the financed premium on a $92,000 loan at 10% for 30 years.

	Up-front/renewal	Financed
PI/MI payments	$844.94: $807.37 PI + $37.57 MI	$827.55
Additional Closing costs	$995.14: $920 (1% up-front premium) + 75.14 (2 months' renewal in escrow)	-0- in closing costs
Savings	None	$17.39 per month

Again, these figures are only for illustration. Call a lender for current rates. If you have the cash to put into equity, you can cut down your out-of-pocket, nonequity expenses by a significant amount.

If you don't have the cash to put down, and you don't have all of the cash necessary for all of the closing costs, there is one more type of mortgage insurance program that might fit. Most mortgage insurance companies offer **the up-front financed program.** It has a normal up-front and renewal premium, except that the up-front premium is financed into the loan, leaving only the renewal premium escrows to be paid at closing.

A final question on mortgage insurance is, Can the borrower drop it when the loan reaches 80% LTV or below? For Fannie and Freddie, the answer is yes. For other investors, you should ask your lender. In general, you must wait at least two years before requesting the removal of mortgage insurance. You must also show either that the value of the property, by a current appraisal, has increased sufficiently to cover the 80% LTV mark or that the principal has been paid down to at least 80% of the original value of the property. If you have a financed premium, a portion of it may be refundable to you. (Some mortgage insurance companies offer two types of financed premium, refundable and nonrefundable.) At one time the only way most borrowers could get rid of the mortgage insurance once they had it was to refinance their loan, a much more expensive alternative. (See information in the Appendix on requirements to remove mortgage insurance.)

5

LOAN TYPES
The ABCs of FRMs, ARMs, GPMs, GEMs, FHAs, and VAs

Although we have looked at many pitfalls and requirements the borrower must understand, we have not yet considered the most important one—the reason that a borrower comes to a lender in the first place—the loan itself. If you think Baskin-Robbins has a lot of choices, start calling all your local lenders. There are so many variations on the loans offered today that even the lenders themselves can get confused. As a result, many lenders emphasize their basic loans plus whatever the special of the moment might be. The special is usually a loan that the home office wants them to market aggressively because it has a lot of money invested in this particular loan program. Sometimes the special is a loan the originator understands and thinks is great. During periods of high interest rate, you will see a tremendous increase in the numbers and types of adjustable rate mortgages (ARMs) and buy-down loans. During periods of low rates, lenders will duel over who can show the lowest rates by raising the discount points. Remember, the lower the rate, the higher the discount points. The borrowers' problem is to decide the following:

1. Which type of loan best suits their situation?
2. What differences in the same basic loan offered by different lenders are worthwhile and are advantageous to the borrower?

3. How much they are willing to pay for the loan?
4. Which lender will give them the best service on the loan they choose?

Some of these questions can be answered only by the borrowers, but a competent lender can give invaluable guidance. To start the process, you must first separate the different types of loans, then compare the advantages and disadvantages.

FIXED RATE MORTGAGES (FRMs)

The plain old stodgy, fixed rate loan is still the best for many people. You know what your payment will be every year. You don't have to worry about interest rate increases. You can budget for it very easily. And, if your loan requires it, your mortgage insurance costs less. When interest rates are low (less than 10.5%) it is hard to go wrong with a fixed rate loan.

These loans can be obtained in just about any amortization period that the borrower could want. The standard periods for mortgage loans are 30, 25, 20, 15, and sometimes 10 years. If a loan has an amortization period of 20 years, it will take 20 years of making the monthly payment to pay it off. The shorter the amortization period, the less interest the borrowers will pay because they will not owe the money for as long a period. A 15-year loan will have almost half the interest payments of a 30-year loan at a comparable rate. If we compare $100,000 loans at 10%, keeping the loans for their complete terms, the interest paid would look like this:

30-year: $215,925.20
15-year: $ 93,429.80

As you can see, 15 years is much cheaper. And, making an even better deal, 15-year interest rates are almost always lower than 30-year rates. The lesson here is that the shorter the amortization period, the less costly the loan. Occasionally someone makes the observation that because mortgage interest is almost the only deductible interest remaining on the federal income tax schedules (at least it was when I wrote this), one shouldn't worry about rates or amortization period. This person also doesn't think the federal deficit is something to worry about either. Everyone is entitled to a personal opinion. That's why there are different loan choices.

One reason someone might choose a 30-year loan over the 15-year is that the payment is much lower. The borrower often can qualify for the 30- but not for the 15-year loan. Let's see what the difference is. Using our $100,000 loan at 10%, the monthly payments (PI) would be:

    30-year: $ 877.57
    15-year: $1,074.61

The difference is $197.04 per month. The obvious reason for this is that payments on the 15-year loan reduces the principal amount much more quickly. (See the loan amortization comparison Appendix.) Without considering tax and insurance escrows and using the 28% ratio, we find that the qualifying incomes for the two loans would be:

    30-year: $3,134.18 gross monthly income
    15-year: $3,837.89 gross monthly income

Or about a $8,500 difference in annual income.

Prepayment

There is a way to have your cake and eat it too. Remember that I referred earlier to a way that you could design your own loan? Most loans, and all Fannie-Freddie loans, have no **prepayment penalties**. That means you can pay off any or all of your loan principal at any time without penalty. There are some loans out there that do have a penalty, so make sure you ask your lender. If your loan doesn't, you can get creative.

Say you want the $100,000 loan at 10% and you want the 15-year payout, but you can only qualify for the 30-year loan. Get the 30-year loan and make the corresponding 15-year payment. That is, pay the extra $197.04 per month and you will have paid the loan off in 15 years. You have accelerated the amortization, and there's no penalty!

There are a few shortcomings. As you remember, 15-year loans have lower rates than 30-year ones. You may have to accept a 10% 30-year amortization, which you pay off in 15 years, instead of a 9.75% 15-year rate. That is a small price considering the fact that you are able to get the loan, buy the house, and pay it off in 15 years.

If you can't make the 15-year payment, compromise on $50 or $100 more a month—whatever you can afford. It will still accelerate the amortization and pay the loan off faster. You are only required to make the 30-year payment. Only you can take the initiative and create the motivation to make the higher payment every month.

Some lenders will require that any extra payments be made to the nearest $10 or $50. A few will only allow payments in multiples of itself. A $500 payment could only be prepaid as $1,000 or $1,500, and so on.

You can also make payments periodically during the year or even once a year. The latter is done by people who may not be able to make regular extra payments, but who get cash (such as tax refunds) once a year that could be applied. Making extra payments monthly is more effective because they are credited toward the principal at the time they are paid and will lower the interest paid more quickly.

In any case, make sure that the lender understands that you are making a principal prepayment. If the payment coupon shows one amount and the check is for a higher amount, the clerk who credits it may put the extra into escrow until your intention is known (late payment, insufficient escrow of taxes, and so on). Most payment coupons today have a space specifically for principal reduction. If there is not a space, I recommend that you make out your regular check for the normal payment. Then, write a separate check for the additional principal reduction and attach a note stating what it is for. This way there is little chance that it will not be properly credited.

One last advantage to rapid principal reduction is that it is **an enforced savings account**. Every dollar that you put into your home is a dollar that you probably can get out later, along with the appreciation that has occurred. A person's residence is usually the largest single investment that he or she will make, and it will also be the largest part of a person's net worth.

BIWEEKLY MORTGAGES

The biweekly mortgage has slowly gained acceptance from borrowers and, even more slowly, from the general secondary market. It is a marketing bonanza for banks and other depository institutions that are set up to service it. It also allows the borrower to pay his loan off in two-thirds the time.

This mortgage is a fixed rate loan in which the normal monthly payment is split in half and paid every two weeks. Voilà! Biweekly! Because the lender receives part of the principal earlier than with a once-a-month payment, the interest charged is less. Also, over the course of a year the borrower makes 26 payments instead of the normal 24 in a monthly payment. At first the principal reduction is very small. But, if it is carried out to term, a 30-year loan will be paid off around the twentieth year.

The lenders that offer this loan have several requirements. The main one is that you must make your payments by automatic debit draft from your bank account. The reason for this stipulation is that it is just about impossible for an individual to get the payment in on time every two weeks. Any tardiness would play havoc with the bank's ability to service the loan and keep the records straight. It also means that the bank will be assured of a regular deposit account and an obligated depositor. But, because of the headaches of keeping track of a large number of rapidly paying loans, some investors will not buy them. If you are interested, check all your local lenders to see not only if they offer them, but also what is required to get one.

One note of caution: There are companies out there today offering to convert your normal fixed rate, monthly payment mortgage into a biweekly. Look at them very carefully. They are not doing so for free. They normally charge a fee up-front of .5% to 2+%, as well as a fee that is built into the payments. So, you are paying a large cost for the service plus a regular fee in each payment. These extra costs could nullify any advantage you might gain. It is often better just to make extra payments each year that go directly toward reducing your loan payment amortization rather than into someone else's pocket as a fee.

BUY-DOWN LOANS
Pay your money and take your choice

Buy-down loans are in 2 different categories, temporary buy-downs and permanent buy-downs. For the money, permanent buy-downs will usually work out to be the better deal.

Permanent Buy-Downs

The permanent buy-down is simple. You pay more discount points to get a lower rate. There is no absolute as to what the cost will be. One rule of thumb says 1 point (1%) for every one-eighth percent (0.125%) drop in the rate. If you check different lenders' rates, you will see that the costs can be much less, depending on how competitive the lenders are at the time. For example, a lender might be quoting the following:

> 10% with 1 + 0 (1% origination fee+zero discount points)
> 9.875% with 1 + 0.25
> 9.750% with 1 + 1.00
> 9.625% with 1 + 1.75
> 9.500% with 1 + 2.25

Don't try to figure out why the pricing is this way, just decide whether you are willing to pay 2.25% of the loan amount at closing for 0.5% less interest.

Most lenders set rates based on the following:

1. Market rates.
2. Local competition.
3. Regional competition.
4. How they feel the rates are going to move.
5. How much insurance they have on their loan pipeline.
6. How much they need the business.
7. If they are making money or losing money.
8. How lucky they think they can get.

The simplest method of choosing which rate you should buy is deciding **how long you are going to have the loan**. (I am assuming that you have the cash to pay the extra points. Of course, if someone else—like the seller—is paying the points, go for the max.) For example, on a 30-year $100,000 loan with the 2.25 points given above, we can make these calculations:

Rate	Payment(PI)	PI difference	Cost of points	Pay back
10%	$877.57	+$440.64/yr	-0-	-0-
9.5%	$840.85	-$440.64	$2,250.00	5.11 yrs*

*($2,250 divided by yearly savings = Time it will take the savings to pay back the additional discount points)

In this example, the borrower would have to keep the loan for about five years for the savings from the lower payment to equal the additional discount points.

Of course, if you as borrower have to buy down the loan to 9.5% just to qualify, then the decision has at least in part already been made for you. The house itself should appreciate $2,250 in a year during a normal economy (3% on a $75,000 house). If you wait for interest rates to drop (which they may not), the cost of the house may have increased (which it probably will)—if it is still available.

The permanent buy-down offers the advantages of a set rate and payment for the life of the loan. It allows you to obtain a lower rate as well as a lower payment. The only drawback is the additional cost.

It is not unusual for the seller to pay some of the closing costs. Make her an offer. All she can say is no. If the seller is asking $100,000, but will take $97,000, offer $100,000 and get the seller to pay 3 points. You get the house and the lower rate, and the seller sells her house and gets what she wanted. In this situation it is imperative that you have working with you a professional Realtor and a knowledgeable lender who know what they are doing.

Permanent buy-downs can also be done on loans other than fixed rate. By paying more points, you can get a lower initial rate on an adjustable rate or a graduated payment mortgage. We will look at these later.

Temporary Buy-Down

A **temporary buy-down** will give the borrower temporary relief in the form of lower payments for the first few years. This is done by several means. In the traditional type of temporary buy-down loan the borrower simply pays the difference between the actual payments and the initial lower payments in cash at closing in the form of points, normally for either two years (2-1 buy-down) or three years (3-2-1 buy-down).

If you want to lower the payment on our 30-year, $100,000 loan at 10%, this is how it is done:

Payment Rate	PI Payment		Yearly Total	Difference	Total diff
10.000%	$877.57×12	=	$10,530.84	-0-	
9.000	$804.62	"	9,665.44	($865.40)	$865.40
8.000	$733.77	"	8,805.24	(1,725.20)	2,590.60
7.000	$665.30	"	7,983.60	(2,547.24)	5,137.84

If you bought the initial payment for the first year down to 8.00% (2-1 buy-down) the sum of one year of payments at 8% plus one year at 9% would be $2,590.78 (difference between two years of monthly payments of 10% PI and 8% and 9%), plus any normal discount points that would be on the 10% rate that was bought down. You then have monthly payments of $733.77 for the first year, $804.62 for the second, and the normal 10% 30-year payment of $877.57 for the third through the 30th. If you really want to pay a lot, consider the 3-2-1 buy-down to an initial payment of $665.30 for a cost of $5,137.84, or 5.13784% of this particular loan amount of $100,000.

These loans are normally done when the seller, usually a builder, offers to pay the buy-down cost to help sell the house. The buyer qualifies at the initial payment. However, nothing is free. The builder has just added the extra cost into the price of the house. For about the cost of that 2-1 buy-down, you can get a permanent buy-down of 0.25% to 0.5% over the life of the loan. For the cost of the 3-2-1 you could get the same permanent buy-down and take a vacation as well. Or, if you were smart you would invest the $2,590 to $5,137.

Another type of temporary buy-down, **the lender funded buy-down**, is initially very cheap. For this, the lender offers a very attractive initial bought-down rate with minimal, or no, points and sometimes pays most of the closing costs. By the time the loan has adjusted back up to its actual rate, the borrower is paying 0.5% to 1% higher than the current market rate. An example would be a 2-1 buy-down with an initial payment based on a rate of 8% with 1% discount point at closing. The second year the payment is based on 9%, and then it levels out for the remainder at 10%. Not bad as long as you knew when you obtained the loan that the current market rate for a comparable fixed rate loan with similar points was 9.25%. This is not to say it's a bad loan. You just need to know what the market is to make a comparison.

The advantage of a temporary buy-down is that it will get you qualified at a lower payment so you can buy more house than a permanent buy-down at comparable cost. Just remember that you will end up making the higher payments.

Buy-down loans are limited to no more than 90% LTV by most lenders.

THE EQUAL LOAN

Another form of temporary buy-down is a very creative loan that starts out with an interest-only payment. Freddie Mac offers one called the equal loan. For this fixed rate loan the payments start low; then the PI payment increases 7.5% per year until it reaches a year when the payment levels off. (The year of level payment can be anywhere from the second to the eighth year, depending on how far you want to buy it down.) The payment then stays the same for the remainder of the loan term. Equal loans are offered in either 30- or 15-year amortization periods. The 15-year loan is by far the better buy. The most appealing features of this loan are that it only costs a fraction of a normal buy-down and you qualify at the first year's payment.

Freddie Mac does require the lender to show why it feels the borrower will be able to make the higher payments in the later years. Likelihood of increased income, lower debts, increase in assets, completion of an advanced degree would all be factors that could show the borrower's continued ability to make the payments.

Using the $100,000 loan and a 10% rate for both the 15- and 30-year equal loans (the 15-year interest rate will in reality always be lower), here is how they compare. (See p. 76.)

The cost is what you pay to buy the loan down! Compared with the $2,600 to $5,100 on the other buy-downs, $510.00 to buy down the 15-year payment to a starting, and qualifying, payment of $790.79 is cheap indeed.

How do lenders do it? They start the payments at a point where the principal reduction is less than normal. In the first 15-year loan example, the first-year payments are actually less than interest-only payments. The 0.510% cost is the difference between the $790.79 payment and the interest-only payment of $833.34. The payments then increase by 7.5% per year until they reach the level payment year. This payment is sufficient to amortize the loan out over the remaining term.

A normal 15-year 10% loan on $100,000 would have a PI payment of $1,074.61, while the equal loan's level payment beginning in Year 8 is $1,261.73. The $187.12 difference is what is necessary to pay the loan out by the 15th year.

Underlying an equal loan is the idea that borrowers can buy a lot more house with less initial income, as long as their income

	EQUAL LOAN		3-2-1 BUY-DOWN		2-1 BUY-DOWN	
	15-year	30-year	15-year	30-year	15-year	30-year
Buy-down cost	$510.00 (.51%)	$1,074.00 (1.064%)	$4,261.00 (4.261%)	$5,138.00 (5.138%)	$2,152.00 (2.152%)	$2,591.00 (2.591%)
First year Interest Rate	5.0%	8.375%	7.0%	7.0%	8.0%	8.0%
PI Payment:						
1st Year:	$ 790.79	$760.07	$ 898.82	$665.30	$ 955.65	$733.77
2nd Year:	850.10	817.08	955.65	733.77	1,014.27	804.62
3rd Year:	913.86	878.36	1,014.27	804.62	1,074.61	877.57
4th Year:	982.40	889.04	1,074.61	877.57		
5th Year:	1,056.08					
6th Year:	1,135.29					
7th Year:	1,220.44					
8th Year:	1,261.73					
—						
15th year	1,261.73		1,074.61		1,074.61	
30th year		889.04		877.57		877.57

will increase to meet the higher payments. A borrower getting the normal 10% fixed payment 15-year loan would need at least $3,838 per month income, but only $2,825 for the same equal loan requiring initial payments of $790.79. That is a difference of over $12,000 per year. The equal has been called the ultimate Yuppie loan. It allows you to buy now and pay later.

The equal loan is limited to no more than 90% LTV. It is considered a nonfixed payment loan for mortgage insurance purposes, meaning you have to use ARM premiums. If you finance the premium, the total LTV including the financed premium cannot exceed 90%.(Thus, you would need to put down about 12% to 13% cash.)

The equal loan's advantages are these:

1. The initial payments for qualifying are low.
2. The borrower can buy more house for less income.
3. It is a fixed rate loan.
4. You know exactly what your payments will be every year.
5. The payments rise slowly enough to avoid payment shock.
6. Its cost structure is perfect for a buyer who will be in the house only three to five years.
7. The buyer whose income will increase in the future can benefit from this earnings potential.
8. It has a low-cost buy-down.

The disadvantages are these:

1. The payments increase.
2. Your income and debts must keep pace with the higher payments.
3. The note rate will be higher than a normal 15-year straight fixed rate.

ADJUSTABLE RATE MORTGAGES (ARMs)

Also known in some areas as Renegotiable Rate Mortgages (RRMs), Flexible Rate Mortgages (FRMs), or Variable Rate Mortgages (VRMs), these are all the same animal. They have evolved to the point that they now have many of the same basic characteristics.

In the United States the original ARMs were not designed to protect the borrower. As time passed, the consumer received more protection, but, because of increased competition, the lenders themselves took on more of the risk in the form of lower initial rates with fewer points. After the S&L crisis beginning in the late 1980s and the resultant restructuring of the mortgage industry, ARMs have come to more of a middle ground. The initial rates may not be quite so low as they once were, so that a profit is more likely, and the borrower has better protection in the forms of caps on movement of the rate, and disclosures on how the loan works.

An ARM gives the borrower an **initial low payment** that then will be adjusted at a given interval during the loan (every six months, one year, and so on) based on a given benchmark, usually a government or lending index, with caps on the interest rate rise, or fall for each adjustment period and for the life of the loan. That's not too hard to understand, is it? Of course it is. That is why a lender must by law give each borrower a written disclosure of the loan at application.

There are several common features in the disclosures to all ARMs:

1. Initial rate
2. How often the interest rate, and payment, is subject to change
3. Index on which the interest rate change is calculated
4. Margin that is added to the index to determine the new rate
5. Cap on the amount the interest rate can rise or fall:
   a. On each adjustment period
   b. Over the life of the loan

To explain the ARM, I will use a normal one-year ARM as an example.

Initial Rate

The initial rate is the actual interest rate that the borrower will be charged for the first period of the loan. Almost all initial rates are lower by about 2%, plus or minus, than the prevailing fixed rates at the time. For this example, if the fixed rate at the time is

10% for a 30-year loan, let's say the ARM initial rate is 7.75%. (To keep it simple we will not use any discount points, but an ARM normally has 0 to 3 + points. As with any loan, you can pay more points to buy down the rate, in this case the initial rate. However, there are limits on how far down one can buy the initial rate.) At 7.75% you are starting at a rate 2.25% lower than the market fixed rate. The 7.75% is the interest on which your payment is based for the first period of the loan until the first interest rate, and payment, adjustment.

In our example, **the adjustment** will come on the one-year anniversary date of the loan. If the loan closed on June 1, 1990, the first change date would be June 1, 1991. Well, actually it would become effective on that date, but the rate change is calculated sooner. Normally, the lender sets the new rate about 45 calendar days before the effective change date in order to make the adjustment, notify the borrower, and send out a new payment coupon book. Some loans will be adjusted within certain quarters of each year, depending on when the loan closed. As a result the first adjustment could occur sooner or later than the given adjustment period, one year in our example. So, you might have an ARM for which all loans closing June through August be adjusted in June of the next year. Ask your lender to explain it fully.

The Index

How does the lender determine what the new rate will be? One might say it was based on the average air pressure of the bicycle tires in China and to many borrowers this answer would not seem too far wrong. In reality, it is based on some **type of index**. The most common is the index of **U.S. Treasury Securities** for the period of the loan adjustment. In our example it would be the One-Year Treasury Securities Index. This is a compilation of the rates on one-year treasury securities adjusted to a constant maturity. There are other indexes such as the FHLBB (Federal Home Loan Bank Board) index, the Cost of Funds (COF) index for FSLIC (Federal Savings and Loan Insurance Corp.)-insured institutions for all districts or just one district such as the Eleventh District, and even a foreign index, the London Interbank Offered Rate (LIBOR). There may be a Chinese Averaged Bicycle Air Pressure Index (CABAPI) for all I know. In any case, the Treasury Securities Index is the one most widely used, and the one we will use in our example.

Many lenders have the history of the index for the past one to five years. Get them to give you a copy, but don't rely on history to provide a key to what the index will be in the future. An index that has been low every year in May could be the highest in its history the May of the year after you get your loan, thereby giving you the highest possible adjustment.

The index itself changes once a week, and the change is reported by the Federal Reserve. In normal times the index moves in increments of 0.125% to 0.25% in any given week, if it moves at all. Of course, it may move 1% or more when the economy experiences a major event like the stock market crash. The amount of adjustment on an ARM is at the mercy of what the index is on the week the lender makes the change. One week it could be 7.5% and the next it could be 6.8% I have seen ARMs that were adjusted within one to two weeks of each other with new rates that differed by over 0.5%.

For our example we will say that our 7.75% initial rate comes up for adjustment on June 1 and the index used is determined 45 days before that date, or April 15. In the week of April 15 the index is 8.375%. Before you congratulate yourself on getting such a great loan that you will only be paying 8.375% in the second year, we need to add to the index rate the margin.

The Margin

The margin is a percentage that is added to the index to determine what the new interest rate will be for the next period, one year in our example. Most ARM margins will be in the range of 2.00% to 3.00%. For our example let us use a margin of 2.50%.

Using the 7.75% initial rate with the One-Year Treasury Securities Index, which we have said is 8.375%, and a margin of 2.50%, the new interest rate will be 10.875%. You don't think that is a very good deal? Just because your rate went up 3.125% in one year and your payment increased over 22%? Luckily, "Let the consumer beware" is not the government credo when it comes to lending. To protect the borrower against huge interest increases and **payment shock**, lenders have been forced to cap the maximum that the interest rate can increase, or decrease, in any adjustment period and on the the maximum that the interest rate can increase, or decrease, over the life of the loan.

The Caps

Depending on the different ARMs, caps can be as low as 1% a year and 3% lifetime or as high as 2% a year and 6% lifetime, or any combination. A loan with a 1% maximum interest rate increase would keep your payment (PI) from increasing more than about 7.5% a year, while the 2% cap could take it up as much as 15% in a year. The lifetime cap can certainly make a difference if you are looking at 3% over the initial rate (10.75% in our example) as opposed to 6% (13.75% in our example). For our example, we will use caps of 2% per year and 5% lifetime, which are fairly standard in the market. That would mean the second-year interest rate could not exceed 9.75% and the lifetime rate could be no higher than 12.75%.

In reconsidering our index of 8.375% plus the margin of 2.50% that totaled 10.875%, we find the cap of 2% would prevent the rate being any higher than 9.75% for the second year (7.75% + 2%). The rate will be adjusted toward the total of the index plus the margin, within the maximum rate set by the caps. If the index had been 7.00% (a decrease from the initial rate of 7.75%), then the total with the 2.50% margin would have been 9.50%, and that is what the second-year rate would be, less than the maximum set by the caps.

How High Can It Fly?

As you can see from our example, you would get one year at 7.75%, one year at 9.75% (maximum), and, worst of all, the third year could be 11.75%, for an average of 9.75%. Not bad when you could have had 10% fixed. And, the rate can go down. But, just to rain on your parade, it can also go up, and stay up if the index doesn't drop. An ARM will move toward the market rate and, once it is near it, will trade up and down toward it within the caps. Like the equal loan, it is good for people who know they are going to be in the house only three to five years. But it can be a very good loan for the long term if interest rates stay low with only an occasional jump for a year or two.

With each interest rate adjustment, the payment is adjusted to pay out on the remaining principal balance at that time, over the remaining amortization period left on the loan, based on the new interest rate to which the loan is adjusted (in our example, 7.75% for 30 years, 9.75% for 29 years, and so forth). This schedule will fully amortize the loan over the payment period. Now, if you want to get more sophisticated, you can take the **prepayment** idea that we discussed for fixed rate loans and apply it to the ARM (as long as there is no prepayment penalty). If you prepaid on the mortgage each month or once a year, the balance would be less at the time the rate, and payment, are adjusted. Thus, the payment would be less than it would have been if you just made the regular monthly payments.

Now that we have been through a typical one-year ARM with 2%/5% caps and a margin of 2.50%, let's take a look at some of the other ARMs that are available.

Shopping at the ARM Store
The Six-Month ARM

This works on the same principal as our one-year ARM except that it adjusts every six months. This is not for the fainthearted, but by law it will have a cap of no more than 0.5% to 1% per six-month adjustment. These are the equivalent, with a normal one-year ARM, of a 1% or a 2% per year cap. The big difference is that you can get the lower, or higher, rate every six months instead of once a year. Is this a good loan? It depends on what the market is doing at each adjustment period, and your luck. It should not be much different from a corresponding one-year loan.

The Three-Year ARM (3/3 ARM).

This resembles the 1-year ARM, except that the interest rate and payment change only once every 3 years. The index normally used for this loan is the 3-year Treasury Securities Index, with caps that are usually 2% per change date (three years) and 5% to 6% lifetime, with a margin of 2.5% to 2.75%.

The initial rate on a three-year ARM will be higher than for the one-year ARM because the lender is stuck with that rate three times longer. In addition, the three-year index is always higher than the one-year index. It is a good loan for anyone who does not need to go beyond the sixth year because even on a worst-case scenario, the rate will be favorable. After the second change, or at the end of the sixth year, it's a gamble.

The Five-Year ARM (5/5 ARM).

This is the same as the three-year ARM, except that it changes once every five years and uses, you guessed it, the five-year index. And, the five-year index will be higher than both the one- and the three-year indexes. If you want a loan for no more than five years, this may be it. Compare it with what is available at the time to see if you will save on closing costs, payments, and qualifying.

3/1 and 5/1 ARMs

Then there are the hybrid ARMs. You can get a three-year ARM that turns into a one-year ARM after the first three years, commonly called a 3/1 ARM. Or, you can get a 5/1 ARM, for which the rate stays the same for the first five years; the loan then turns into a one-year ARM. These loans give you the advantage of a stable payment and rate for an extended period of time, followed by the lower rates and indexes of a one-year ARM.

Fannie Mae Stable Loan

Then there is the new (1991) Fannie Mae product called the Fannie Mae Stable Loan. This loan combines "some of the stability of a fixed rate with the adjustability of an adjustable rate mortgage" (quoted from the Fannie Mae Announcement #91–05). Right now Fannie has two different stable loans, the 50/50 and the 75/25. Basically, the loans have a much higher margin and a much lower index than other ARMs at present. Both are 30-year loans that use the one-year Treasury Securities Index. Here is how they work.

On the 50/50 loan the lender takes 50% of the one-year index and adds it to the margin. Let's use 6.0% as the index and 5.5% as the margin. This means half of 6% = 3.0% index +5.5% margin = 8.5% as the rate. The caps on the 50/50 are 2% yearly and 6% lifetime.

The 75/25 loan uses as an index 25% of the one-year index and then adds the margin. Using the 6.0% index and a margin of 7.625% (the margin will be higher on the 75/25 because the index is lower) we find the rate works out to be 9.125% (25% of the 6% index plus 7.625%). The 75/25 caps are 1% yearly and 4% lifetime.

In addition, the margin can change as the interest rates move up or down. So, you do not know exactly what the initial rate and margin will be until you decide to apply. Once you have locked in your loan, the margin does not change.

The whole idea of manipulating the index and margin is to make the ARM more like a fixed rate loan, with less payment shock. The stable loan does as good a job as any loan available. You just have to remember that it is an ARM.

Overview

To summarize, the intervals for adjustment on ARMs can be any of the following:

1. Six months
2. One year
3. Three years
4. Five years
5. Every one year after an initial three- to five-year level period

And, ARMs are adjusted based on Indexes such as the following:

1. One-, Three-, or Five-Year U.S. Treasury Securities Index
2. One-, Three-, or Five-Year FHLBB Cost of Funds Index (COF)
3. One-, Three-, or Five-Year 11th District COF Index
4. Other, more exotic indexes

A margin, ranging from 1.0% to over 3% (higher for the stable loan), is added to the index to determine the rate toward which the loan will be adjusted. Caps are added to protect the borrower from unacceptably high rate and payment jumps. The caps vary from 0.5% to 2% per year, and 2% to 6% lifetime.

No law governs how low the rates, indexes, margins, and caps can be on any ARM. But, the secondary markets do set certain minimums and maximums that they will allow if they are to buy the loans. Because most lenders today want the loans to be salable, they will adhere to these guidelines. If you find an ARM with abnormally low characteristics, it may well be a special "in house" portfolioed loan; perhaps it has been purchased by a special investor. In either case, the holder of the loan is taking a much higher risk.

We're not through with ARMs yet. There are still conversions, LTVs, qualifying, and extended lock-ins to cover.

Conversion Feature   Into a Prince or a Toad?

A conversion feature on your ARM allows you to convert it into a fixed rate loan. It is available during the early life of the loan, usually after the first change date, for a period ranging from one year to six years. Some loans charge a one-time fee of $100 to $500 at the time of conversion, and others have no fee at all. Even with a fee, conversion is a much cheaper alternative for getting a fixed rate than completely refinancing the loan and paying all of the closing costs, including points, again. This feature is good to have on your ARM, whether you ever have the opportunity to use it or not. Most ARMs today do have it as a regular feature. Those without it may have a slightly lower initial rate and/or discount points.

ARMs with a conversion option have been one of the most innovative and consumer-oriented features to come onto the market in some time. This option is also one of the most misunderstood and least disclosed feature of an ARM. What most borrowers do not recognize, and often are not told, is that the rate to which the loan is converted is neither the current rate on the ARM nor the current fixed rate being offered in the market. Instead, most conversion rates are based on the Fannie Mae or Freddie Mac 30-day or 60-day mandatory delivery rate, priced at par (that means without any discount points), plus some additional interest, similar to a margin, of 0.25% to 0.75%.

The mandatory delivery rate is usually slightly less than the market interest rate quoted by a lender by 0.25% to 0.125%, but not always. The 30-day delivery rate will usually be cheaper than the 60-day rate. And the Fannie and Freddie rates can differ. In essence, the mandatory rate is the net interest yield required by the investor, before a servicing fee is added, that will be accepted as long as the loan is delivered within the mandatory period—that is, 60, 30, or 15 days. Almost all lenders can tell you what these rates are, and they can change daily.

The lender will take the mandatory delivery rate and add the additional interest when you choose to convert your ARM to a fixed rate. Part, or all, of this is for the servicing of the loan. Here is an example:

Current 30-year fixed rate at par (no discount)	10.00%
Current 30-year 60-Day Mandatory Rate at par	9.77%
Plus 0.625% additional interest added to mandatory rate (rounded up to the nearest 0.125%)	10.50%
Or, plus 0.375% additional interest (normally the lowest)	10.25%

The 10.50% or 10.25% interest rate is the fixed rate to which your ARM will convert, depending on the additional interest.

As you can see, the rate to which the loan is converted would be higher than the current market fixed rate.

The period during which the borrower can convert the loan depends on the loan and the lender. On most one-year ARMs, the conversion period is any time from the thirteenth through the sixtieth month (second through fifth years). Others only allow conversion at a given date once a year from the second through the fifth or sixth year. On three-year and five-year loans conversion is normally allowed starting from the first adjustment date; it is then available for a three- to five-year period, either monthly or once a year.

The borrowers get the conversion by calling the lender servicing the loan (the lender to which they make their payments) during the specified time period. The lender will quote the rate available, and if the borrowers want to convert, the rate is locked in at that time. If there is a fee, it must be sent to the lender within a certain time. The lender will advise the borrowers when their loan will convert, usually within 60 days of the commitment. New documents for the fixed rate must be executed, and the borrowers will receive a new payment book.

In general, a borrower will not benefit from converting the ARM unless the fixed rates have fallen far enough that the new converted rate will be 10% or less. (This statement assumes that rates do not rise to 12% and stay there for a protracted period of time.) As long as the market rate stays around 10.5% to 11%, the ARM rate will hold close to if not below these rates. On the other hand, when the rates get down to 9.50% and lower, converting may make sense because the normal market does not usually stay that low for long periods. Now, just as I say that, the market will fall to 7.5% to 8.0%, as it did in 1991 and 1992, and everyone will be angry with me for getting them to convert to a 9.75% to 10% rate when they could have had 8% to 8.5%. But you get the idea. Convert when the rate is low enough that you will be happy with it as a fixed rate.

Qualifying with an ARM

One of the main reasons that people consider ARMs is that they hope to qualify using the lower initial interest rate and payment. Because of changes in the industry, qualifying may not be so easy as it once was. It really depends on several factors: the amount of cash the borrower puts down (LTV), the yearly cap, and/or the length between rate/payment changes.

Under standard secondary market guidelines on a one-year ARM, **the borrower must put down at least 25% cash to qualify at the initial payment.** With less than 25%, the borrower will qualify at the maximum second-year rate. With a 2% per year cap and using a 7.75% initial rate, you would qualify at the payment based on 9.75%.

Let's make our computation a little more complicated. If the annual cap is 1% or less, or if it is a three-year, five-year, 3/1, or 5/1 ARM, then you would qualify at the initial rate. The rationale for this is that the payment does not change significantly or for a prolonged period of time.

In qualifying, you would use the standard **28%/36%** ratios, up to the maximum 90% LTV. With the exception of the stable loan, Fannie and Freddie no longer accept 95% ARMs as of 1991. However, there may be other investors who still offer them.

When considering an ARM, the most important thing that you can do is to get a copy of the complete **Disclosure Statement** from the lender, which explains the loan. Then, make sure this loan is the best way for you to finance your home. It is not hard to become confused by the multiplicity of products available. And, you have to remember that lenders are trying to sell their products (that is, loans), just like any other business.

The first lender for whom I worked came out with an ARM that no other lender could touch. Fixed rates were running 12.5%

to 13%. Our loan had an initial rate of 9.75%, 1 + 2.75 points, 2% yearly cap, and no lifetime cap. A later version even had negative amortization, which we will discuss later. We qualified borrowers based on the initial payment rate, even on 95% LTV, using very liberal standards. Everyone came to us. It was the best deal in town. The problem was that it was a very high risk loan, and it ultimately created an unusually high incidence of defaults and foreclosures. Also, most of the borrowers eventually refinanced as soon as better loans came onto the market. And, from the lenders' perspective, it was a bust because they lost money on that loan product. In the long run, this loan was not a very good deal for many of the borrowers, or for the lender. Today, ARMs are designed to benefit both the borrower and the lender.

Long Lock-in ARMs   The Meter Is Running

One more thing that needs to be explained on ARMs is the long lock-in offered by some lenders. The lender will lock in, or guarantee, the initial interest rate for as long as 9 to 12 months, until you close on the loan. This is very attractive to people who are building or cannot close within the normal 60-day lock period. You do not have to worry about interest rates rising before you can lock in. What most people do not realize about these extended locks is that the initial rate's adjustment period begins with the lock-in. That is, if you lock in 7.75% on a one-year ARM, it will adjust one year from the lock-in date, not the closing date. If you don't close for nine months after you lock in, you will get the benefit of the lower rate and payment for only three months; then it will go to the higher rate and payment. This is not to say that it isn't worth locking in early. You should just make sure that you understand the consequences.

GRADUATED PAYMENT MORTGAGES
For the high and desperate times

GPMs, or Gipp Em's as they are called in the industry, were originally offered by the Federal Housing Administration (FHA). They help people qualify by starting out at a lower payment than would normally be required. They are similar to the equal loan in that the payment starts out very low and increases 7.5%

(usually) per year until it reaches a level payment that is sufficient to pay the loan off over the remaining term of the loan. The big difference is that it is not a buy-down, but that it is a fixed rate loan. What this means is that you are making a payment that is less than the interest being charged on the loan. This is called **negative amortization.**

To give an example, say that you get a fixed rate loan on $100,000 at 10% for 30 years. The PI payment would be $877.57 and the interest only payment would be $833.34. But, using a GPM, the first-year payment is $567.80 (the equivalent of a 5.5% interest rate payment), meaning there is negative amortization of $265.54 per month ($833.34 − $567.80). That is, you are paying $265.54 less than you are being charged in interest each month. That unpaid interest is added to the principal amount of the loan. The payments then increase each year (normally 7.5%) until they reach a level payment that will pay off the principal plus the additional unpaid interest within the remainder of the amortization period. GPMs are set up according to formulas that specify the lowest starting payment, the year the payments level off, and the exact amount of negative amortization (or unpaid interest) that will accrue.

If a GPM doesn't sound like a very good deal, it isn't—for most borrowers. But when fixed rates are high, and you don't qualify unless the payment is significantly lower, this may be the loan for you. It isn't pretty, but it will get you into the house. Your biggest concern with a GPM is that the property appreciate enough at least to keep pace with the accrued unpaid interest.

Most GPMs will not allow the total principal and interest to exceed 125% of the original loan balance. If your house appreciates 3% per year, which is minimal, that increase would cover the excess unpaid interest in about six to seven years. If you end up having to sell your home during the negative amortization period, the house must have appreciated sufficiently to cover the increased principal balance to prevent a loss on the sale. With appreciation of 6% to 10% a year, you should be able to start making payments on the principal after three or four years.

With a GPM you know exactly what the total accrued interest will be and, therefore, what the total loan will be with the maximum amount of negative amortization added. You also know when it will begin to amortize positively. There have been negative amortization ARMs whose rates bounced around like a rubber ball. You had no idea if and when the loan would ever completely amortize out. With those ARMs, you could get stuck at the end of 30 years with a balloon payment. Or, along the way you could get hit with very nasty payment increases.

Most negative ARMs have disappeared from the market, at least until rates climb again; the few left are usually paid off by sale of the house or refinancing. They also have had more safeguards built into them. My advice is not to get one unless you have explored all the alternatives and it is the only way to purchase the house.

Here is an example of an FHA GPM: On a $100,000 purchase, with an interest rate of 12% for 30 years, the maximum loan amount would be $92,700 plus FHA mortgage insurance premiums financed into the loan, for a total of $96,200. On a normally amortizing (fixed-rate) loan, the PI/MI payment would be $989.53. The GPM would be as follows:

Year	PI/MI Payment	Loan Balance	Negative Amortization
1	$ 761.31	$ 98,745.34	$2,545.34
2	818.40	100,889.36	4,689.36
3	879.78	102,526.82	6,326.82
4	945.76	103,535.14	7,335.14
5	1,016.70	103,771.73	7,571.73
6–30	1,092.95[a]		

[a]The loan will cross the original balance with the 147th payment.

GROWING PAYMENT MORTGAGES OR GROWING EQUITY MORTGAGES
Loans for the upwardly mobile

Commonly known as **GEMs,** these loans are designed to force the borrower to pay off the loan quicker than the normal amortization. A GEM works on the same principal as the equal loan; however, it does not start at a lower initial payment. If it is a 30-year GEM, it will start at the normal payment and then increase the PI payment 7.5% per year until the payments reach a point that they will pay off the loan in some specified time, such as 20 or 15 years. A GEM will usually have a rate lower than the normal fixed rate. There is nothing wrong with this loan as long as the borrower can make the required higher payments. Neurosurgeons and lawyers who work on a percentage basis would fit this description. Otherwise, get the normal fixed rate and pay it down according to your ability.

BALLOON LOANS
Exercises in stress management

Balloons offer the advantages of **lower rates and lower points.** They also offer the potential for personalized financial panic. A balloon loan is set up like a regular amortizing loan, usually for 30 years, although you can get them for shorter periods. You make the regular monthly payment until a set time, when the balance of the loan comes due, or balloons. The balloon period is usually between three and ten years, five- and seven-year periods being the most common.

As an example let us use a $100,000 loan at 9.0% for 30 years, ballooning in seven years. The monthly PI payment would be $804.62. The balloon balance due at the end of the seventh year would be $93,600.

If you sell the house, refinance, or pay off the loan within the seven years, you have no worries. If you get to the end of the seven years and you can't pay off the loan, then you have to hope the interest rates are favorable and you can qualify for a new refinance loan. Some lenders offer balloons that have a provision allowing for a cheap refinance. Other balloons allow you to continue at the fixed rate available at the due date. Balloon loans are attractive to borrowers who know they will not be in the house until the end of the balloon, know they can pay it off when the time comes, or need the lower rate to qualify.

Fannie Mae and Freddie Mac are now offering a balloon loan, called the two step or 7/23 loan, that gives you some of the advantages of a lower rate coupled with the security of not being stuck with a large payment due at the end of the balloon. You received a rate that is around 0.375% to 0.75% lower than the current fixed rate with a balloon at the end of either five or seven years. However, you have the option of renewing the loan for the remaining 25 or 23 years for a rate that is similar to an ARM conversion rate. That is, the renewal rate will be about 0.375% to 0.75% higher than the current fixed rate at the time you renew the loan. This type of balloon loan gives you the advantages of a lower initial rate without the uncertain short-term fluctuations of an ARM. It is perfect for anyone who will be selling or refinancing within seven years. There may be a small fee for the conversion.

Another type of balloon loan offered in some parts of the country is **the mortgage bond.** These are usually offered by private individuals or bank trust departments. They are loans of low LTV (usually 70% or less) that are made up of a series of bonds in denominations of $500 or $1,000 multiples. These bonds provide for interest only payments, usually every six months. At the end of the loan period, typically five years, the principal balance comes due. The advantage of these loans is that you deal directly with the loan maker; there are less rigid guidelines, lower closing costs, and a quicker closing time. All you have to do is make sure that the lenders receive their interest every six months and that you can pay off the principal at the end of the term.

SHARED EQUITY LOANS
Sharing the wealth

With the higher cost of housing today, many first-time homebuyers do not have the resources to make a down payment on a home. Bringing in someone who will put down part of the money in return for a share of the equity has become an acceptable practice, especially in high cost areas like California.

These arrangements can become very complicated, but for the most part they are a simple deal whereby the borrower gets money from a person who will in turn get a specified percentage of the net equity in the house when it is sold. Many agreements will state that the investor gets his or her equity by a certain date or when the appreciation reaches a set level. Others stipulate that the equity will be divided upon sale of the property, whenever that may occur. In areas of high appreciation, this kind of loan can be advantageous for everyone. It gives the investor a good return and it allows the borrower to pay relatively little money down in order to get into a house. The borrower hopes to come out with enough money to put down on another home.

JUMBO AND NONCONFORMING LOANS
For the mansion and the little grass shack

These loans exceed the maximum loan limits set by Fannie Mae and Freddie Mac. Or, they may be within the limits, but they do not fit the Fannie-Freddie conforming guidelines for property or borrower qualification, so they are **nonconforming.**

They can be any type of loan, from a fixed rate to an ARM. The big difference is that the many investors who buy them set the guidelines to which they are subject. Most will use Fannie and Freddie guidelines as the basis and then diverge from there. The qualifying can be more liberal, or more conservative.

Most will set the maximum amount that they will loan for any given LTV. This is further restricted by the maximum loan amounts that mortgage insurance companies will insure at specific LTVs over 80%. Many investors will require two or more appraisals for loans over certain amounts.

The differences in jumbo or nonconforming loans are as varied as the number of investors who buy them. If you are in the market for one, do what you would do for any loan—check out all of them, compare them, ask the lender pertinent questions such as these:

1. How long will the loan process take?
2. Who will be processing the loan, the lender or the investor?
3. Who will underwrite, or approve, the loan, the lender or investor?
4. Exactly what will be required for approval?
5. Is there a prepayment penalty? (Some jumbos do penalize.)

It is very important that the lender be comfortable with the investor and familiar with the way it works. Most jumbos are underwritten by the investor, which can lead to many misunderstandings and problems.

One jumbo that I did was an absolutely perfect loan. The borrower had single-digit qualifying ratios, he was putting down $200,000 on a $500,000 house, and he had enough assets that he could have paid cash. The borrower locked in the rate when it was low. Subsequently, the rates rose. After the loan was approved, and about one week before closing, the borrower decided he wanted to reduce the loan for which he was approved by $30,000. The investors insisted that they must reappove the borrower, which would take at least five working days. Never mind that the loan package they had approved showed the borrower capable of putting down the extra

$30,000 and that the borrower would qualify even more easily. What was obvious was that the lock-in on the low rate was due to expire before the reapproval and closing could occur. The investor refused to extend the lock and would only give the current rate. The borrower was upset, I was outraged, my company was in disbelief, and the borrower's attorney was ready to sue. As it turned out, the attorney's written threat to sue gave the investor a little clearer perspective. The loan closed on time, without reapproval, and with the lower rate. Not all loan stories turn out this way. When you are dealing through a second party (that is, the lender) to get a loan over which the lender has little or no control, there is always the potential for problems.

CONSTRUCTION LOANS

When you are building a house, one of two things will happen: either the builder pays for the costs until it is finished, or you pay the costs. If the builder pays the costs, you have to be able to pay these costs at the end either by cash in hand or by proceeds from a permanent mortgage that will close after the house is 100% complete. If you have to pay the construction costs while the house is being built, chances are that you will need to borrow on a short-term basis to get that money. This short-term loan, secured by the real estate, is called a construction loan.

The process usually works in this fashion:

1.   The borrower will get a commitment to a permanent mortgage.

2.   The lender will then commit to a construction loan. This lender may or may not be the same one that gives the permanent mortgage. Sometimes a normal mortgage lender will commit to the permanent loan and then a bank will give the construction loan. Most construction loans will not be granted until there is a permanent loan commitment.

3.   The construction loan will be between 70% and 100% of the permanent loan amount (depending on the borrower's needs and the lender's rules). Any equity in the land is counted as cash, i.e., it can go toward both the permanent mortgage and the construction loan. If you buy a lot for $25,000 and put $10,000 down, then that $10,000 is part of the money counted as equity. Most lenders take into account the value of the land

as a function of how long you have held it. If you have held it for less than six months, they use the purchase price as value; if you have held it for six months or more, they will use the appraised value. However, some will use the appraised value only after you have held the land for at least one year. Therefore, if the $20,000 lot is appraised for $25,000 after whatever time period the lender requires, then that is the value, and you have $5,000 more in equity.

4.   The builder will request **draws** or payments, during certain phases of construction. Draws will be for the costs of labor and materials during that phase. A normal draw schedule is, after the foundation is done, after the house is under roof, after the mechanical systems (heating, plumbing, electric) are roughed in, after the dry wall is complete and ready for paint, and upon completion. The lender will require that the builder submit evidence of the work completed and signed **lien waivers** (which protects the borrower and lender against liens that could be placed on the property by any of the builder's subcontractors or suppliers who the builder did not pay). The lender also will inspect the house before each draw.

5.   Upon completion of the house, the lender will close the permanent loan, which will pay off the construction loan balance and any remaining balance due the builder.

A construction loan can take many forms. Interest can be based on the prime rate plus extra interest from 0.5% to 2%. Interest can be at a fixed rate. The lender may or may not, but usually will, charge 1 or 2 points. The lender may charge interest on the entire amount from the beginning of the commitment, although this is very seldom done today. The lender will generally charge interest on the money as it is used. In figuring out exactly how much the house will cost and how much you need to borrow, it is important that you add in the cost of the construction loan. A prime rate of 10% plus an added 1% can run into a significant interest cost after three to six months.

Using our $100,000 loan, let us calculate the costs of the interest expense, based on an 80% LTV (of the permanent loan) with a 1%($800) upfront fee, a simple draw schedule of four draws a month (equals $20,000 per month at 11% [prime of 10% + 1%]) and completion at the end of the fifth month. Those costs would be $800 + $1,835 approximate interest = $2,635 in additional building costs.

Most construction loans run for six to nine months, renewable up to one year. This is plenty of time to build any normal house. Most are built in six months or less.

The lender who makes the permanent loan will have less risk than the construction lender because the permanent loan will only close when the house is finished, if it was built according to the plans, and if the borrower has sufficient cash to close. The construction lender is a partner with the borrower from the beginning. If the completed house turns out to be trapezoidal instead of rectangular, the construction lender will find itself "holding the bag" without a permanent loan to pay off the remaining construction debt.

Situations like this are why almost all lenders will require the general contractor to have a track record. Contractors must at least show knowledge and a background in building that will assure the lender that they are competent. Borrowers who want to act as their own general contractor will find it very difficult to get a lender to commit on a construction loan, unless it is a low LTV.

The best way to approach building, and the least complicated for the borrower, is to have the builder take care of financing the construction. Financing costs will then be added into the price of the house, but that is not any different from when the borrower has the construction loan. The procedure also allows the borrower to have a set cost for the house, as long as the contractor gives a set price bid. Some builders will build based on cost plus. That means you pay the cost of the house plus a stated percentage as the builder's gross profit. Cost plus 15% to 20% or more is normal.

One of the products that has come onto the market to keep lenders competitive and to provide more loan revenue is the permanent-construction single loan package. The borrower applies for the permanent and gets the construction as part of the package. The rate for the construction loan is the same as for the permanent, and you pay points once, not for each loan. The biggest difference is that you pay one set of closing costs. At closing, you will then have a construction loan in place to build the house. Upon completion, the construction loan turns into a permanent loan with regular monthly payments. Depending on the lender offering this combination loan, it is possible to get 15- or 30-year fixed rates, or an ARM. Also, you may be able to lock in your interest rate at application, or, at the very least, you may be offered some type of rate protection such as guaranteeing that your permanent rate will not be more than 0.5% higher than at time of application.

After reading this section, you can see that there are many different loans and variations available because of the competitive and changing nature of real estate financing. As time goes on, other new and innovative products will come along to provide the borrower with even more choices. In making a decision, take it one step at a time. Decide which type is best for your needs, and then look at all the extras. So far we have discussed Fannie, Freddie, and all the mutants created by the conventional market. Now we need to look at government loans.

GOVERNMENT LOANS

What lenders refer to as government loans are those loans that are either insured, guaranteed, held by, or in some way created by the federal government. We will look at FHA (Federal Housing Administration) and VA (Veteran's Administration) loans.

Federal Housing Administration (FHA)

To get an idea of what you are dealing with in the FHA, you must first know that it is part of and controlled by **HUD (Department of Housing and Urban Development),** one of the largest and most bureaucratic of the federal agencies. This fact doesn't mean that it is a bad loan, it simply means that at times it can become incredibly paper intensive, rule bound, and subject to political grandstanding. Despite the shortcomings, the end product is worth the effort.

FHA was intended as a means by which borrowers, usually moderate income and/or first-time buyers, could get a loan with **less down payment and liberal qualifying.** Because most lenders would be reluctant to make a loan like this, **the federal government insures the loans through FHA.** If your loan is going to be insured, you cannot find a stronger way to do so than by the full faith and credit of the United States government.

The government, through FHA, insures these loans by means of a **mortgage insurance premium (MIP),** just like mortgage insurance companies. FHA does not provide the money, only the insurance. The M.I.P., as of July 1, 1991, is now **divided into two parts.** The **up-front MIP** is financed into the loan amount. The second part is a **renewal (periodic) premium** that is escrowed into the monthly payment, just like the renewal premium on private mortgage insurance (PMI). (See the FHA MIP Chart on page 100). The proceeds are held to pay any claims on foreclosed FHA-insured loans.

The FHA sets the guidelines under which these loans are approved, closed, and insured. The rules are similar to the conventional ones, except that they are more liberal and have several significant differences. The loan applications are taken by lenders approved by FHA. Then, the lender can approve the loan and close it if the lender is designated "Direct Endorsement" (D.E.)-approved by F.H.A. Otherwise the loan is submitted to the FHA for approval. It is to the borrower's advantage to use a D.E. lender because the entire loan is done in-house, without having to submit anything to the FHA. The lender then applies for insurance coverage from the FHA. With that insurance in place, the loan can then be sold to the secondary market as a government-insured loan.

Ginnie Mae, Fannie and Freddie's little sister, was created by the government to purchase and/or guarantee government loans as part of the secondary market system. That is why you hear about buying "government-backed Ginnie Maes" from stockbrokers. For the borrower, knowing about Ginnie Mae's is not really important so far as the borrower is concerned, except to know that Ginnie exists and she does set some guidelines on government loans herself.

The advantage of an FHA loan is that you can put down less cash and qualify under liberal guidelines. There is **no maximum limit on income to qualify** at this time (although Congress has been trying to put a limit on income and it may eventually happen); but there is a **maximum on the loan amount.** Unfortunately, it is not nearly so high as conventional loans. The FHA sets these limits by region, based on the median sales price and other statistical data. As of 1991 the maximum loan amount on a single-family dwelling that the FHA will allow is $124,875 compared with $202,300 (as of December 1991) for conventional conforming loans. This amount represents a high-cost region. In most areas it is more likely to be in the range of $68,300 to $90,000. The reason its loan amounts are less is that the FHA is geared toward first-time buyers or borrowers who cannot afford higher-priced homes and the cash down payments they would require. Loan amounts on duplexes, triplexes, and quadraplexes are proportionately higher, just like Fannie and Freddie. To find out what the maximum loan amounts are in your area, call a lender who does FHA loans.

FHA determines the maximum loan that can be obtained on a home by a formula based on a maximum LTV; this formula is adjusted downwards by either a set percentage or the amount of closing costs that are financed and/or paid by the seller (or other third party). Determining the basic amount for the simplest loan is not hard. But, as you add variables such as seller paid costs, the determination becomes much more difficult. For you, the borrower, to try and master these calculations would be a waste of time, unless you are a math and brain-teaser freak. What I will do is first explain what goes into figuring the loan amount, and then I will show you some examples of how they are calculated.

Many people have heard that they can "finance their closing costs" with an FHA loan and not have to pay them at closing. This assumption is made because of the "closing costs" that are added to the sales price to determine the maximum loan amount. Although the government will pay for a lot of things, like $500 screw drivers and $1,000 toilet seats, they do not pay your closing costs. They are allowing you to add these costs into the total to determine how much cash you will have to put down. By doing this, you can put less cash down so that you will have more cash available to pay your closing costs. (In my examples, I will show you the difference between loans with and without financed closing costs. These allowable financed closing costs are further restricted by any amounts that the seller pays toward the purchaser's closing costs. This restriction makes sense when you consider that otherwise the borrower is not only getting the seller to pay these costs, but is also getting the government to allow him to "finance" them. (I will show how this works in my examples.) Remember, I am just telling you what is involved so that you will be better informed. You will need an experienced FHA-approved lender to show you the exact figures.

The next step is to figure the MIP that will be financed into the loan amount. The table of factors is shown below. Based on the new, revised (read "political") FHA "risk-based premium payments," the up-front premium and the length of time for which the borrower will pay the renewal premium will change yearly between 1991 and 1995, depending on the LTV.

| Year of origination | Up-front premium | Term (years) | | | Renewal premium |
		Below 90% LTV	90% to 95% LTV	Above 95% LTV	
1991–1992	3.80%	5	8	10	0.5%
1993–1994	3.00%	7	12	30	0.5%
1995+	2.25%	11	30	30 years[a]	0.5%

[a]The renewal premium for loans with less than 0.5% down during or after 1995 will be 0.55%.

Now we are ready to dive into the murky waters of FHA loan-amount calculations.

Two separate calculations must be performed to determine the maximum loan amount. First, take the **appraised value** of the property and multiply it by **97.75%** if the value is over $50,000 (use **98.75%** if the value is $50,000 or less). This is the easy part. Second, take the sales price and,

1. If there are any **seller-paid closing costs,** excluding discount points, subtract them from the sales price. (The seller-paid costs are not subtracted from the 97.75%/98.75% calculation so long as the seller does not pay more than 6% of the total mortgage with MIP.)

2. If the seller did not pay any closing costs, other than discount points, ignore Point 1. If the **lender pays any of the closing costs,** none of these are subtracted from the sales price.

3. **Determine your closing costs.** (You will need a lender for this unless you can sufficiently master the section on closing costs. Then you can use the FHA Maximum Loan Worksheet, in the Appendix, page 196). Take all of the closing costs, subtract the discount points and pre-paid items (prepaid interest, first year's homeowner's insurance premium, and escrows for homeowner's insurance and taxes), multiply this figure by 57% (FHA will not allow more than 57% of the closing costs to be financed, as of 1991), and add this amount to the value.

4. Subtract $25,000 from the value determined in Point 3 and multiply the remainder by 95%. Then take 97% of $25,000, or $24,250. If the cost of the house is $50,000

or less, just use a straight 97% of the total from Point 3. (A shortcut to this calculation is to take 95% of the total after adding allowable financed closing costs and subtracting seller-paid closing costs. Then simply add $500 to this amount. See calculation #1 on the Maximum Loan Worksheet in the Appendix).

5. Compare the 97.75% (or 98.75%) figure with the figure that you determined in Point 4. The maximum loan amount is the lesser of the two. If the appraised value is less than the sales price, this fact will obviously affect the maximum loan amount.

After reading this, you may wish to call a lender to help determine the maximum amount that you can borrow. Adding to the confusion, the government is considering still more changes to the FHA rules.

Example 1:

Sales Price: $90,000   Appraised value: $90,000
Estimated closing costs
    (without discount or prepaid items): $2,450
      No seller-paid closing costs. (Seller may pay
discount points without affecting the loan.)

1. $90,000 (appraised value) × 97.75% =   <u>$87,975</u>
2. $2,450 (closing costs) × 57% = $1,396
    $90,000 (sales price) + $1,396 = $91,396
      $91,396
      −25,000
      $66,396 × 95% = $63,076
      $25,000 ×97% =   <u>$24,250</u>
                       $87,326

(Shortcut: $91,396 × 95% + $500 = $87,326)

The maximum loan amount is $87,326 (97% LTV). Most lenders will round the loan down to the nearest $50, so this would be $87,300.

3. $87,300 × 3.8%
    up-front MIP
    (until 1993) = $ 3,317.40

Total loan with MIP = $90,617.00

Again, most lenders will round down the MIP to the nearest $50, with the difference paid at closing. Thus, our loan becomes $90,600 total, with $17.40 MIP paid in cash at closing. (Notice something peculiar about the loan amount? It is more than the sales price. This is normal when you add a 3.8% premium onto a 97% loan, and the FHA allows the loan to exceed the price.)

Example 2

Sales price: $90,000   Appraised value: $90,000
Seller paying $1,000 in closing costs (not including discount points.)

1. $90,000 × 97.5% = $87,975
2. $90,000 − $1,000 (seller-paid costs) =
   $89,000 + $1,396 (57% of total closing costs) =
   $90,396
  −$25,000

   $65,396 × 95% = $62,126
              +   24,250 (97% of $25,000)
              = $86,376

The maximum loan amount is $86,376. With the MIP added it would be $89,600 (rounded).

What would the loan amount in the first example be if the 57% of closing costs were not added, or financed? It would be $86,300, or $1,000 less (1% more cash down).

As you put more cash down, the advantage of an FHA loan over a conventional loan may disappear. As you remember, conventionally financed private mortgage insurance is cheaper than 3.8%. Also, on FHA loans it does not matter how much cash you put down, there will always be a MIP, and the MIP percentage does not change, even on a 50% LTV. To insure the loan is the reason for FHA. The only time you would want to use FHA with more than the minimum cash down is when you need the more liberal qualifying to get a loan. And, with Fannie Mae's 3-2 loan that came out in 1991, there is an alternative to FHA (see section on the 3-2 loan). While there are pros and cons to both loans, borrowers may still need some F.H.A. guidelines in order to qualify for loans that the 3-2 does not offer.

Now that we have figured out how to get the maximum loan amount, we need to know if it exceeds the **maximum allowable loan limits** for your area. If the house in our Example 1 above was in an area where the maximum loan limit was $86,000, the borrower would not be able to get the $87,300 loan. The borrower would have to put down an additional $1,300. If the maximum loan limit was exactly $87,300, then the loan would qualify. And, the up-front MIP ($3,300 in Example 1) that is financed can be added beyond the amount of the loan limit, for a total of $90,600 in this example.

If you think that you can use a second mortgage (see section on second mortgages in Chapter 4) with an FHA loan to reduce your down payment, you don't understand the system. The FHA will allow second mortgages, but only to the extent that the first and the second combined do not exceed the maximum loan that FHA would otherwise normally allow. If we consider our $87,300 loan, the first and second cannot total more than $87,300. So, unless the second is a real bargain, there is little incentive. Once you have the mortgage, your FHA lender has no restrictions on obtaining a second mortgage.

Qualifying with FHA

FHA used to qualify by a residual income method that only a statistician could appreciate. Now, they use gross qualifying, just like conventional loans, but with the following higher ratios:

29% of gross monthly income for housing expense (PITI/MIP/HOA)

41% of gross monthly income for housing expense and all monthly debts with over six months to pay off (PITI/MI/HOA/LTD)

While they do not encourage it, the FHA will allow lenders to go above these ratios if there are good compensating factors. What is considered a compensating factor and how high lenders will go vary from region to region (administration of the FHA is divided into regions) and lender to lender. Regional offices will sometimes interpret guidelines differently from what the national office intended. A higher housing expense ratio is more acceptable than a total debt ratio. If you need to go much above 29%/41% you may be beyond your ability to pay anyway.

Using our example of the $90,000 purchase and loan amount of $87,300, let's see what the payment would be and the approximate income to qualify.

$$\$87,300 \times 3.8\% (\text{up-front MIP}) = \$3,317.40$$

The UFMIP is financed into the loan, so the total is $90,600 (the UFMIP was rounded down and the $17.40 will be paid in cash).

1. Using 10% with a 30-year amortization: $90.6 × 8.776 per 1000 (factor from table on page 218 in Appendix) = $795.11 P & I.

2. $87,300 × 0.5% (renewal premium) = $436.50. This premium, which is calculated on the basic loan before the UFMIP is added, is escrowed into the monthly payment by dividing it by 12 months. $436.50/12 = $36.38.

3. $795.11 + 36.38 = $831.49 PIMIP.

4. One twelfth of the yearly taxes and homeowner's insurance is also added for a PITIMIP payment. Because this is just an example, I will use $20 for insurance and $75 for taxes. The insurance figure is probably within a few dollars of what it actually would be, but the taxes can vary considerably. Thus, $831.49 + $20 + $75 = $926.49. $926.49 divided by 29% = $3,195 gross monthly income necessary to qualify. (This computation depends on the borrower's total debts and the flexibility of the lender. It is possible to qualify with less income).

The 0.5% renewal premium was added effective July 1, 1991. It is being used to keep the MIP insurance fund solvent. Just like the S&L fund, it too suffered huge losses. While adding another 0.5% to your loan is not the best thing to happen, it is better than the alternative, no FHA loans at all.

On FHA-acceptable **energy efficient homes,** lenders will allow the ratios to increase by as much as 2% each. The rationale is that you will save money on your utility bills, so you will have more to spend on your house payment. This compensating factor will apply mainly to newer homes that have been built with more insulation and more efficient heating and cooling systems. The house must be certified as energy efficient, normally by the power company or the builder.

If we use our example one more time, we can see approximately **how much cash will be needed** to get into the home.

Cash down	$2,700.00
Estimated closing costs(without prepaids)	$2,450.00
Estimated prepaids (with 15 days' interest)	$878.00
Total cash needed (give or take $100)	$6,028.00

That is, just over $6,000 to buy a $90,000 house. Not bad when you consider that the total down payment and closing costs will be about 7%.

The FHA is also more lenient toward houses that don't fit the mold of what is common in the market as a whole. They will consider properties such as two-bedroom homes and rural properties, which conventional loans might not be so inclined to finance if the property has a high loan-to-value. If you are considering a house in a rural area, the Farmer's Home Administration guaranteed loan program may fit your needs better. (See section on Special Loans).

Another thing that FHA has is **different loan types**—Over 30 of them at last count. There are the normal fixed rates, an ARM, the GPM that we discussed earlier, loans for veterans, loans for people who want to fix up a house, loans for people with no money, loans for people with bad credit. You name it and they probably have it (and they designate each one by section numbers: 203b for fixed, 234c for condominiums, and so on). The trick is to find a lender that will do the more exotic ones. Most FHA lenders do the fixed, GPM, ARM, and maybe the rehabilitation loan (203k). They don't get into the others because either they are not familiar with the loan, there is little or no demand in the area, the loans are so time-consuming that there is very little profit in them, or there is no secondary market source that will buy them.

The FHA used to have loans for nonowner-occupied investment property. But, as of December 14, 1989, these loans are no longer offered. What you might find is an investment property with an existing FHA nonowner loan on it that you can assume.

FHA loans have always been **assumable.** However, for loans on or after December 1, 1986 and before December 14, 1989, time and qualifying restrictions were added. Depending on whether the loan was originally taken as an owner or nonowner-occupied property, the requirements are different. (See the FHA assumption chart on page 200 in the Appendix).

With the HUD Reform Act of 1989 (December 15, 1989), all FHA loans approved from that point on require that at least one of the assuming borrowers be qualified and have a full credit check.

Any time an FHA loan is assumed, the MIP goes with the loan. The seller cannot request a partial refund. If the buyer who assumes the loan later pays it off, they can request a refund of any remaining MIP.

Something that is disclosed to every borrower in writing, but few borrowers remember, is that if you pay off the loan early, part of the MIP will be refunded to you. (See the Homeowner's Fact Sheet on Mortgage Insurance Premium Refunds and Distributive Shares, on page 198 in the Appendix). The longer you hold the loan, the less that is refunded. But in order to get the refund you have to request it, on an FHA form. If you don't, as of the time this was written, FHA just keeps it.

Have you ever seen those newspaper and television advertisements in which the huckster says that he can show you how to get rich for only $49.95? What he will tell you for that amazingly low price is that you can go down to the courthouse and search the records for the payoffs of all FHA loans. Then, you check with the FHA to find out if the MIP refund was ever requested. If it wasn't, you call up the former borrowers and tell them that you know about some money that they can get from the government. And, you will get it for them for 50% of the total. Not bad for a little research.

The ability to assume the FHA loan can often make the difference in whether the property will sell or not. Or, it may affect how much the seller can get for the property. Assuming a loan without having to pay much in closing costs will appeal to many potential buyers.

For investors looking for rental property, an assumption can allow them to build up a portfolio. But, there are some restrictions. The FHA will not allow a loan to be assumed if that buyer already owns at least seven properties in any specific neighborhood or development. And, a borrower cannot have more than one high LTV loan (over 75% of value plus closing costs) at a time. The only way that they could have a high LTV would be if it was their personal residence, or they were co-borrowers with someone else (like a child) who is living in the property.

FHA will allow **co-borrowers.** Either the borrower or co-borrower must live in the property. They are qualified based on their joint incomes and debts. The co-borrower must be a relative or someone with a demonstrated close relationship.

One last note on assumability: If the seller has an FHA loan that can be assumed without the buyer qualifying, and if the seller does not request a release of liability, you will remain liable for a period of five years in case of default and/or foreclosure. (See page 197 of Appendix for Notice to Homeowner: Assumption of HUD/FHA Insured Mortgages.) It is better to have the assuming purchaser qualify for the loan and to request the release to protect yourself. And, on assumptions FHA has no restrictions on second mortgages.

In many parts of the country **the seller pays part of the closing costs.** And, this is great as long as you remember a few rules that I have noted before:

1. If the seller pays the discount points, nothing is affected.

2. If the seller pays any of the other closing costs, other than the prepaids (which he cannot pay anyway), then the allowable loan amount is going to be lower. Example 2 above shows how $1,000 in seller-paid closing costs (not including discount points paid by the seller) will affect the loan amount. Although you will have to put more cash down, a better way of looking at it is that you will be putting that money into equity and not closing costs. The seller can contribute up to a maximum of 6% of the total loan amount with the MIP financed (including discount points). If you find someone willing to do that, that person is an extremely anxious seller.

In summary the advantages of FHA loans are these:

1. Liberal qualifying.
2. Less down payment required.
3. Assumable.
4. Can make the resale higher and/or quicker.
5. Insured by the full faith and credit of the U.S. government

The disadvantages are these:

1. There is a MIP regardless of the LTV.
2. The MIP is higher than on conventional loans.
3. The loan limits are lower than conventional.

As you may have noticed, FHA loans tend to go through periods of significant changes, especially in connection with the parent agency, the Department of Housing and Urban Development. While the primary role of FHA, to provide low-cost liberal qualifying loans, should remain relatively unchanged, politics has a way of altering how these goals are accomplished. Always check to make sure the rules have not changed. Assume nothing. And *always* use a competent, established FHA lender.

Veterans Administration (VA)

VA loans benefit borrowers who are eligible veterans. The **VA guarantees the loan.** The guarantee, known as the veteran's **Entitlement or Eligibility,** acts in the same function as the FHA's MIP, except that it is not insurance. A veteran can find out if he or she has this entitlement by calling the local VA office. You will then receive a Form 26-1880 (Request for Determination of Eligibility and Available Loan Guaranty Entitlement) to fill in and return. (You may be out of the service, but you will never escape the government forms.) Many lenders also have this form available.

The basic criteria are that the veteran must have served a minimum number of days in active service, depending on whether the veteran served during World War II, the Korean conflict, the Vietnam war, or other conflicts, during peacetime, or after certain dates. The veteran must also have other than a dishonorable discharge if he or she is no longer on active duty.

V.A. Entitlement

Enlisted after   September 7, 1980 (enlisted personnel)
                      October 16, 1981 (officers)

Veteran needs two years' active duty, or the full period for which they were called, but not fewer than 181 days. For Operation Desert Storm, the requirement is 90 days. Prior to 9/7/80 and 10/16/81, the veteran must have served at least 90 days in wartime and 181 days during peacetime. A borrower on active duty must have served at least 181 days before being eligible. The two-year requirement is also reduced to 181 days if the veteran was discharged early for disability or hardship. Spouses of service personnel who are officially listed as missing in action or as a prisoner of war can receive entitlement after 90 days.

The dates for wartime and peacetime are:

WW II	9/16/40 - 7/25/47
Peacetime	7/26/47 - 6/26/50
Korean	6/27/50 - 1/31/55
Peacetime	2/1/55 - 8/4/64
Vietnam	8/5/64 - 5/7/75
Peacetime	5/8/75 - 8/1/91
Operation Desert Storm	8/2/91 - the end had not been established as of 4/1/92.

A qualifying veteran will receive a short green or blue form that is called a Certificate of Eligibility (Form 26-8320). This form will show how much entitlement the veteran has, if the veteran has had VA loans in the past, and if they were paid off.

The Entitlement is different from your everyday mortgage insurance or mortgage insurance premium. It is a given dollar amount that is raised periodically as the cost of housing increases. The current entitlement (1991) is $46,000 for loans over $144,000, and $36,000 for loans up to $144,000. (Call your local VA office or a VA-approved lender to find out what the entitlement is at the time and if you qualify). Using the Veteran's Entitlement, VA says that it will guarantee that portion of the loan up to 50% on $45,000 or less, and up to $22,500 on loans in excess of $45,000, but not over $56,250, and not exceeding the dollar amount of the entitlement. On loans over $56,250 up to $184,000, the lesser of 40% or $46,000 is guaranteed. This confusing method that VA uses to determine the percentage that it will guarantee is not as important as knowing how much the lender (that is, the secondary market) requires.

The secondary market, and Ginnie Mae specifically, says that it will buy the loan only as long as the entitlement and/or cash covers at least 25% of the loan. That way, Ginnie's risk is limited to 75%, just like mortgage insurance (if the loan goes to foreclosure, the lender only has to get 75% of the loan amount and the VA will pay the remaining amount). A word of warning here: if the veteran defaults and is foreclosed upon with the VA having to pay part of the loss, the veteran will still be liable to the VA for that deficiency.

A VA loan is just about the only one that will allow the borrower to get a 100% LTV, no cash down loan, although the government is trying hard to change the rules to require around 2% to 5% minimum cash down. As long as there is sufficient entitlement to cover the top 25% and the loan does not exceed the maximum allowable amount, the veteran borrower does not need any down payment. If a veteran has $25,000 in entitlement, then upon qualification he or she could buy a $100,000 house with no cash down. The table below shows what the entitlement has been in the past and how it has risen.

The maximum entitlement is $46,000, so for the purposes of the secondary market this means that a qualifying veteran could get up to a $184,000 loan ($46,000 × 4). At the time the $46,000 amount was approved by VA, Ginnie Mae had not agreed to purchase loans over $144,000. This discrepancy made it very

Original (1944)....................$ 2,000
December 28, 1945   4,000
April 20, 1950   7,500
May 7, 1968 12,500
December 31, 1974 17,500
October 1, 1978.................. 25,500
October 1, 1980.................. 27,500
January 1, 1988.................. 36,000
December 18, 1989 46,000

difficult to allow the veteran to use the new entitlement amount. Ginnie finally agreed to purchase loans up to $184,000 but it just goes to show that the secondary market can even tell the government what to do.

VA loans are for owner-occupied dwellings up to a quadruplex, and the veteran can only have one VA loan at a time. If he sells the house and pays off the loan, his entitlement is restored. If he allows the loan to be assumed, and the loan is **assumable** if the buyer qualifies, that entitlement is tied up until that loan is paid off. If another qualifying veteran who has sufficient entitlement wants to assume the loan, she can substitute entitlement (called **Substitution of Entitlement**), which will free the selling veteran's entitlement by replacing it with the buying veteran's entitlement.

The requirements for assuming a VA loan depend on when the loan commitment was issued. Any VA loan that was committed before March 1, 1988, is assumable by anyone without qualifying. If the commitment date was on or after that date, anyone assuming the loan must first qualify. The qualifying requirement carries for the life of the loan. An important part of the assumption process is that if the loan is assumed without qualifying, the original borrower remains on the note and is liable, along with the assuming buyer, if the latter defaults. If the assuming borrower is qualified, the original borrower can request a release of liability. However, the veteran must request this release, or he will continue to be liable, even with the assuming borrower having been qualified. A good lender will make sure that the liability is released. But don't assume that it will happen. Regardless of whether there is a release of liability or not, the assumed loan is not counted against the original borrowing veteran as a debt when she qualifies for another loan.

Partial Entitlement

In the good old days, if you sold your house, let your entitlement go with the loan, and VA subsequently raised the entitlement levels, you got the full amount of all new increases. For example, let us say you bought a house in 1976 when the entitlement was $17,500 and then sold it by assumption of the VA loan; the $17,500 was tied up until that loan was paid off. But, over the period since the entitlement was $17,500, it has been raised to $46,000, $36,000 for loans up to $144,000. That increase meant you had partial entitlement of $28,500 ($46,000 − $17,500) or $18,500 ($36,000 − $17,500). No more. Using the VA Exhibit A (Worksheet for Computing Guaranty under Public Law 100-198) on page 202 in the Appendix, it could be much less.

An example would be an $80,000 purchase using the above scenario with the original $17,500 entitlement still tied up in the old assumed loan. By following the directions on Exhibit A, you would find the partial entitlement to be only $14,500. That would only buy a $58,000 house with no cash down. Using our example, the maximum usable entitlement up to a $144,000 loan would be $18,500. Not a very good deal either way. To avoid loss of entitlement, I recommend that a veteran allow his or her loan to be assumed without substitution of entitlement only if it is an absolute financial necessity.

If you have only partial entitlement, you can use it plus cash to make up the 25% coverage. If you end up putting down 10% or more, you may need to decide if the VA loan is more advantageous than a conventional loan. However, this decision may be moot if you need VA to qualify or if you want to pay a smaller VA Funding Fee, which we will cover later. In our example above, you would need to put down $5,500 cash. The $14,500 partial entitlement plus the $5,500 equals $20,000, or 25% of the loan amount ($20,000 × 4 = $80,000). That would mean a little less than 7% cash down.

You can use a second mortgage in combination with a VA loan, with two restrictions. The VA will not allow a second to make up the difference between the sales price and a low appraised value. The secondary market will not allow a second to make up a shortfall in entitlement, as in our example above.

The VA is very liberal in its qualifying. It does not use straight gross qualifying ratios (at this time), but a **net residual** qualifying method. This subtracts the following from the gross monthly income:

1. Federal income tax withholding on earned income
2. State income tax withholding
3. Social Security withholding
4. Child care expense, if applicable
5. Long-term monthly debts with over six months to pay off. (Debts with less than six months, but that are large enough to affect the borrower's ability to make the mortgage payments, will normally be counted.)
6. Total proposed housing expense (PITI)
7. Maintenance expense from regional VA charts based on finished square footage
8. Utilities expense from regional VA charts based on type of heat, square footage, and construction

What is left is called the **Residual Income.** This is what the veteran has left with which to buy everything unrelated to the house. The VA sets these minimum residual income amounts by region, based on family size and loan amount (see Table 5.1).

If the veteran has at least the minimum required residual income, half the battle is won. Having excess residual can help overcome other deficiencies.

Table 5.1 Minimum Residual Income

Family Size	Northeast	Midwest	South	West
Loan Amounts of $69,999 and Less				
1	$375	$367	$367	$409
2	629	616	616	686
3	758	742	742	826
4	854	835	835	930
5[a]	886	867	867	965
Loan Amounts of $70,000 and Above				
1	$433	$424	$424	$472
2	726	710	710	791
3	874	855	855	952
4	986	964	964	1074
5[b]	1021	999	999	1113

(Note: As of 1991, These figures change periodically.)

[a] Add $75 each for additional family members numbers 6 and 7.

[b] Add $80 each for additional family members numbers 6 and 7.

Likewise, compensating factors can lower this residual income figure. It is up to the individual lender and underwriter to determine if the veteran qualifies.

The VA also requires that the veteran's total housing expense (PITI/HOA) and long-term debt payments (over six months) **not exceed 41%,** just like FHA. This 41% ratio can be exceeded with compensating factors. It is up to the individual lender to justify the higher ratio.

On page 201 of the Appendix is a copy of the form used to qualify the veteran. You only need to know the withholding amounts (look on your pay stub or get them from an approved VA lender), and to get the maintenance and utility figures from either a local VA-approved lender or the regional VA office near you. It would be a good idea also to make sure the residual figures are still current.

The VA's guidelines for self-employed and part-time income are similar to those for conventional loans. The VA will tend to be a little more flexible in some respects. At worst, it will allow the income from those sources to be used to offset long-term debt in qualifying. Again, check with your local VA-approved lender to find out what you will be allowed.

The VA Interest Rate

The maximum VA interest rate is set by the VA. If the maximum is 9.5%, the veteran cannot get a 10% loan (except in certain limited instances). This limitation sounds like a good deal for the borrower, and superficially it is. However, if the going rate is at 10%, the market is not going to buy a 9.5% loan without adding more discount points so that the actual yield is 10%. And on VA loans, **the veteran cannot pay the discount points** (again, except in certain limited instances not involving a purchase). They must be paid by someone else, usually the seller. When the market says that it wants 3% discount points on the maximum allowable VA rate, it can be hard to get someone to agree to sell his or her house and pay 3% of the borrower's loan amount.

Actually, 3% or less is not hard if you use the strategy we discussed in Chapter 2, under cash needed, by offering full price or at least enough above the seller's acceptable price to cover the cost of the points. That way, the sellers get the minimum price at which they will sell.

The VA will usually raise the rate when it is evident the market is rising and will not be coming down any time in the near future. When discount points rise to 3% or 4% and stay there, the market is surely rising. But, because the federal government is involved, politics can have a role in the decision. No president wants to recognize that interest rates are rising if it is avoidable. During the Carter administration the prime rate reached 21% and fixed-rate loans hit as high as 16%, but VA loans never went above 12.5%. Bureaucrats could control the rate, but not the points. They went over 10.

VA Funding Fee

The VA does not have a mortgage insurance premium as such; what they do have is the VA funding fee. The fees as of October 1, 1991, are as follows:

1. 1.25% of the loan amount on loans with less than 5% down payment (100% − 95.01% LTV)
2. 0.75% with 5% down, but less than 10%
3. 0.50% with 10% or more down
4. 0.50% on assumptions

In this way the government collects money for one reason and calls it something else. The VA has tried in the past to raise the funding fee to 3.8%. If that looks suspiciously like the FHA MIP, there is a reason. Luckily for the veteran, politics has prevented the government from pushing through a higher funding fee at this time. This fee can be paid in cash at closing, or the borrower can finance it into the loan, just like a MIP. If you buy a $100,000 house with a 100% loan and finance the funding fee, the total loan will be $101,250. The only time you cannot finance the fee is when it will exceed the maximum allowable 100% loan ($184,000 based on entitlement of $46,000; $144,000 with $36,000 or, 4 × current entitlement). This prohibition arises not because VA won't let you do it, but because Ginnie Mae (that is, the secondary market) won't buy it.

There are a few instances when the veteran does not have to pay the funding fee. Obviously, the seller can pay it. Or, if the veteran has a service-related disability, he or she is exempt from the funding fee. If a veteran dies from a service-related injury or disability, the surviving spouse retains the entitlement and does not have to pay the fee. If you think you may qualify, call your local VA office.

Besides being a no cash down loan, VA has another benefit. The seller, or anyone else, can pay all of the borrower's closing costs—if you can convince the seller. Usually, it will be a very motivated seller. I have done three VA loans for which the borrower put no cash down and got the seller to pay all the closing costs. The borrower literally bought the house with no cash out of pocket. But, in addition to having a motivated seller, the borrower must have strong qualifications. Few lenders are willing to make a loan to someone who has no cash in the property and is not well qualified.

The **seller concessions** are divided into *two categories* by VA. The *first* includes costs on which there are no limits, such as closing costs (excluding prepaids) and normal discount points. The *second* is limited to 4% of the value of the property and includes such items as prepaid taxes and insurance, the funding fee, temporary or permanent interest rate buy-down discount points above the normal discount, and any other inducements to buy such as microwave ovens or helping to pay off the buyer's debts in order to qualify easier. I have never had a seller offer to pay off some of the purchaser's debts, but then again, I don't think anyone knew to ask. A word of caution: Just because the VA will allow it doesn't mean that the lender will. Remember that each lender and investor can modify guidelines to make them less flexible.

Land Limits

And, for the gentleman farmer, the VA has no maximum land limits (see Chapter 6 for other loan types). You can buy a farm or build a residence on a large parcel of land. If you are going to use income from the farm to qualify, you must be able to show that you have a background in farming.

Loan Lock-ins

Because the VA sets the maximum interest rate, and because that rate can go up or down during the loan process, the VA has set rules governing when the lender can charge a higher rate. Basically, if the lender locks in the rate and then the VA lowers it, the veteran must pay the higher rate as long as the **written lock-in agreement** contains the following:

1. The interest rate and/or points being locked.

2. A statement that the interest rate at the time of the lock-in does not exceed the maximum VA rate current then.
3. The legal description of the property being financed.
4. A reasonable lock-in period.
5. The signatures of both the borrower(s) and the lender.

Otherwise, the lender must give the borrower the new, lower interest rate.

The VA Appraisal

VA appraisals are called **Certificates of Reasonable Value (CRVs),** and they are performed by VA-approved appraisers. The normal process has been that the lender requests the appraisal, the appraiser sends the finished appraisal to the VA regional office for VA review, and then the VA mails it back to the lender. This system can add a week to the processing time of the loan. Fortunately, the VA is beginning to change. It is now starting to allow approved lenders to review and approve the appraisals without going to the VA. If the veteran borrower uses one of these approved lenders, he or she can save time, and, in some instances, avoid possible problems. The VA has been known to lose appraisals.

The advantages of a VA loan are these:

1. Liberal qualifying
2. Little or no cash down
3. Relatively high maximum loan amount
4. The fact that the seller pays discount points, and can pay any or all other closing costs, including prepaid taxes and insurance
5. No mortgage insurance (other than the funding fee)
6. No maximum land limits

The disadvantages of VA loans are:

1. Relatively high funding fee costs
2. Somewhat bureaucratic
3. A little longer to process

OTHER "SPECIAL" LOAN PROGRAMS FOR
MODERATE INCOME AND/OR FIRST-TIME HOMEBUYERS

These loans are meant to help the low- to moderate-income buyer and, in some programs, the first-time homebuyer. The federal government has mandated that lenders must make programs of this type available to meet the Community Reinvestment Act. As a result, many lenders will have at least one of these programs.

Fannie Mae's 3-2 Option Loan

To meet the call for affordable housing, and to help take up the slack created by new FHA requirements, Fannie has developed the Community Home Buyer's Program with the 3-2 option (CHBP). (This program is similar to the Revenue Bond Authority Mortgages discussed below.) This program is for owner-occupied single family residences, with approved condominiums (condos) and planned unit developments (P.U.D.s) eligible. The borrower's income cannot exceed 115% of the area median income; this requirement satisfies the goal of providing financing for moderate- to low-income borrowers. (A participating lender will have the income figures for your area.) The loan terms can only be 15- or 30-year fixed rates.

The down payment works like this:

1. *The borrowers have to put down at least 3% of their own funds.*

2. *The other 2% (for a total of 5% down) can come from the following:*
   a. A gift from a family member, nonprofit organization, or public authority. Don't forget that you will need a gift letter and full gift verification as required by Fannie Mae (see section on gifts in Chapter 2)
   b. A grant or unsecured loan from a nonprofit organization or public authority. These loans are typically deferred and forgivable; since they have no required monthly payment, they do not count in the qualifying ratios.

3. *A secured second mortgage can be used for additional financing, but it cannot be used as part of the 5% down*

(3% + 2%). With the second mortgage, the maximum TLTV is 95%. This loan must be counted in the qualifying unless it is fully deferred, forgivable, and has no required monthly payment.

The cash for closing costs also should come from the borrower's own resources. If the buyer does not have sufficient cash, a gift from a family member or a gift or unsecured loan from a nonprofit organization or public entity can be used. Fannie Mae has also **waived the normal reserve requirement of two months' payments** that their other loans have as part of the total cash needed.

You are probably wondering about **the nonprofit organizations and public authorities** that are giving all this money away. Yes, they really do exist for moderate- to low-income borrowers. Many local governments have set up Housing Authorities or Foundations, in one form or another, that will help supply cash, up to a maximum amount, to a borrower who may not have much cash. These loans, or grants, are usually set up so that there is no required payment. If the house is sold before the first mortgage is paid off, the borrower has to pay back the grant plus moderate interest. If the borrower keeps the house until the first mortgage is completely paid off, then the loan is forgiven. Check with your local government housing agencies to see if there are programs available. They should be usable for any of the moderate-income loans discussed in this chapter as well as FHA and VA loans.

The qualifying ratios go well beyond the standard Fannie Mae ratios. They will allow the housing expense to be **33%** of the stable gross monthly income (GMI) and the total expense ratio to be **38%** of GMI. Fannie will allow the total expense (housing and monthly debt) ratio to go up to 40% if the borrowers can show they have previously paid a higher portion of their income toward debts.

When figuring for yourself how to qualify, don't forget that there will be mortgage insurance. Several mortgage insurance companies are participating in this program. Using the highest up-front and renewal premiums in the mortgage insurance comparison chart on page 195 in the Appendix, one should be able to make a close approximation of the actual premiums.

This is a great loan for anyone who falls within the maximum income limits and has only a minimum amount of cash.

Many lenders who offer normal Fannie Mae loans will have this program.

Mortgage Revenue Bond Authorities

The federal government has granted state and local authorities the power to issue tax-free mortgage revenue bonds. The proceeds are used to make low-interest mortgages to borrowers who are, with few exceptions, **first-time homebuyers with lower incomes.** Because the bonds sold are tax-free, they carry **a lower interest rate,** which then allows the authority to offer lower rates on its mortgages. These loans are subject to a multitude of rules, based on the federal law governing them. There are **maximum sales prices,** not loan amounts, that a borrower can pay for a house, and **the borrower cannot make a gross income over certain limits.** The house must be occupied by the borrower. It must be a single-family residence. And, the property cannot be used in any way to earn income, either by rent or by running a business from the property (this restriction includes businesses such as Amway™ and the like). The limits on sales price and gross income will vary from area to area, usually within a Standard Metropolitan Statistical Area (SMSA). Each year, the Internal Revenue Service provides data to set the new limits based on incomes and housing costs in each SMSA.

Each state has its own authority. An example is the Virginia Housing and Development Authority, or VHDA, which approves and funds the loans. The mortgage lender receives the application and processes it. The loan is then submitted to the Authority. The lender will normally get the 1% origination fee and the servicing rights. The Authority gets the discount points. As in a VA loan, the borrower cannot pay the discount points.

The borrower must be a first-time homebuyer, or not have owned a residence within three years. There are exceptions to this rule, mostly within certain targeted areas. The personal net assets of the borrower also are limited. The object is to help people with limited cash and income.

In line with that goal, these loans offer **liberal qualifying** based on several different sets of loan types. The basic loan is the conventional loan with a minimum of 5% down and mortgage insurance. The ratios for qualifying are 32% for housing expense and 40% for housing expense plus monthly debts with over six months to pay off. The lender needs to have a mortgage insurance company that recognizes the more liberal standards and will approve higher-risk loans.

Another option is for the borrower to get an authority-issued loan that is FHA insured. In this type of loan, the income and sales price limits are still set by the authority, but the qualifying and cash down are the same as in a normal FHA loan. That is, the borrower can put as little as 3% down and finance the MIP. The maximum loan amount with the MIP financed can never exceed the maximum sales price set by the authority.

Or, the borrower can get a loan that is guaranteed by the VA if he or she has sufficient entitlement. As in the FHA loan, the qualifying and cash down are done according to VA standards, but the authority income and sales price limits must be met. The loan with the funding fee financed cannot exceed the maximum sales price.

The Farmers Home Guarantee program, discussed below, now participates in guaranteeing revenue bond mortgages. A local lender can tell you if it is available in your area.

Because the guidelines between the lender and the insurer overlap, using a lender who is familiar with bond authority loans is important. Some authorities may not offer FHA or VA loans.

The authority given by Congress to issue these bonds has time limits. Each time the authorization nears expiration, Congress must extend it. Otherwise, the revenue bond authorities cannot issue new bonds. There seems to be a yearly struggle between those who hate to see all that interest income go untaxed, and those who recognize that there must be some way for low- to moderate-income borrowers to purchase a home.

The Farmers Home Administration
Guaranteed Rural Housing Loan

This new form of financing functions differently from the way Farmers Home has in the past. It was created by the same National Affordable Housing Act of 1990 that gave us the major changes and additional costs in the Federal Housing Administration program. Note that we are now discussing the Farmers Home Administration (FmHA), not to be confused with the FHA.

This program is designed to provide **financing for rural housing for first-time owners** or for those who do not own a "structurally sound or functionally adequate home." The house must be on a publicly maintained road. *Rural* is defined by the FmHA as outside a standard Metropolitan Statistical Area. To find out which areas qualify, call your lender or the FmHa. **The loan amount can be up to 100%** of the lesser of cost or appraised value and the seller can pay all closing costs (that's right, no cash down). There is **a 0.9% guarantee fee,** which is much cheaper than the comparable FHA or VA fees. The loan is obtained from an approved lender, which will process and close the loan with FmHa underwriting. The loan can be sold into the secondary market, with Fannie Mae being the first investor agreeing to purchase this program.

Some of the limitations to this program include **maximum allowable adjusted gross income** (similar to the revenue bond authorities) and **maximum loan amounts** based on the area's current FHA maximum loan limits. The adjustments to the borrower's gross income are these:

1. $480 per year for each child under 18 years, or over 18 years if the child is a full-time student
2. Actual child care expenses up to $4,800 per year
3. $400 per year for an elderly family

Other deductions may be published by the FmHA in the future.

For the most part, these limitations are not so low as to preclude a large segment of moderate-income borrowers from qualifying. The interest rate, according to the FmHA rules, cannot exceed the current VA or Fannie Mae rate. The meaning of this rule is unclear, because these rates are not always the same; but it probably means the Fannie Mae pricing on the current VA rate (example: a maximum VA rate of 9.5%, which Fannie agrees to purchase with 2% discount points). Also, similar to a revenue bond authority loan, it must be for a single-family owner-occupied home from which no income can be derived.

The biggest obstacle, however, will probably be the requirement that **the borrower must be "unable to secure the credit necessary to finance a home without FmHa assistance"** (all of these quotations come from the FmHA Information for Lenders booklet). That means, of course, that the borrower must be turned down by or be unable to qualify for any other available loan program, such as conventional, FHA, or VA.

This loan is not for those with a spotty credit history. The credit standards are very strict. Consider:

1. No more than one payment over 30 days past due in the past 12 months. This includes credit cards.

2. Less than two rent payments 30 days or more past due in the last three years.

3. No unsatisfied judgments within the past 12 months

4. No collections within the past 12 months.

Just like FHA, qualifying is based on ratios of 29% for housing expense and 41% for housing and debt expense. However, these ratios cannot be exceeded for any reason (as of the time the program was started).

Not being able to qualify for any other loan program, being in a designated rural area, falling within adjusted gross income slots, and meeting the absolute credit and qualifying guidelines are quite a gauntlet to run. The government is counting on these guidelines to weed out most of the problem borrowers. While this is a very laudable idea, it may also weed out many otherwise qualified and deserving borrowers, in effect, denying loans to those it was intended to help.

This loan also has a subsidized payment program for borrowers who do not have sufficient income to qualify for the standard plan. FmHA uses a formula to determine if the borrower fits. If you do not qualify under the normal program, ask if you can get the subsidized one. This loan, however, still requires that you have good credit.

This politically motivated program has many gray areas. As a result, it undoubtedly will undergo numerous revisions within the first one to two years (it became effective in May 1991). You should consult with several bond authority approved lenders and the FmHa to find out exactly what is currently required to qualify. Note that I said "several lenders and the FmHA." I think it will be a good while before any one person or lender, much less FmHA, will know enough to be considered a "one stop" authority.

6

THE APPRAISAL

The appraisal is one of the four main parts of a loan application. Because the property to be financed will be the security for the loan, the lender must be certain that it has sufficient value. The loan amount is based on the lesser of the sales price or appraised value, called the **Value.** Otherwise, the lender could make a 95% LTV loan on a $100,000 purchase when the house is really worth $90,000. That would be a loan of over 106% LTV. If that happened, the lender had better hope the property appreciates quickly and that the borrower doesn't default.

The art of appraising residential property has evolved over time into a very sophisticated yet subjective science. The secondary market has developed guidelines with which it expects the appraiser to comply in order to come up with a fair and reasonably certain value. Also, to cover themselves in case of foreclosure, investors in the secondary market want assurance that it is a marketable property. Lenders always look at the worst case scenario.

Lenders want to know whether the property is in an area that is growing, stable, or declining. Is it in a predominantly residential area? Is the area in transition, for example, from residential to industrial? Is the house in good repair? Does it have the minimum number of bedrooms, bathrooms, and the like to give it marketability in the area? In short, is this a property on which it would be safe for the lender to make a loan.

The appraiser's responsibility is to provide the lender with the necessary information to make this decision. A good appraiser will make an independent judgment, uninfluenced by any of the parties to the transaction. If she feels any or all parts of the property do not meet the minimum guidelines, she is obligated to inform the lender. Although the borrower usually pays for the appraisal, it is done for the lender.

Let us say that an appraiser reports a roof needs to be re-placed, or the surrounding properties are declining in value. Then the lender would require that the roof be replaced before closing, or, in the case of declining values (known as economic obsolescence), the lender would probably not make the loan un-less the LTV was so low as to present minimal risk. If the house had only one bedroom and was located in an area where most houses had three bedrooms and there was no demonstrated de-mand for one-bedroom houses, then the lender would probably decline the loan because the property would be functionally ob-solete. However, certain lenders and loan types, such as FHA, may be more lenient.

Appraisers use the rooms that are aboveground (that is, not in the basement) in determining the total number of bedrooms and bathrooms—even if the basement is a walk-out. This rule can present some special problems. If the house is a ranch style on a full basement with one bedroom on the main level and two bedrooms in the lower level, the property is considered a one-bedroom house by Fannie and Freddie. If this type of house cannot be shown to be common in the area, then the secondary market may decline to buy the loan. That is, the lender won't make the loan.

The value of the land without the improvements is another key part of the appraisal. Most lenders do not want the land to represent more than about 30% of the total value, unless the ap-praiser can show it is common in the area for the land to exceed that percentage. In Virginia is an area where the land is averag-ing $150,000 per lot, or 40% to 45% of the value. By showing that other properties in the area have similar land values, an ap-praiser can convince the lender to make loans on these homes. The FHA will vary from region to region, but generally it will use the same guidelines as Fannie and Freddie, except their rules are more flexible. Tax-exempt bond authorities normally limit their loans to a very small amount of land, two to five acres or less. The VA, as we noted earlier, has no land restrictions. Jumbo and nonconforming loans set their own guidelines for land values. There are lenders who will do special loans for farms and estates. If you have a property that you feel might not meet a lender's normal requirements, call around and find out if it will present a problem. Each lender can be different.

Most important of all, the appraiser must establish the value of the property. In the *Market Value* method of establishing value, the appraiser compares the property in question with three recent comparable sales. A second method of establishing value, the *Cost* approach, calculates the value of reproducing the property. The Market approach is used in the majority of appraisals. The comparables must be within a reasonable distance of the subject property, be similar, and have sold within the last six months, 12 months at the very latest. The comps (comparable values) are adjusted (value added or subtracted) based on their overall similarity to the subject property. If the subject property has a garage and one of the comps does not, then the comp is adjusted by adding the value of the garage to it, or, vice versa. The total of these adjustments on each comp should fall within a certain percentage of the value, or sales price, of that particular comp. If the percentages are too high, that fact indicates either that the appraiser used excessive adjustments to justify the subject property's value or that the comp may not be similar enough to the subject property to use as a comparable. The latter reason is why some recent sales that the borrower or the Realtor thinks are perfect comps will not be used by the appraiser in determining the value of the property. Another point that may confuse the borrower is the lender's rejection of certain comparables because they are too far away from the subject property. In suburban or urban areas, the lender expects the comps to be within blocks of and no more than a mile from the subject, and in a similar neighborhood. In a rural area, depending on the lender, the comps can be 5 to 15 miles away. However, most lenders will want at least one comp to be in close proximity to the subject property. Because of the difficulty in determining an accurate market value on rural properties, and because they tend to take longer to sell, most lenders will not lend more than 90% LTV on rural properties. Fannie and Freddie will not buy 95% rural property loans. As I said, the lender is looking at the worst case scenario.

The majority of loan appraisals will have few problems, and most of those can be cured. However, the appraiser can act much like an underwriter, by approving or rejecting the property as acceptable security for the loan.

An example of an appraisal that did affect the loan occurred when a borrower came to me wanting to refinance his house in a very nice area of the city. He had done some renovation work and wanted to recover the cost by refinancing. Based on the preliminary value of what he originally paid for the house and the cost of the renovations, the LTV would be around 60%. The borrower was well qualified, and the loan, all in all, looked like a sure bet — until the appraisal arrived.

The borrower had hired what is known as a jackleg contractor to do the work, that is, someone who is unskilled or untrained to do independent work. This "contractor" had wired and plumbed the house and added interior partitions. The wiring and plumbing were not done according to the local building code. In fact, a permit had never been obtained and the work had never been inspected. If it had, it would have been rejected. The owner was not aware of these defects. He didn't even know that a permit and inspection were required. He was not completely innocent in this mess, however. He designed the changes, which turned the third bedroom into more of a passageway and created a bathroom with such a low ceiling that anyone taller than 5'2" had to stoop in it.

The appraiser, seeing that things weren't quite right, checked the city building department, where he found that the permits had never been issued. Being a competent professional, he knew several things. First, the city could require that the work be torn out and redone. Second, the lender would not like a bedroom in a hallway and a bath in which people cannot stand erect. The appraiser literally stated in his report that the property was not good security for a loan. Because the borrower was not willing to make the corrections, the loan was denied. Only a lender willing to take a risk and hold the loan in portfolio would have considered this property.

In arriving at the value, one other thing should be mentioned: personal property. That is, things like stoves, refrigerators, blinds, rugs, and lawn mowers that the seller has included in the sale. For purposes of evaluation, most lenders will accept the major appliances if the appraiser states that it is normal for them to be included in the sale, and that no value was given to them in arriving at the final value of the property. Short-lived, readily replaceable things like lawn mowers and Oriental rugs should not be part of the purchase contract. If the purchaser will not buy the house without them, they should be purchased by a separate bill of sale that states the items will convey upon the closing on the real estate.

When I was still selling real estate a couple that was interested in buying a house that I had listed came to me. There was one problem. They had already contracted to purchase another property, which they ultimately decided they did not want (a case of Buyer's Remorse). The contract stipulated they would apply for a first mortgage. It also stated that the seller was throwing in the lawn mower, two rugs, and a horse. As I told them, all they had to do was apply for the loan and they would be turned down. Mortgage lenders do not make 30-year loans on horses.

Most of the appraisals done today will be acceptable. The majority of borrowers have little to worry about. Too often the borrower gets upset over something the appraiser noted about the property which the borrower takes exception to—as, giving the condition of the property as average, when the proverbial "everyone" knows that it is in mint condition. If the lender doesn't comment on it, don't take it personally and don't worry about it. Worry about the big stuff like old wiring or leaky basements. And be happy that it was noticed by the appraiser, because appraisers are not usually expected to catch the less obvious structural and mechanical problems.

7

THE DIFFERENT TYPES OF PROPERTIES

Most borrowers don't consider the property that they are purchasing in terms of how it appeals to the market as a whole, as long as it appeals to them. Sellers usually have a definite emotional attachment, while borrowers are trying to justify the purchase and the price in their own minds. Lenders have a less emotional and a more proprietary interest, in the form of large sums of cash. These business and personal emotions can collide when the relative merits of the property are discussed.

Lenders want to make loans on properties that appeal to as wide a market as possible. Borrowers want to own property with character—property that is different from the rest of the houses on the block. The appraisal will define just how unique this property is, and the lender's guidelines will judge whether it is acceptable for the type of loan for which the borrower has applied. Most properties are broken down into different types and then classified according to whether their features, such as number of bedrooms, are common for the market area.

THE SINGLE-FAMILY DETACHED HOME

The single-family home is what almost every American dreams of owning. Most people think of this as being a single, free-standing structure, a single house by itself, on its own lot. The construction style of the property adds further to its definition. There are the standard ranch, the colonial two-story, the split-level, the tri-level, the contemporary, the log home, the dirt-covered energy-saving home, the dome house, and the ones that look as if someone lost the blueprints. The more offbeat or bizarre the construction, the more difficult it is to obtain regular financing. For example, Fannie and Freddie require that log homes have three comparable sales of log homes on the appraisal (sometimes two comps will be acceptable). Unless you live in a community of log homes, there is little chance of finding three, or even two, recent sales of comparable log houses to support the value. This property will require a nonconforming loan, or FHA or VA; these are more liberal in financing this type of property.

THE SINGLE-FAMILY ATTACHED HOME, OR TOWN HOUSE

Attached homes or **town houses** are becoming more prevalent as the costs of land and materials rise. Each of these houses, joined together at a common wall, sits on its own lot. The only difference between the attached and the detached house is that they are—attached.

Town houses generally are built as part of a development that has covenants and restrictions to protect the properties as a whole and that provides certain basic services such as trash removal and snowplowing. With this type of property you often are subject to homeowner's association fees (HOA) and Road Maintenance fees (when the roads are not public). These fees add another item that the lender must approve. There are lending guidelines for acceptable HOA and Road Maintenance Agreements. Most builders today work with Realtors or lenders who make sure that the covenants and restrictions are acceptable. Also, most state and local governments will have requirements that meet or exceed lender requirements on homeowner's association agreements. It is always advisable to get a copy of the recorded Covenants and Restrictions before committing to the purchase of any property governed by them. Some states now require that the purchaser be notified that there are covenants and restrictions on the property and that these Covenants and Restrictions be provided within a given period of time after acceptance of the contract to purchase.

CONDOMINIUMS

Condominium was the buzzword of the 1980s. It has also been a dirty word for much of the market, and lenders in particular. Condos are basically apartments that are owned instead of rented (not to be confused with co-ops). They come in many forms, from detached or attached housing in a complex to multiple units. The main distinguishing feature is that everything except the unit itself is owned in common by the entire complex. There are no individual lots. Most condos consist of a complex much like an apartment building in which the units are owned individually. (Many condos today are actually apartments that have been converted.) This sounds great for those who cannot afford a house or who are not interested in cutting grass.

The problems start when not enough units sell to make the complex viable. Then the developer may either abandon it or declare bankruptcy, which leaves the poor souls who got in on the "ground floor" sitting in a mostly empty complex that is not being maintained or managed. Or, the units are sold as investment properties and become run-down because the tenants trash it. In either case, the properties will decrease in value, if indeed there is a market for them in which you can establish a value.

Condos are not all bad. They have their place in the market as long as they are properly designed, marketed, and managed. The secondary market, and almost every lender, feels the same way. But, they will thoroughly scrutinize the development, its covenants and restrictions, condo fees, homeowner's association budget, and bond coverage before they will make loans there. Fannie and Freddie will not buy loans on any of the units unless they have approved the development beforehand. After the project has been in existence for several years and it has demonstrated market demand, it is often easier to get some lenders to make loans there.

When it comes to condos, be very careful! Make sure the one you want is approved by either Fannie or Freddie so that it will have more potential mortgage money available for purchasers when you decide to sell. If only one or two lenders are making loans on the condos, you may later find yourself trying to sell a property on which purchasers cannot find adequate financing. If the original lenders stop lending there, you may have no available financing. Don't buy where more than 20% to 30% of the total units are nonowner-occupied. (Most secondary market investors will not buy loans when over 30% are nonowner or investment units.) Check the covenants and restrictions to make sure there is nothing that could adversely affect your investment. Look at the homeowner's association budget to make sure there are adequate reserves for repairs and maintenance. And, most importantly, check around the area to see if there really is a demand for the condos you are considering. Do not get suckered in by the initial low price and the health spa in the basement. The lender won't.

TWO- TO FOUR-FAMILY HOMES

Then there are the two- to four-unit multifamily dwellings: duplex, triplex, and quadruplex. The secondary market, and most lenders, recognize properties from two to four units as multifamily residential properties. These can be financed as either owner- or nonowner-occupied homes. A multifamily property will require a more detailed appraisal and comparables that are also multifamily. And these mean a more expensive appraisal.

Anything over four units is considered a commercial property and will need a loan from a specialized lender, usually a bank, insurance company, or a nonconforming secondary market investor. Mortgage lenders for home loans do not get involved with commercial lending.

LOCATION, LOCATION, LOCATION

Once you know what you want, where do you want it to be? Is it downtown, in the suburbs, out in the county, in the woods, or up on the mountain? Lenders categorize homes as being urban (in town), suburban (on the edge or close to town and all of the amenities such as schools and shopping), and rural (not close to other developments, schools, shopping, and generally not convenient to much of anything).

As a rule, the more accessible, the more urban, and the nearer to a desirable area your property is, the easier it will be to obtain normal financing. It is no fluke that Realtors always say that location is the primary factor for being able to sell a property and to get top dollar for it.

A rural location presents the most problems because it is harder to establish market value and there may be much less demand for a rural property (as we discussed earlier). Lenders will make certain allowances for rural properties when the appraiser looks for comparable sales. And, as the LTV goes down, the lender's requirements also go down. The comps can be 7 to

15 miles from the subject instead of one block to one mile. But, they do have to be similar, and they still must have sold within the past 6 to 12 months. These can be very hard to carry out when there is little around to compare with. On top of that, much of the rural property has **extra acreage.**

The normal mortgage lender, in particular those dealing with the conforming secondary market, is interested in financing residential properties, not mini-farms. There are other loans and lenders for that type of property. Nonconforming loans, commercial banks, and the Federal Land Bank are a few lenders who will finance your place in the country.

SECOND HOMES

If you want a place in the country or on the beach or on the river as a getaway, you are talking **Second Home.** There is a very large market for these properties, and most lenders offer some type of second-home financing. The secondary market will buy second home loans as long as they meet the standard guidelines. The normal standards are that the cost of your personal residence should not be more than 28% of your gross monthly income; and the total expenses, including the second-home mortgage payment, should not exceed 36%. No rent income from the property can be used in qualifying. You also have to put down at least 20% cash. Check your lenders for their programs. Some of them may charge a higher rate or more points for second homes.

8

INTEREST RATES, POINTS, AND LOCK-INS

As we discussed earlier, lenders set rates based on what the current market is, or what they think the market will be. They also charge points to buy the rate down and/or to get extra fee income. The borrowers' mission is to find the best loan, the best rate and points, and the best service, and to be assured that they will get all of these at closing.

When you call around to the various lenders you find that their rates are not the same. Some will be 0.125% to 0.5%, or more, higher or lower than the rest. Why is that?

WHY ARE LENDERS DIFFERENT?

The rates and points of each lender are based on various methods of dealing in the secondary market, plus any additions or subtractions that the lender includes. There are innumerable ways to derive pricing from the secondary market. I will cover the most basic methods, and how they can help or hurt the borrower in his quest for the best rate and lender. While this description may not seem very pertinent to getting the loan, it will help the borrower to understand the different pricings of lenders, and to avoid being taken advantage of in certain circumstances. It can also make the borrower's choice of the best, most reliable lender easier.

First, lenders can sell loans by either of two methods, called *mandatory* or *optional deliveries.* They are exactly as their names imply. If a delivery is mandatory, the loan, or loans, must be delivered within a given period of time. If the lender cannot fulfill the commitment, the lender is required either to pay a stiff penalty or even to replace the shortfall with cash. Most lenders doing a mandatory delivery will make sure that they can fill it before committing, and they will also be less likely to allow any renegotiating of locked rates if interest goes down (see next section). For an idea of how a typical mandatory delivery works, here is an example.

The lender agrees to deliver $20 million in 30-year fixed rate loans to the investor at a rate of 10% with 1% discount (commitments can also be for a range of loans, say from 9.75% to 10.25% with corresponding points to give the investor the interest rate that was agreed upon, 10% in our example). The lender then has a specified number of days in which to deliver this package of closed loans. We will say 90 days for this example. If the lender provides the package at the agreed time, everyone should make a profit. If the lender does not fill the commitment and ships only $15 million within the 90 days, then it will have to pay a penalty on the $5 million shortfall, or else pay the $5 million in cash. In the latter case the investor still makes money and the lender has a serious cash problem. Or, if the lender thinks that the market will go down even further than the rate agreed upon, it might lock in loans for more money than the amount committed for delivery, say $30 million, or $10 million more than the commitment. If the rates do drop, the lender can negotiate a sale at a premium because it has loans at a rate above the current market, and it will make lots of money. If the rates go up, the lender has $10 million in uncovered loans which it cannot sell, unless the lender wants to lose a bunch of money by selling the loans at a discount to their actual cost. (If the market rose to a point where a 10% interest rate required 2 discount points, the lender would have to sell its 10% and 1% discount point loans at a loss of 1% of the $10 million in uncovered loans, or $100,000). Faced with this potential loss, the lender has several options. It can portfolio the loans (use its own money to hold the loans) until the rates drop, if it has the assets to do this. It can sell at a loss, if it can afford to do this. Or, it can refuse to honor the locked-in loans that it cannot cover, by either outright refusing to close at the agreed interest rate or delaying the closing until the lock-in expires. Either way is unethical and illegal.

The advantage of mandatory deliveries is that the lender can get lower pricing from the investor because the investor knows he will get the loans and pricing on which they agreed.

Optional delivery is safer for the lender because it is only *optional* that they deliver the loan(s) to the investor. On groups of loans, called pools or packages, the lender will pay an up-front, nonrefundable fee to the investor for the privilege of not having to fill the commitment if the lender cannot fill it or does not want to fill it. On single loans, there usually is no fee, except in certain instances where the investor requires a lock-in fee at the time the borrower decides to lock the rate and points. The lender will get better pricing on a commitment for a package of loans than it will for single loans. Smaller lenders and brokers will normally use the single loan delivery because of its low risk. Optional deliveries will sometimes have features allowing the lender to offer a relock option when interest rates go down. For the borrower, rates for loans with optional delivery will be higher than mandatory rates. Do not expect the lender to divulge how it sells its loans. Most branch offices and loan officers have little idea of how the loan is handled once it is closed. I have included this information to give you an idea of how pricing fluctuates and why a lender may try not to close the loan.

Next, consider how the servicing is handled in these deliveries. In Chapter 2 we talked about how the lender can get more income by selling the servicing; that is, the lender receives a servicing-released premium as additional income. If the servicing is released, this premium, paid to the lender, can be used to offer even lower rates to the borrower. Also, most investors offer premiums on a sliding scale, paying a higher one for higher loan amounts. Some lenders will offer pricing that has fewer discount points as the loan amount goes up, that is, if the lender wishes to pass on all or part of this premium to the borrower instead of holding it as fee income. An example would be pricing of 10% with 1 discount point to the investor, and an additional 0.375% servicing-released premium to the lender for selling the servicing to the investor. The lender could choose to pass this on to the borrower and offer the loan at 10% with 0.625% discount to the borrower (1% required discount − 0.375% premium rebate = 0.625% discount). Or, the lender could keep part of the premium, say 0.25%, and pass the remainder on to the borrower (0.125%, or 0.875% discount). Of course, as we have discussed, the lender can keep the whole thing for itself. If the loan is being sold and the servicing will be transferred at the time the loan is closed (this fact must be disclosed at closing or shortly afterward), you can bet the rent that the lender is receiving some type of premium.

Now that you are confused by these multiple manipulations of interest rate pricings, let us consider another common way for lenders to sell loans into the secondary market: issuing their own **securities, or bonds,** backed by the loans that they have taken.

Without going into great detail (that would require a book unto itself), a lender can package or pool its loans in large amounts, usually millions, and sell securities that are secured by the loans it holds. In this way it can get back the money invested, it still holds the loans and the servicing, and it can often offer an even lower interest rate. The big drawback is that the lender can lose its shirt, and sometimes the whole company, because of the high risk involved in setting its own rates and trying to make sure that it can then sell the bonds into the market before interest rates jump. Under such circumstances the integrity of the lender is tested. Just as in a mandatory delivery, the lender may be forced to honor interest rates that cost it money.

As you may have noticed, the pricing and marketing of mortgage loans is legalized gambling. How competent and conservative a lender chooses to be can make a tremendous difference in the overall costs to the borrower. The difference between a commitment of a large pool of money and the rates on a per loan basis can be 0.5% or greater on the interest rate. Most lenders will employ some combination of the methods described to devise competitive products and minimize risk. Each lender (and each investor in the secondary market) can have pricing for any particular loan type that will be different from that of the next lender (or borrower) because of how it is buying or selling that loan. Pricing gets much more complicated than this, and there are many variations on how loans are bought and sold, but the explanation gives you an idea of why rates differ. What it means to the borrower is that there are multiple opportunities to get the best rate through this competitive marketing structure.

LOCKED-IN RATES

Lock-Ins reserve the money for the borrower at a given rate and points for a set number of days. Most lock periods are determined by the lender and are for 10, 30, 60, 90, 120, and sometimes 180 days. The most common period is 60 days. The shorter the lock-in period, the lower the discount points, and vice versa. A lender may, or may not, choose to pass this savings on to the borrower. If you are locking in 45 days or less before closing, ask if the lender will give you lower points. Here is a simple example.

The investor is offering to buy 30-year loans at 10%, with 1 discount point, for delivery in 90 days. The lender then offers to make a loan at 10%, with 1 discount point, or even more if it wants additional fee income. The borrower wants to close 50 days from now and wants to lock in the rate. The lender will lock it in for 60 days, knowing that 60 days will provide enough time to process, approve and close the loan; after that, the lender will have at least 30 days to get the completed documents together, straighten out any problems that might have come up (like attorney mistakes), and then deliver the loan to the investor. (Remember, while this example uses a 90-day delivery, others may have much shorter periods.) If everything goes according to plan, the borrower gets the rate, the lender gets the loan closed, and the investor buys the loan. But, as we know, "The best laid schemes o' mice and men" will often come undone.

What happens if the borrower doesn't qualify or backs out of the contract? If the commitment to deliver the loan to the investor was an optional one, the lender has no problem. If it was a mandatory delivery, then the lender has two choices: Find another loan that can close and be delivered on time to replace it, or pay a stiff penalty. Pay enough penalties, and you can go out of business. To protect themselves, many lenders will hedge, or cover part of the loans in their pipeline with a commitment, and leave the others uncovered based on the normal percentage of loans that do not close. You begin to see the balancing act the lender has to accomplish to be competitive and profitable.

It is not required that borrowers lock in a rate at application. They can wait until several days to do so. By waiting, they are obviously taking a chance, much like playing the stock market. There will always be borrowers who think they can wait until the market is at its lowest and get the best rate. Chances are better that they will wait so long that the market will have gone back up. Don't worry about whether you are getting the absolute lowest rate possible, or you will go crazy trying to outguess the market.

On the other hand, borrowers who lock in a rate may then see the market go even lower. Although they have been guaranteed a rate, and the lender has made commitments to ensure that that rate is available, the borrowers will insist that they get the lower rate. As you saw from what we discussed before, the lender may not be able to give the lower rate without taking a loss. If you, the borrower, are concerned about the possibility of getting the lower rate after locking, ask the lender if it offers that option. Some lenders have programs that will allow the borrower to lock in a rate, and then relock at a lower rate if interest rates go down. Typically, the rate must go down at least 0.25% to 0.50%, and the borrower may have to pay an extra 0.25% to 1.0% in points to get the lower rate. If the lender does offer this feature, make sure it is in writing as part of the lock-in agreement you sign. (Many states require that lenders disclose their lock-in procedures, in writing, at the time of loan application.)

Some lenders will not allow the borrower to lock in the rate until after the loan has been approved. This way the lender limits its risk in committing to an investor and then having the loan not close because the borrower did not qualify. A few will not give a rate until the day of closing, but this alternative is not prevalent. While both of these policies are conservative and unattractive to the borrower, the chances of these lenders staying in business and being profitable are much greater than for those who play the market.

As you probably recognize by now, rates and lock-in periods may not be the determining factor when choosing a lender. Instead, look for one that is established and known in the community, one that has a reputation for honesty and fair dealing. Avoid any lender that has been known not to honor a lock-in, or has allowed too many loan lock-ins to expire before closing. A good lender will stand behind a commitment, even if it means taking a loss.

DISCOUNT POINTS
Money talks

In Chapter 2 we discussed discount points and how they are used to buy down the interest rate. Points are interest in advance. There is a book published that gives equivalent yields resulting from paying additional discount points to get a lower rate, but not all lenders use these formulas. There is no absolute formula that can be applied to all lenders to determine what they will charge. (The basic theory is that 1 discount point, 1.0%, will lower the rate one-eighth percent, 0.125%. But, as I have noted, not all lenders are reading from the same page.) They will often undercut the market or set prices over it because they are anticipating changes, they are trying to earn extra fee income, or their particular method of selling loans fixes the price that much higher or lower.

For example, if a 10% loan is at par, with no discount points, different lenders may charge 0.50% to 2.50% discount points for a 9.75% rate. The actual market may require 1.00% or more. The lender must decide whether to risk lower points in anticipation of lower rates or add points in expectation of a rising market. The lender must also decide whether to add to its fee income.

Some borrowers reading this might conclude that they can negotiate points with the lender to get something lower than what is being quoted. They are right, so long as the lender has excess points built in and the lender is willing to forgo this income to get the loan. Most lenders are not willing to set a precedent that would require them to consider negotiation for everyone, so it is not widely practiced. And, if it were, they wouldn't tell you. It is much more likely that the lender will do it as a favor to the Realtor in order to ingratiate themselves for future business. Or, if business is slow they may have a limited-time "special" to help bring in business. One company I worked for had regular weekend specials for contracts to purchase written from Friday afternoon to Monday morning.

THE ORIGINATION FEE
Loan originators have to eat, too

The origination fee is fee income to the lender that helps to pay the cost of originating, processing, closing, and shipping the loan. Unfortunately for the lender, it often will not pay for all of these things. But, as the loan amount gets higher, it begins to cover more of the expenses. While 1% of a $40,000 loan ($400) does not come close to paying costs, 1% of $180,000 ($1,800) takes care of all, or at least a significant part, of them.

Part of this fee goes to the loan originator, either in the form of salary or commission income. Most loan officers are paid a commission. It can be a set percentage, 0.5% of the loan amount being fairly typical. Or, they can be paid on a sliding scale depending on the value of the loans they close in a month. An example would be 0.40% for $500,000, 0.45% for $750,000, 0.50% for $1,000,000, and 0.55% for $1,500,000. On commission income, the originator can get rich (I have seen loan officers make six-figure annual incomes easily), or she can just barely survive. It depends on whether the lender is competitive, provides good service, and has a good reputation in the community. And, of course, whether the loan officer is competent.

What do these observations have to do with the borrower, other than the fact that someone, most likely the borrower, will have to pay the origination fee? Usually nothing. Unless the lender or the originator fouls up to the detriment of the borrower. If a rate was not locked as requested, if the lender did not process the loan correctly, if the originator failed to disclose certain important and costly facts about the loan, or if the originator disclosed facts that later proved to be incorrect, the borrower could be left holding a very expensive bag. If any of these should happen, borrowers can consider several things.

They can threaten to sue, which might yield some money and satisfaction, but it does not get the loan closed. They can pull the loan application, but that would only give them satisfaction. Or, they can negotiate with the lender and/or originator. A lender or the originating loan officer would probably be happy to give up some fee income in order to keep things from getting more embarrassing, and giving them a bad name in the community. Cutting the origination fee to compensate for the mistake is always an option.

I am not suggesting that borrowers insist that lenders cut their fee for every little problem that comes up. Many glitches are not directly the fault of the lender, and borrowers cannot expect to be compensated because they feel things did not go smoothly. I am suggesting that if the lender did make a mistake to the borrower's detriment, the origination fee is one source from which restitution can be made. Using a good, experienced lender will help to avoid this potential problem.

One more note: Some lenders will offer loans that have no points at all. That means no discount OR origination points. In addition, some will also pay part of the allowable borrower's closing costs. How do they do it? And why? By offering a rate that is a good bit above the current market rate, the lender will be able to make significant premium income when the loan is sold—as much as 2% to 5% or more. By taking part of this windfall and rebating it back to the borrower in the form of no points and/or closing costs, they have generated one more way to market loans. This offer is good for a borrower who is short of funds (see Chapter 10 on closing costs). It is not so good for a borrower who wants or needs a low-interest rate. Unfortunately, you can't always have it both ways.

9

THE TYPES OF LENDERS

The point should be clear that there are all types of lenders. What we will look at now is exactly how different ones operate, and how these differences can affect the borrower.

THE BANKER

The normal, everyday retail bank is what most people think of when they need money. You go to the bank to put in money, and when you don't have any to put in, you go to get a loan to take some out. Banks make loans on cars, computers, horses, people—and on real estate. Unless you are dealing with a bank that has a mortgage department or subsidiary (see below), you will find mortgages are done a little differently by the retail, or commercial, end of banking.

Retail banks use their own money to make loans, which they do not sell. They set their own guidelines and rates. These guidelines can be less demanding than those of the secondary market, but their rates are often significantly higher. They also are less interested than other institutions (which we shall discuss shortly) in making long-term loans. Most bank mortgage loans will balloon or, at best, not go beyond a 10- or 15-year amortization. Every bank will be different. Each has its own rules.

The terms of the loan, and whether the bank will do it or not, will often be based on the relationship the borrower has, or will have, with the bank. If you keep large deposits with the bank, you stand a good chance of being approved, and quickly. If you already have significant debt with the bank, it may not be so interested in adding to that obligation, unless all of the debt is renegotiated so that more of it is secured by the real estate.

The advantages of dealing with a retail, or commercial, banker are that you can get an answer quickly, closing costs are normally less, and the requirements are less rigid. The disadvantages are that the rate will often be higher, the loan term will be short, and the LTV is usually lower.

THE MORTGAGE BANKER
Dedicated to the secondary market

A mortgage banker can be a freestanding company, unaffiliated with any other entity. To be accepted by the investors in the secondary market it only needs to have substantial capital enough to sell, buy, and service loans. For that reason, there usually is some connection with another capital-rich source, such as banks, insurance companies, credit unions, or any large company like General Motors and Sears.

Mortgage bankers work closely with the secondary market, using its guidelines and selling the resulting loans or securities backed by the loans. They can fund and close their own loans, and hold them if necessary until the loans are sold. They will also buy loans from other sources to be pooled with their own loans for sale in the secondary market.

Buying loans from other lenders, which is done by a Wholesale Division, allows the lender to acquire loans at an acceptable price without the cost of paying for an originating branch office. A mortgage banker will buy loans from other mortgage bankers and from mortgage brokers.

THE MORTGAGE BROKER
The independent loan source

Mortgage brokers do what the name implies, they broker loans for other lenders directly to the borrower. Brokers will normally have access to many different wholesale lenders. The broker gives the borrower the wholesaler's price to which they have added their fees in the form of the origination fee, additional discount points, and other miscellaneous fees. Because the wholesaler does not have the overhead of the broker's office, it can discount the price to the broker so that the broker can add a fee and still be competitive. Brokers can offer a wide range of products, including commercial loans.

The importance of brokers has grown in recent years because of the increase in wholesale mortgage buying. The need to make sure they are properly regulated has also increased. There are many stories about borrowers going to a broker who promised a loan that did not exist and who collected an application fee that was nonrefundable. Or, more commonly, these tales recount dealings with a broker who did not know enough about mortgage lending to process the loan correctly. The results have been disastrous. A few brokers have been known to take a loan application without knowing whether they will be able to place it or not. The problem is that this fact is not disclosed to the borrower, at least not until the last minute, when the broker has run out of options. Check out the broker carefully before making application. The best ones can be a cornucopia of loan products, and the worst ones can cause you misery.

THE THRIFT
Created to finance your home

The majority of mortgage loans are done by the thrift industry. These are the Savings and Loans (S&Ls) or Savings Banks. They originally made loans with their own money and held them, just as a commercial banker does today. They are depository institutions that are in business principally to make mortgage loans.

They function much the same as a mortgage banker, and in fact, are mortgage bankers. They price, process, fund the closings, and then sell the loans to the secondary market. Like banks and other mortgage bankers, they can also portfolio some of their loans.

For a time during the 1980s, changes in federal regulations allowed thrifts to stray from their main business of making home loans into the domain of the commercial banker. Too many thrifts made loans on high-risk ventures and other projects for which they had little background or capital. The resultant massive failure of many thrifts led to a taxpayer bailout costing hundreds of billions of dollars. The liquidation and absorption of these failed thrifts has caused a shift back into the business of mortgage lending, but with only half the original players.

THE CREDIT UNION
Using your money

Similar to commercial banks, credit unions have historically used the money of the members to make loans. This means (1) the approval process is usually easier, (2) the interest rate is usually higher, (3) the LTV is lower, and (4) the amortization period is shorter.

Within recent years some credit unions have begun dealing in the secondary market, meaning that they are taking on the same role as a thrift. Only a small percentage of credit unions are currently doing loans under these guidelines, but many of them will be offering secondary market mortgages through programs offered by the Credit Union National Association (CUNA). Access to the secondary market will also offer the credit union member a wider selection of mortgages. If you belong to a credit union, check out its rates.

LIFE INSURANCE COMPANIES
You bet your life

Life insurance companies have made mortgage loans for a long time, either as investment instruments for their cash or as loans against an individual policy's cash value. Because of their huge amounts of available premium deposits, life insurance companies are one of the prime sources of mortgage money, often at very attractive rates. They are one of the larger investors in the secondary market.

Many life insurance companies target jumbo loans and commercial projects. They can also set guidelines that may not be found in the standard Fannie or Freddie loan. Most of these loans are done through mortgage bankers or brokers, but some insurance companies, such as Prudential, have opened their own lending subsidiaries.

If you have a whole life policy that has accumulated significant cash value, you can borrow against it at a very low interest rate. The loan is cheap, simple—and it is your money. This is one of the few times you get the money before you die.

Call some of the local insurance agencies to find out if their parent companies offer mortgage products. These are sometimes available, even if you do not have a policy with them.

MORTGAGE LENDERS OF LAST RESORT
If it sounds like a good deal, it isn't

A growing number of "lenders" prey on people who, for whatever reason, do not have good credit or enough income to qualify for a normal mortgage. The "Bad Debt Lender" will make a loan with little or no cash down, or refinance the borrower's house and finance the cost of the loan into the mortgage amount. The cost often is equivalent to a large number of points. I have seen instances of 10 to 15 points being added to the loan amount. On top of this, most of the interest rates on these loans are in the range of 18% and higher.

The loans done by these lenders tend to be smaller, between $5,000 and $20,000. If you take a $20,000 loan at 18%, the lender is already getting a nice return. Add 5 to 10 points financed, and the borrower's costs soar.

Another ploy of these lenders is to lure the borrower in to make application and pay some type of nonrefundable application fee, knowing that they cannot make a loan. The borrowers are then out some money they usually cannot afford, and the lender has picked up some quick income.

The saddest part is that most of these borrowers cannot afford any additional debt, much less a mortgage with stratospheric rates. What happens is that the borrower will ultimately default and this "lender" will all too gladly foreclose on the property. Because the loan amount is usually low, the lender can then resell the property at a profit. It is loan sharking with a legal, and highly unethical, face.

However, there are loan companies that are very aboveboard in their practices. Many of the finance companies will offer mortgages. Because they deal with higher risk borrowers, their rates will be higher. But, they will not consciously try to overcharge the borrower. If you are thinking of using one, check them all for the best rates. Also, some of their loans will have prepayment penalties. That is, if you pay off the loan early, you will still have to pay a portion of the interest that you would otherwise have paid if you kept the loan to maturity.

10

CLOSING COSTS
The Bottom Line

"What will this cost me?" This question always comes right after "What are your rates and points?" Nothing in life is free, least of all mortgages. However, some loans and/or lenders are more expensive than others.

At loan application, or within three working days afterward, the lender must give to the borrowers a **Good Faith Estimate of Closing Costs** (see page 191 of the Appendix) on the loan for which they have applied. While closing cost forms may look different, each has the same itemized costs that must be disclosed. A good lender will disclose this information at application and explain each line. The U.S. Department of Housing and Urban Development (HUD) has helped to make this explanation easier by requiring the lender to give the borrower a booklet called *A HUD Guide to Closing Costs.*

At closing the borrower and the seller will get a detailed closing cost statement, which is generally put on **HUD-1 Form,** or settlement statement (see pages 205–206 of the Appendix). It will have the actual costs that must be paid, and it will seldom be exactly what was disclosed at time of loan application. This discrepancy arises because the lender cannot know what the final fees will be for all of the items. But, the Good Faith Estimate should not be off by more than several hundred dollars at most, assuming the rate, points, and loan amount do not change. What the borrower should get from the lender is a worst-case estimate. You would much rather be told up-front that the cost will be $4,000 and find out it will actually be only $3,000, than the other way around.

A borrower who is shopping for the best rate will do well to check each lender's closing costs. All of them will charge the basic costs, such as appraisal, credit report, points, and so forth. What the borrower needs to be aware of are the ubiquitous **"garbage" or "junk" fees.** A lender may also add onto the cost of an appraisal or other standard cost so as to collect more fee income. These additions are made part of an **Application Fee** that is nonrefundable. If an appraiser charges $250 for the appraisal, the lender might collect $300 or more from the borrower, keeping the extra. These fees can more than make up the difference between one lender's lower rate and another's higher rate when the higher rate does not include the additional cost. My advice is this: at time of application do not pay any application or other fee that is not directly, and solely, a cost of processing the loan (such as the appraisal), unless it is refundable and unless you are shown very clearly that you qualify for the loan for which you have applied. There are still dishonest lenders who will take your money and run.

In this chapter we will look at the basic closing costs and some of the more prevalent garbage fees. Because costs in different regions can be significantly higher or lower, my example will only be a representation of these fees. In addition, government loans set maximum allowable fees for costs such as the appraisal and do not allow lenders to charge garbage fees to the borrower.

For each item that I cover, there is a number that does not seem to bear a relationship to anything. These numbers correspond to numbers on the HUD-1 Form and are referred to in *A HUD Guide to Closing Costs.* Now, let's see just where all this money goes.

1. *The loan origination fee* (801). The lender charges this fee for processing the loan. It is usually 1% of the loan amount, but it can be more, or less. On FHA loans, it is based on the loan amount before the MIP is financed. On VA loans, it is based on the total with the funding fee financed, if it is financed.

2. *The loan discount points* (802). This fee is charged to yield the given rate of interest. The base rate, or par rate, will have no discount points. The lower the interest rate below the par rate, the higher the discount points. Points go to buy down the interest rate and are considered as interest in advance. They can be as high or low as the borrower is willing to pay. They are also a tax-deductible expense. On a purchase, the points are completely deductible in the year they are paid. For refinances, they must be amortized over the life of the loan ($1,000 in points on a 15-year loan would be $67 deductible per year). If the refinanced loan is paid off early, the remaining undeducted points can then be claimed in the year it is paid off.

3. *The appraisal fee* (803). The lender will always require that an appraisal (see copy of the Uniform Residential Appraisal report on pages 209–211 in the Appendix) be done to determine that the value of the property is high enough to secure the loan. The appraisal fee can vary from $150 to over $400, depending on the type of property, its location, the loan type, or any combination of these. Check lenders in your area to get an idea of the cost. Many lenders will collect this fee at time of loan application.

4. *The credit report* (804). Every lender will require that a Standard Residential Mortgage Credit Report be prepared by an approved credit bureau for each borrower. Married couples' credit will be incorporated into one report. The cost will depend on the type of loan and whether a business credit report will be needed for self-employed or incorporated borrowers. Credit reports range from $25 to over $50. This is another fee that most lenders will collect at application.

5. *Lender's inspection fee* (805). This fee is charged when the lender must inspect the property before closing. It is usually for new construction or renovation work. However, some lenders require that they inspect all properties on which they make loans. The inspections are usually done for the lender by the appraiser who did the appraisal. On FHA and VA loans a separate inspector may be assigned by the FHA or VA.

6. *Other loan fees* (806–811). Included in this group are assumption fees, mortgage insurance application fees, and space for the lender to list "garbage" fees. Some of the fees listed here are: Application Fee, Processing Fee, Underwriting Fee, Document Review or Preparation Fee, Commitment Fee, and Tax Service Fee. Some of these may also be listed under numbers (1303–1307).

7. *Prepaid interest* (901). This is the interest that the borrower will pay for the first month of the loan. It is simple interest based on the number of days remaining in the month from the date on which the loan closes.

As an example, let us consider a $100,000 loan at 10% that closes on June 15. The interest is calculated as $100,000×10% = $10,000, divided by 360 days (365 for government loans) = $27.78 per day (per diem) interest. The per diem interest is then multiplied by the number of days remaining in the month from the date of closing, 15×$27.78 = $416.70. This is the house payment for the month of June. It is the only time that interest on the loan will be paid in advance. The next mortgage payment on this loan will be due August 1, and will represent the interest that accrued during July plus a principal reduction.

Many borrowers try to close toward the end of the month to lower their closing costs. For estimating purposes, it is always safer to figure on a full 30 days of interest ($833.40 in our example). If you plan on closing on the last day of the month, and for some unforeseen reason, you don't close until the next day, you would be looking at the full $833.40 instead of only one day at $27.78 as shown in our example.

8. *Mortgage insurance premium* (902). This is the up-front premium or any portion of it that will be paid by cash at closing. If it is being financed, most lenders will show it on the Good Faith Estimate and not add it into the total. This is obviously required only when there is mortgage insurance involved. The cost can be from hundreds to thousands of dollars, depending on the type of loan and the amount. There is a table of premiums on page 195 in the Appendix, or a lender can give you the premiums of different mortgage insurance companies. The FHA MIP up-front premium would be shown here.

9. *Hazard insurance premium* (903). The lender will require that the first year's hazard (homeowner's) insurance be paid up in full by time of closing. You can find out this cost by calling your insurance agent, or you can use $2.50 per $1,000 of sales price (value) as an estimate. The lender is interested only in the hazard portion of the insurance, but almost every borrower will get full coverage. The $2.50 should approximate the full coverage cost.

10. *Flood insurance premium* (904). If the property which you are purchasing has any improvements that are in a federally designated flood plain, you will be required to purchase this federally funded insurance through your insurance agent. The appraiser will state on the appraisal if this insurance is necessary.

11. *Other prepaid items* (905). These spaces are for items not specifically listed that the lender may require to be paid in advance. The *VA funding fee* is often put in this space.

12. *Hazard insurance reserves (escrows)* (1001). Most lenders will require that the hazard insurance be escrowed into the monthly payment. At closing they will normally escrow two months' worth of the yearly premium. From our example above, on a $100,000 house the yearly premium would be $2.50 × 100 = $250. The yearly premium of $250 divided by 12 = $20.83 monthly × 2 months = $41.67 to be escrowed at closing. The reason for the two months is that, if you close in June and the first payment is in August, you could be two months behind by the time of the first payment. Then, a year later when the insurance premium renewal comes up, there would not be enough money in escrow to pay it for the next year.

13. *Mortgage insurance escrow* (1002). On mortgage insurance that has a renewal premium, this cost is handled the same as the hazard insurance. For example, consider a $95,000 loan on a $100,000 property with a renewal premium of $0.49 per $100 of loan amount. The yearly renewal premium would be $0.49 × 950 = $465.50; dividing by 12 yields $38.79 per month × 2 months = $77.58 escrow at closing. On mortgage insurance that does not have a renewal premium, such as the one-time financed mortgage insurance, there would be no escrow.

14. *City or county real estate taxes* (1003–1004). Most lenders will also require that the taxes be escrowed into the monthly payment. Since delinquent taxes can be collected by selling the property, and take priority over mortgage liens, lenders protect themselves by escrowing the taxes and paying them directly. A borrower can find out the assessed taxes from the listing Realtor or the government real estate office. Two or more months' taxes will be escrowed. If you are within two months of when the taxes must be paid to the taxing authority, the lender may require that you pay the two months' escrow and the last two months' taxes so that they can be prepaid for the year in advance. Otherwise, the lender will not have enough time to set up the loan and make sure that it receives the tax bill in time to avoid a late penalty. Check with the lender to find out what the requirements are.

15. *Other escrows* (1005–1008). These items are for other reserves that the lender may require to be escrowed, such as annual assessments for homeowners' associations', road maintenance, and flood insurance.

There are certain fees called *prepaid items* that most loans will allow only the borrower to pay. They cannot be paid by the seller, Realtor, or lender. These include the following:

1. Prepaid interest

2. Mortgage insurance premium

3. Hazard insurance premium

4. Mortgage insurance escrows

5. Hazard insurance escrows

6. Tax escrows

Note: As of 1991 the mortgage insurance premium can again be paid by the seller. This is the third time the secondary market and M. I. companies have changed this rule. If you are interested in pursuing this, check with a lender to make sure the rule has not changed again.

VA loans are the only loans that allow someone other than the borrower to pay the prepaids, and these are limited to 4% of the value. Most loans will allow these to be paid from the proceeds of a gift as long as the borrower has at least 5% of the down payment from their own assets or they are putting down at least 20% cash, even if the down payment came from a gift (the Fannie Mae 3-2 loan discussed in Chapter 5 is an exception). Some lenders, or secondary market investors, may have different guidelines. Check with the lender.

16. *Settlement or closing fee* (1101). This fee is paid to the settlement agent. Depending on your area, it may be an attorney or a title insurance company. The fee can vary tremendously, as much as hundreds of dollars. Charged by the lender, this is a "junk" fee.

17. *Abstract or title search* (1102). This is done to ensure that the title to the property is clear and does not contain any potential defects, or "clouds," on it. Liens, claims by relatives, undefined boundaries, and easements are a few of the problems that could appear. This search is normally done by either the attorney or the title insurance company. The cost can be $2.00 to $4.00 or more per $1,000 of loan amount. Check with the lender or attorney for the average cost in your area. This cost is often included in the Title Insurance (#1108).

18. *Title examination* (1103). This is a continuation of the title search to make sure that the final title is clear and acceptable. This fee is usually part of the search or the settlement fee. Most attorneys or title insurance companies will search and examine the title for one fee and put it on either line 1102 or 1103.

19. *Title insurance binder* (1104). This is a commitment by the title insurance company to insure the title. Most commitments are included in the final title insurance policy fee (1108).

20. *Document preparation* (1105). Some attorneys, and some lenders, will charge this fee in addition to the normal fee for closing. You will often see it combined with the settlement agent's fee. Charged by the lender, it is a garbage fee. The cost can range from $25 to over $350.

21. *Notary fees* (1106). Most loan closings will require that certain signatures be notarized. More often this fee is included in the closing agent's fee.

22. *Attorney's fee* (1107). Most lenders require the use of an attorney, and most title insurance companies use an attorney to inspect the title. When the attorney is the settlement agent, this fee will normally include Items 1101,1105, and 1106 above. The fee depends on the loan type, property, complexity of the title, and the attorney. For a good idea of costs in your area, ask your lender or Realtor for the names of three to five good attorneys and get their fees. They can go from $150 to over $500. Note: The closing agent represents both the borrower and lender at closing even though the borrower is paying the fee.

23. *Title insurance* (1108). This fee pays to insure the title against defects to the title of the property, or defects that existed but were not found in the normal title search. This insurance is issued after the title search and review. The fee usually includes Items 1102–1104 above. For example, let us say a Native American tribe claims that your house is on top of their ancestral burial grounds, and after adjudication the court tells you to move your house. Title insurance would protect you against this by either paying the Native Americans for the land, or paying off the mortgage.

There are two types of title insurance. One insures the mortgage, or **mortgagee (lender's) insurance,** and the other insures the borrower's equity, or **mortgagor (owner's) insurance.** Title insurance is a one-time premium.

1.   Lender's insurance covers the mortgage in case there is some type of defect. For instance, I know of an incident in which the seller was a relocation company that had taken over the property for a transferred employee. The borrower closed the loan and moved in. About a year later the lender sent in the tax escrow to pay the taxes that were coming due. The county sent back the taxes for the current year, stating that it could not accept them until the previous year's taxes were paid. Lo and

behold, the employee had not paid his taxes, the relocation company was not aware of this fact, and the closing
attorney had not caught it in the title search. The title
insurance company paid the back taxes and then went
to the attorney to collect them because he was at fault.
Without the insurance, the borrower would have had to
come up with the money and then sue the attorney.

2. Owner's insurance covers the mortgage and the equity
   that the borrower has in the property. In the case of
   the Native Americans, the insurance would pay off the
   mortgage and return the equity to the borrower. This
   policy will also cover any losses to the owner that are
   not covered in the lender's policy.

Policy premiums can vary by area and by insurance company. A rule of thumb rate would be $3.00 per $1,000 of loan
amount for lender's coverage and $4.00 per $1,000 for owner's
coverage. Check with your lender or attorney for actual costs.

24. *Other title charges* (1111–1113). These may need to be
listed separately from the other fees. However, these items are
usually incorporated in the other fees. A form required by the
secondary market called the ALTA 8.1 Environmental Endorsement is an example.

25. *Government recording fees* (1201). The local government where the property is located will charge a fee to record:

1. The deed (to show ownership)

2. The mortgage (to show a lien on the property)

To find these fees in your area, ask a lender or attorney.

26. *City/county tax/stamps* (1202). Each locality can also
charge a tax on the deed and mortgage in addition to the recording fees.

27. *State tax/stamps* (1203). The state can also charge a
fee on both the deed and the mortgage.

Note: If there are recording fees plus local and state fees,
the lender will sometimes combine them when giving the Good
Faith Estimate of Closing Costs. The HUD-1 Form at closing will
show them separately. Ask your lender if these fees are not clear.

28. *Other government fees* (1204–1205). These spaces are
for any other fees that taxing agencies might want to charge.

29. *Physical survey* (1301). Most lenders will require that a physical survey be done before closing. This survey will show the property boundaries with measurements, the outline of the house and outbuildings from a bird's-eye view, all rights of way and easements, driveways and roads, and any water located on the property. It will also state if the property is in a flood plain. If the house is in a flood plain, then flood insurance will be required. (It will also show under Items 904 and 1006). The survey is done to make sure that the property is in compliance with local setbacks and that it is not encroaching on or being encroached upon by another property. I have seen a number of properties where the house or an outbuilding is over the property line by inches or feet. More common is a roof overhang or a fence that goes over the line.

A normal complaint is that the property has been surveyed before and since it has not changed, why do it again? Because the previous owner may have transferred a small piece to a neighbor; he may have added a deck since the last survey; or there may be a mistake that the last survey did not catch.

Back in my construction/development days we were doing the site preparation for an industrial building. The site was a square area located at the end of a pipestem from the highway to the property (a pipestem is a narrow part from the main road back to the main body of the property, wide enough for the access road). The surveyor had set a bench mark, or point from which all points on the property could be referenced by a transit. I was trying to set the corners of the building by the bench mark, but I could not get the corners to align. I called in the architects, who called in the surveyor, who discovered he had perpetuated a mistake that had been made three surveys ago. The pipestem was not 25 feet wide, but 60 feet wide. I hope that the adjacent property owner had title insurance.

The cost of the survey will depend on the size of the property and where it is located. Your lender can give you an estimate. Some problems found on a survey can be insured by the title insurance so that they will not have to be corrected.

30. *Pest inspection* (1302). Lenders will require that the property be inspected for termites and other property-destroying pests. In many areas it is customary for the seller to pay this cost. If infestation and/or damage is found, most purchase contracts will specify who is responsible for the cost of treatment, usually the seller. The lender will not close the loan until the property is clear of pests and any damage has been repaired. Costs for the inspection can range from $25 to over $100.

31.   *Additional settlement charges* (1303–1307). For a property served by a **septic field** most lenders will require that a person knowledgeable in this type of waste disposal inspect it to make sure it is functioning properly. Likewise, **well water** must be tested to make sure that it meets the minimum safe drinking water standards. (The main feature that is tested is the content of coliform bacteria, which should be less than 1.0 per 100 milliliters.) These septic and water fees can range from $25 to over $60 each. The sales contract should specify who pays for these fees.

32.   *Total settlement charges* (1400). Here it is, the bottom-line estimate of what you should be expected to pay to close the loan, in addition to the down payment. (Remember, on all conventional loans except the 3-2 loan the lender will also require that you be able to show liquid assets equivalent to two months of house payments in addition to the down payment and closing costs).

I would always recommend that you ask the lender to give you a **Good Faith** Estimate before committing to the loan and paying any fees. If there are fees that seem to be out of the ordinary, check with other lenders to see what they charge. A difference of $20 or $50 may not be significant, but if one lender is charging $300 or more than another lender, that could be the same as paying 0.25% and more in extra points. I cannot stress too strongly the need to check the lender's charges. You may go through the entire application and never be aware that you are actually paying hundreds more than necessary.

An additional note on escrows: I am often asked if the escrows that the lender holds for taxes and insurance earn interest. The answer is that they will always earn interest, but where the borrower lives will determine whether the borrower or the lender gets that interest. Some states require that the lender pay interest on this money. Where the lender does not have to pay interest to the borrower, it is taken as additional income. I find that the small amount of interest that would be earned by the borrower is more than offset by not having to come up with large sums of money all at one time to pay the taxes and annual insurance premium. Paying one twelfth of it each month is much easier on the budget. If you are adamant about not paying escrows, check with the various lenders to see if they have that option. It is sometimes available with LTVs of 70% or less.

Another fee which is now becoming an issue is the *Buyer-broker fee*. In this case the real estate agent represents the purchaser instead of the seller. (Many people do not realize that the usual agency relationship is for the agent to represent the seller.) If you are buying and retain an agent to represent you, know who is paying the commission. The VA requires the seller to pay it. The FHA will only allow the purchaser to pay it. And Fannie and Freddie have not stated a position. These rules were effective as of April 1992. Check with a lender before assuming that you can get the seller to pay *your* agent's fee.

11

REFINANCING YOUR MORTGAGE

Anyone who has a mortgage will at some time give thought to refinancing it, for many different reasons. Whether it is a sound idea depends on what the borrowers want to accomplish, and how long they plan on keeping the loan.

LOWER RATES
Get them while they are hot

If the current rates are lower than what you have now, the temptation is to refinance. The basic rule is, if the current rate is at least 2.0% and sometimes as little as 1.5% lower, it will pay to refinance. Doing so will lower your payment significantly enough to save on your payments and pay back the cost of refinancing (the only cost of a normal refinance that you save over the cost of the original loan is the recording of the deed). Here's an example.

If you currently have a $75,000 loan at 12% for 30 years with a PI payment of $771.46, the new payment at 10% would be $658.18, or a monthly savings of $113.28 ($1,359.36 per year). If it costs you $3,500 to refinance, it will take slightly over 2.5 years for the savings to pay back the cost ($3,500 divided by $1,359.36). So, if you plan on staying in the house for over 2.5 years, it is worthwhile.

If you have an **ARM,** there is a different problem. When fixed interest rates go down, ARMs will also often adjust downward. The dilemma is, you don't know if the fixed rates—and your ARM rate—will go back up enough to make refinancing now a smart move. And no one can accurately predict where the rates will go. When you refinance an ARM, your immediate response is to hope that rates go higher, so that your decision is quickly justified. If the rates don't rise, either you justify the refinancing by saying that not having to worry about those periodic adjustments was worth the cost, or you spend your time agonizing over what you could have done with the money it cost you to refinance. My advice is, if you are happy with your ARM and how its rates have adjusted, keep it. If you really want a fixed rate and you will have the property long enough to make it worthwhile, refinance. Of course, if you have **a conversion feature,** the change will be much less expensive, which can make the decision easier (see section in Chapter 5 on ARMs).

Some people will want to refinance from a 30-year to a 15-year loan. If the rates are low enough, it may be a good idea. However, remember that if all you want to do is pay the loan off quicker, you can make an additional principal reduction payment each month that will accelerate the amortization and achieve the same result without paying any closing costs or having to go through the loan application process. You can determine the payment for whatever amortization (payoff) period you want by asking your lender to calclate this based on the remaining principal balance. Or, if you have access to a computer, you can compute this yourself with one of the readily available programs for amortizing loans.

REFINANCING FOR CASH OUT
Using your equity

Other borrowers want to refinance just to gain access to the equity that has built up over the years. If there is a legitimate need and the interest rate is reasonable, it is there to be used. Just remember that you are borrowing savings, and the loan is secured by your house. It took a while for the equity to build. Inflation may not be so kind in the future.

A second mortgage may be a more practical and much less expensive alternative. We discussed these loans earlier in the context of using them to lower the down payment on a purchase. For the purposes of refinancing lenders will allow you to take the equity, without the larger expense and paperwork of refinancing the original first mortgage. However, second mortgages are usually for shorter periods and at slightly higher interest rates, hence a higher payment.

TO GET RID OF MORTGAGE INSURANCE

With Fannie and Freddie you can now have the mortgage insurance removed, without refinancing, after a minimum of five years from the date of the original mortgage with a current appraisal showing at least 20% equity, or after two years if the appraisal shows at least 25% equity. Alternatively, it can be removed after a minimum of 2 years if you can prove by a current appraisal that improvements have been made to increase the equity to at least 20%.

If you refinance and the LTV is 80% or less, as supported by an appraisal, there will not be mortgage insurance. Not having to pay for insurance is an attraction byproduct if you are refinancing for the lower rate. The savings on the mortgage insurance alone, though, will not make up the closing costs on the refinancing.

Depending on the type of mortgage insurance that you obtained, refinancing may not be worthwhile from another standpoint. When we discussed this topic in Chapter 4, we considered the single premium financed method. Some mortgage insurance companies have two types, refundable and nonrefundable. The refundable premium will be more expensive. If you refinance or pay off the loan within a given period of time (check with your lender), you can get back part of the refundable type. The nonrefundable is, well, nonrefundable.

If you have an FHA mortgage, you can refinance with a conventional mortage and have a portion of the MIP refunded to you, depending on how long you have had the loan. Remember, you have to request the refund. It is not done automatically (as of the time this was written). Refinancing back into another FHA loan will only replace the old MIP with a new MIP, including the annual premium, and should be done only if the rate is low enough, *and* it is the only way you can qualify.

THE MAXIMUM AMOUNT THAT CAN BE REFINANCED

Depending on the type of loan that you are using to refinance, rules (which are subject to change) limit how much you can borrow.

Fannie Mae and Freddie Mac

With no cash out, the maximum LTV is 90%. With cash out, it is 75% LTV. The value is established by appraisal. If the refinance is closed before the original note is six months old, the value will be the original cost, not the appraised value (unless the appraised value is less than the original cost). Closing costs may be financed into a no-cash-out mortgage. Most lenders will require that the borrowers have two months' payments in assets and that the prepaids be paid in cash, not financed. Some may also require a seasoning period before the loan may be refinanced for cash out. That is, the loan must be on the property for a minimum amount of time before the lender will refinance the property when the borrower wants to take equity out.

FHA

For cash out, the maximum LTV is 85% of the acquisition cost ([value plus allowable closing costs] × 85%). Otherwise, the borrowers can get up to the maximum allowable FHA loan amount for their area. FHA will allow all closing costs to be financed into the refinanced loan amount as long as they do not exceed the maximum allowable loan amount.

A Streamlined Refinance program exists for borrowers who have an FHA loan and just want to get a lower rate and payment. In this loan there is no cash out except to pay closing costs. A 30-year loan can be refinanced into a 15-year loan if the payments do not increase by more than $50. There is no credit check or appraisal. The mortgage cannot be delinquent at application. If the original loan was assumed, it is not eligible for the streamlined refinance until it has been held at least six months.

VA

VA loans can be refinanced up to the lesser of appraised value or the remaining principal balance plus closing costs if there is no cash out. If the borrower wants to take cash out, the LTV is limited to 90% of value. The maximum Funding Fee of 1.25% will have to be paid.

Construction Loans

Most lenders recognize that paying off a construction loan with a permanent loan is not a refinance transaction. But some loans do have time limits, after which paying off is considered a refinance. If the construction loan has been on the property for over 180 days, check with your lender; it may be subject to certain additional refinance rules.

12

WRITTEN DISCLOSURE TO THE BORROWER

Federal and state laws require the lender to disclose certain information to the borrower at various times during the application process, or even before. Some loans will require more disclosure than others. The increase in paperwork is in direct proportion to the involvement of the government. Conventional loans have basic disclosures, while FHA, VA, and Tax-Exempt Bond Authorities have, on average, twice as much in the form of disclosures.

THE STANDARD CONVENTIONAL LOAN DISCLOSURES

1. *The Equal Credit Opportunity Act Statement— (E.C.O.A.):* This statement discloses that the lender will not discriminate. Most lenders are only interested in the color of your money.

2. *A Good Faith Estimate of Closing Costs:* An example of this form is included in the Appendix on page 191.

3. *A Truth-in-Lending (T-I-L) Statement* of loan costs (see page 207 in the Appendix): This form gives the **Annual Percentage Rate (APR),** the total of all interest and prepaid items for the life of the loan, the amount of the loan minus the prepaids, and the total of all the payments for the life of the loan. It also discloses any prepayment penalties, whether the loan is assumable, the payment schedule, and what the late payment charges will be. The lender must provide this statement within three working days of loan application; and the borrower will invariably call the lender for an explanation, usually because the APR is higher than the rate for which the borrower applied. The APR is made up of the loan interest rate plus the prepaid items and is based on the idea that these items (including discount points) increase the actual yield to the investor above the note rate. If you ask for an itemization of the T-I-L Statement, you will find it much easier to understand. It breaks down each amount disclosed into the following individual items:

• APR (Annual Percentage Rate)

• Finance Charge. This represents the total of the interest that will be paid over the life of the loan plus the prepaid items. The prepaid items listed on a T-I-L form are (a) origination fees, (b) discount fees, (c) other fees, (d) per diem interest, (e) escrows, and (f) initial premiums.

• Amount Financed. This equals the loan amount minus the prepaids. This is the item that most borrowers do not understand. They applied for a given loan amount and the T-I-L statement shows an amount that is significantly less. Do not worry. You will get the amount that you requested. The federal government just wants you to know that because the prepaids are fees, they can reduce your borrowing power by their total. Also, many lenders will "net out" the prepaids from the loan proceeds so that the settlement agent gets a check for the total loan minus the prepaids. "Netting out" is done so that the settlement agent does not have to write a check to the lender for these fees at closing. Thus, the lender gets its fees quicker. The settlement agent will then add in the fees that the borrower pays at closing to the net check to make the full loan amount. An example would be a $100,000 loan with 1% origination, 1 discount point, $240 in escrows, and $417 in per diem interest, a total of $2,657. The net amount at closing would be $97,343. The $2,657 that the borrower brought to closing to cover those items would then be added to get the $100,000 needed to close.

• Total of Payments. This item represents the total of the loan amount and the interest that will be paid over the life of the loan. It is a real eyeopener. If you made all your monthly payments on a $100,000 loan at 10% for the full 30 years, the total of payments would be over $300,000.

• Number and Amounts of Payments and When They Are Due. On a fixed rate loan, these are simple to understand. On a 30-year loan you will have 359 payments plus the last payment, which will be slightly less. On a 15-year loan it will be 179 plus 1. With ARMs it is different. The T-I-L statement will give a worst-case adjustment for the first two or three periods, and then the remainder is based on the current index plus margin at the time the T-I-L statement is done.

5. *Loan disclosure form:* If the loan is an ARM, the lender is required to give written disclosure about how the loan works. Some other types of loans also must be disclosed if they are sufficiently complicated.

6. *A Consumer Handbook on Adjustable Rate Mortgages (C.H.A.R.M.):* You must receive this booklet and a form to be signed stating that you received it. It is only for borrowers getting ARM loans.

7. *Lock-in and Processing Disclosures:* After the financing frenzy of 1986, many states now require that the lender give written disclosure on locking in the loan and the estimated processing time.

FHA REQUIREMENTS

In addition to those for conventional loans, the FHA requires these disclosures:

1. *A Homeowner's Fact Sheet on Mortgage Insurance.* This tells the borrower about the MIP and how it can be refunded to the borrower. (See Appendix pages 198–199.)

2. *A Financial Privacy Act Notice.* This informs the borrower that HUD has the right to check the borrower's financial records held by the lender without further notification.

3. *An Interest Rate/Discount Point Disclosure Statement.* This notifies the borrower that neither HUD nor FHA establishes the interest rates and points on FHA loans. These are set by the lender and can affect the borrower's ability to qualify. (See Appendix page 219.)

4. *A Notice to Homeowner on the Assumability of FHA Loans.* This explains the rules for assuming FHA loans and the original borrower's liability after the assumption.

5. *An amendatory statement* that must become part of the Sales contract. This statement tells the borrowers that the property must appraise for the sales price, or they are under no obligation to complete the loan. The borrower does have the option of proceeding with the sale, but the loan will be based on the lower value. Many Realtor contracts already contain this statement.

6. *The Watch Out for Lead-Based Paint Poisoning Notification* (see page 203 in the Appendix). This is required for all houses constructed before 1978. It cautions the borrower against the consumption of lead-based paint; if house does have lead-based paint it must be removed.

7. *A Final FHA Application Form,* known as the 2900 form. The borrower must sign this before the loan can be approved. It is simply a form that lists all of the verified information about the borrowers. This typical eight-page, front and back, government form is currently slated to be scrapped. Sometime in 1992 it will be replaced by the standard industry-wide application form to be used on FHA, conventional, and VA loans. (See pages 185–187 in the Appendix.)

VA REQUIREMENTS

VA requires the following, in addition to the conventional disclosures:

1. The *Financial Privacy Act Notice.*
2. The *Amendatory Statement.*
3. A *Federal Collection Policy Notice,* which lists all the bad things the government can do to you if you default.
4. A *VA-Related Indebtedness Questionnaire,* which asks if you have any debts owed to the U.S. government (they check on this, so it does not help to lie).
5. A *VA Assumability Notice,* which explains how your VA loan can be assumed and what that means to you.
6. A form giving the *Veteran's Nearest Living Relative.* This is required in the event the government needs to contact the original borrower and he or she has moved.

OTHER REQUIREMENTS

Revenue bond authorities require all of the disclosures listed for conventional loans. If the loan is insured or guaranteed by FHA or VA, they also require all of the disclosures for that particular loan. And, they also have about four to six additional disclosures that are just for the bond authority loans.

While these disclosures may seem like a nuisance, they do make it easier for the borrower to understand what is going on as long as you read the forms and ask questions when you do not understand what is being disclosed. Take the time to read what is given to you.

13

THE LOAN
Now That I Have It,
What Is It?

A loan made on real estate is **a mortgage,** a lien against the property securing the loan. That is simple enough to understand, except that there is more to it. You can get a loan on real estate, but if it is not secured by that real estate all you have is an unsecured loan as evidenced by a note, the proceeds of which are used to purchase the property. To be a mortgage, the property must be the security for the loan. The lender will make you sign **a note** showing that you are in debt, and then the mortgage instrument (mortgage or deed of trust) to secure the debt with the real estate.

You **default** on the mortgage any time you do not meet any of the terms of the loan. If you are one day late on the payment, you are technically in default. If you do not pay the taxes when they are due, you are in default. When you default on the loan, the lender will give you notice that the default must be cured within a certain time or it can recover its funds by foreclosing on the property. When a lender forecloses, it takes legal action to force the sale of the property. Depending on where you live, the lender can foreclose by either a mortgage or deed of trust mortgage.

States that use a plain mortgage require that the lender go to court in order to be allowed to proceed with foreclosure. This is a time- and money-consuming process. Many states give the lender power of sale, or the right to sell the property after default and with due notice to the borrower. A **Deed of Trust (D/T)** mortgage appoints **a trustee** to act in the lender's behalf to foreclose on the property by power of sale without going to court.

As long as you meet the terms stated on the mortgage (read your mortgage instrument), you need not worry. Lenders do not want to foreclose, and they do not want to own your property. They would rather cure the problem. If the lender feels it is reasonable to expect that the borrower will be able to fix whatever problem has placed them in default, the lender will work with the borrower to correct the default. For example, if you lost your job for a long period of time and you have just started in a new one, the lender will work out some type of plan to catch up any late payments. The key, as in any credit transaction, is to communicate with the lender when you know there is going to be a problem. And the sooner, the better.

Now that I have properly scared you, don't worry about the bad things that can happen with a mortgage; think about all the good things—such as owning your home.

14

QUALIFYING YOURSELF
Everyone Is Different

Now that you have all the basic information, you can get a very realistic idea of how well you qualify for a loan. But, in case you have forgotten, here is a short course.

INCOME, DEBTS, AND CASH

1. What is your base **gross monthly income?**
2. What other **reliable, recurring, verifiable income** do you have that will continue into the next three to five years, minimum?
3. List each **debt** that you have:

    Who is the creditor?
    What is the approximate balance?
    What is the monthly payment?
    How long does it have left to pay off?

On **credit cards and revolving debt,** use 5% of the balance as the payment. Make sure you get ALL of your debts. Any debt with over 10 months (6 months on FHA and VA) left to pay off is a long-term debt and will be used in qualifying. If you put down less than 10% cash on a conventional loan, all of the monthly debts will be used. Revolving debt is always used when there is a balance. VA may require a minimum payment based on past average balance even if there is a zero balance on a revolving credit account.

4. How much **cash** do you have for the down payment and the closing costs (and two months residual house payments on conventional loans)?

Where is it (bank, stocks, sale of property, gift, and so on)?
Will there be any cash left after closing, and if so, how much?
What other liquid assets do you own?

It is a good idea to get a blank application form from a local lender and use it to fill in all of the above information. There is a copy of the Uniform Residential Loan Application on pages 185–187 in the Appendix.

QUALIFYING RATIOS
Conventional Loans

1. Take the total gross monthly income (GMI) and multiply it by **28%** (for loans with less than 10% down payment, start at **25%,** and never exceed 28%). This number will be the approximate maximum total monthly house payment that you can afford (PITI/MI/HOA). On ARMs with a 2% yearly cap, use the maximum second year payment if the down payment is less than 20%. ARMs with a 1% yearly cap and three- and five-year ARMs qualify at the initial rate.

2. Multiply the GMI by **36%, (33%** for conventional loans with less than 10% down payment) This number will be the maximum total house payment and long-term monthly debt payment that you can afford (PITI/MI/HOA/LTD). Subtract your monthly debts from this total (on 95% LTV conventional loans, all short- and long-term monthly debts are used). If the remainder is less than 28% of GMI, the lower amount will be used for the maximum allowable total house payment. (That is, if your debts are more than the 8% of your GMI allowed by the 28%/36% ratios, the house payment for which you will qualify will be less than 28%. For example, let us say you have qualifying ratios of 24% and 36%. The 24% is the maximum percent of GMI that you can use for the house payment.) Remember, some lenders and/or loans will allow higher ratios, such as 33% and 38% for the Fannie Mae 3-2 loan.

FHA Loans

1. Use **29%** of GMI for the total housing expense (PITI/MIP/HOA).

2. Use **41%** of GMI for the total housing expense and long-term debt. FHA uses any debt with over six months to pay off as long-term debt.

3. Qualifying ratios for energy efficient homes can go up to 31% and 43%. In most areas the local electric company will certify the house as energy efficient. Otherwise, FHA has a formula, available from a lender, that can be used to determine if the house is energy efficient.

Use the Conventional/FHA Qualifying Form in the Appendix on page 190.

VA Loans

1. Use the VA Net Income Residual Qualifying sheet (page 201, Appendix) to determine if you have sufficient income. You will need to know the federal and state tax and social security withholding information for your income, and estimates of the maintenance, utilities, and residual figures. You can get the withholding information from your pay stub. A local lender can give you the current maintenance and utilities figures as long as you know the approximate finished square footage of the house and the type of heat. The lender can also provide the withholding figures if you give them your gross salary and number of dependents.

2. Use **41%** of GMI to determine the total housing expense and long-term debt payment. The VA uses all debts with over six months remaining. This ratio does have some flexibility if there are sufficient compensating factors.

COMPENSATING FACTORS

Remember, almost all loans have some flexibility, but for basic qualifying, assume none. Then, list everything that you feel might be a compensating factor to help you qualify. Here is a short list that lenders will consider:

1. No debt or little debt.
2. Excellent long-term credit, including previous mortgage and/or rent payments.
3. Proven ability to pay debts in excess of allowable ratios.
4. Large amount of liquid assets left after closing.
5. Proven ability to save.
6. Long-term job stability.
7. Good potential for increase in income.
8. Possess an advanced degree, or are working toward one.
9. Large down payment, low LTV loan.
10. Ability of nonworking co-borrower to obtain a job in which he or she has a background.
11. Potential for a large amount of overtime or a bonus.
12. Shorter loan term.
13. Little or no increase in housing expense.
14. Other income not used in qualifying.

THE MAXIMUM LOAN AMOUNT

To calculate the maximum amount of loan for which you qualify, you must first answer two questions:

1. How much cash do you have for down payment after closing costs?
2. What will be the LTV?

CONVENTIONAL LOANS

1. The maximum Loan-to-Value (LTV) is **95%** (5% down).

2. There will be mortgage insurance on loans with less than 20% down payment (over 80% LTV).

3. Conforming Fannie Mae and Freddie Mac loans have maximum loan limits that depend on the number of dwelling units (single, duplex, triplex, quadruplex). The loan limits can change each year. Ask a lender for the current amounts.

4. Nonconforming or jumbo loans are any loan amounts over the conforming limits. They are usually limited to no more than 90% LTV.

FHA LOANS

1. The FHA sets maximum loan limits for different regions of the country. Just like conventional loans, the maximum loan amount will depend on the number of dwelling units up to a quadraplex. They change periodically. Call a lender for the limits in your area.

2. Use the FHA Maximum Loan Worksheet (page 196, Appendix) to get the minimum down payment, or call a lender. Get the current closing cost figures and MIP amounts from your local lenders, or use the charts provided in Chapter 10 and the Appendix.

3. FHA loans will always have Mortgage Insurance Premium (MIP) regardless of LTV. This is financed on top of the loan amount, plus the annual premium escrowed into the payment.

VA LOANS

1. The VA will guarantee a 100% no-cash-down loan if the veteran qualifies. To determine the maximum 100% loan, multiply the veteran's available entitlement by 4, or use VA Exhibit A on page 202 in the Appendix if there is only partial entitlement. The usable entitlement will be on the Certificate of Eligibility. If you do not have one, call the nearest VA office to request it.

2. The VA Funding Fee can be financed into the loan as long as the total does not exceed the maximum loan amount (full entitlement × 4). Entitlement and/or cash down must equal 25% of the loan.

16

USING YOUR HIGH SCHOOL MATH

TO FIND THE HOUSE PAYMENT

If you know the maximum payment you can afford, how do you translate that into a maximum loan amount? You use a very simple equation:

$$A \times B = C$$

where

A = Loan amount (in thousands of dollars)
B = Factor for interest rate amortization per thousand dollars (from tables)
C = Principal and interest payment

Let us consider an example of $100,000 purchase with an $80,000 loan at 10% for 30 years. The per thousand payment factor for 10% 30-year amortization is $8.78 (from the amortization tables).

$$A \times B = C$$

$$80 \times \$8.78 = \$702.40 \text{ PI}$$

TO FIND THE LOAN AMOUNT

What if you know the payment, and you want to know the loan amount it represents?

$$C \div B = A$$

$$\$702.40 \div \$8.78 = 80 \text{ (or } \$80,000)$$

TO FIND THE PER THOUSAND FACTOR

Or, what if you know the payment and loan amount, but want to know the factor?

$$C \div A = B$$

$$\$702.40 \div 80 = \$8.78.$$

TAXES, HOMEOWNER'S INSURANCE, MORTGAGE INSURANCE, AND HOMEOWNER'S ASSOCIATION FEES

Remember, you have to add an estimate for monthly taxes and insurance to the full house payment. Use one twelfth of the taxes on the property and $2.50 per thousand dollars of sales price, divided by 12, for the monthly homeowner's insurance.

If there is mortgage insurance, use factors (per hundred dollars of sales price) of 0.5 for 95% LTV, 0.34 for 90%, and 0.29 for 85%. Divide this amount by 12. (For example, consider a $90,000 loan on a $100,000 house. $0.34 \times 900 = \$306$ annual renewal premium, divided by 12 months = $25.50 escrowed into the monthly house payment, PITI/MI). These figures will be higher or lower than what you may actually pay, depending on the mortgage insurance company and the loan type, but they should get you within $5–$10 of the true amount. These are based on up-front and renewal mortgage insurance premiums. Financed premiums are different. Get a lender to help you with these (see Chapter 4).

Also, add any required monthly homeowner's association or condo fees. These fees are not escrowed by the lender, but they are counted in qualifying, PITI/MI/HOA.

AN EXAMPLE

To carry our example out to the full PITI payment, we start with the principal and interest:

$$\$702.40 = \text{PI}$$

In our area, taxes are $0.72 per hundred dollars of assessed value, which would be 1000 (based on our sales price or assessed value of $100,000) $\times$ 0.72 = $720/year taxes, divided by 12 months = $60 per month.

$$T = \$60.$$

The estimate of homeowner's insurance would be $2.50 $\times$ 100 (per thousand dollars of sales price) = $250/year, divided by 12 = $21.

$$I = \$21$$

Thus,

$$PITI = \$702.40 \; PI + 60 \; T + 21 \; I$$

$$= \$783.40 \text{ total house payment}$$

The qualifying is based on this total.

ADDITIONAL CONSIDERATIONS

Now, let's add a few more factors into the qualifying math game:

A = Gross monthly income (GMI)
B = Housing ratio (28% conventional loan, 29% FHA)
C = Maximum house payment (PITI/MI/HOA)
D = Total payments ratio (36% conventional loan, 41% FHA)
E = Total long-term monthly debts

To find the *maximum allowable house payment* (PITI/MI/HOA),

$$A \times B = C$$

$2,798$ (income) $\times$ 28% = $783.44 PITI/MI/HOA

To find the *necessary GMI* for a given house payment,

$$C \div B = A$$

$783.44 PITI $\div$ 28% = $2,798 per month minimum income

To find the *borrower's housing ratio* for a given house payment,

$$C \div A = B$$

$$\$783.44 \text{ PITI} \div \$2{,}798 \text{ (income)} = 28\%$$

To find the *borrower's total payments ratio* for a given house payment,

$$(C + E) \div A = D$$

$$(\$783.44 \text{ PITI} + 223.84 \text{ [debt]}) \div \$2{,}798 \text{ (income)} = 36\%$$

The value $223.84 is the maximum monthly debt to stay within 36%.

To find the *borrower's maximum allowable total payments* (house + debts),

$$A \times D = C + E$$

$$\$2{,}798 \text{ (income)} \times 36\% = \$1{,}007.28$$
$$= \$783.44 \text{ PITI} + \$223.84 \text{ debts}$$

To find the borrower's *maximum house payment when the total payments exceed 36%,*

$$A \times D - E = C$$

$$\$2{,}798 \text{ (income)} \times 36\% - \text{(debts payment)} = \$1{,}007.28$$
$$-\$400 \text{ (for this example)} = \$607.28$$
$$\text{PITI/MI/HOA}$$

If the long-term monthly debts were $400, the total debt would be $1,183.44 (= $400 + $783.44). But $1,183.44 PITI/MI/HOA/LTD divided by $2,798 income equals 42%. To get the total debt ratio back to 36%, you determine the difference between $1,183.44 and $1,007.28 as excess monthly debt, or $176.16. This excess debt would have to be eliminated, or the total house payment reduced.

C (Proposed PITI/MI/HOA) + E − A × D (36%) =

C (Maximum allowable PITI/MI/HOA)

Because the total payment ratio of 42% is over the maximum of 36%, the maximum allowable house payment will be lowered until the house payment and total monthly debts are no more than 36% of the borrower's GMI. This is done by calculating 36% of the borrower's GMI and then subtracting the monthly debt payments. The remainder is the maximum allowable house payment.

CALCULATIONS FOR YOUR OWN CASE

Just substitute your income for A, your proposed house payment for C, and your monthly debt payments for E to find your own qualifying ratios, payments, and necessary income. The ratio you use depends on the loan type (conventional or FHA) and the LTV (95% conventional loans use 25%/33%).

The more monthly income, the more debt that the borrower can have, or the more the borrower qualifies for if there is less debt. Don't worry about getting it to the dollar. As long as it is within $10–$15, more or less, you will be safe. You can also round up or down to get rid of the cents. No lender is going to worry about being 40 cents over. I kept the cents in the example so your answers would come out to the penny if you tried it with your calculator.

17

IF YOU ARE TURNED DOWN FOR THE LOAN

What can you do if the lender turns you down? There are several options available.

Just because you were denied the loan does not mean that your chances are absolutely finished. Ask the lender to detail exactly why you were turned down. It may be something that can be corrected so the loan can be resubmitted to the underwriter and approved. If the lender is not willing to try to correct the problem, or if it is not correctable, you will receive a written statement of credit denial that will give the reason(s).

If you feel that you can still get the loan, go to another lender and give them the facts and the reason why you were denied. The original lender may even help you to find another source. If another lender thinks the loan can be done, you can request that your original loan package be transferred from the first lender. Except for FHA and VA loans, the lender is not obligated to transfer the package. But if the lender values its good name in the community, it will do everything possible to assist you.

As a mortgage banker, I had to reject one loan that I knew could be approved by another lender. I called the other lender and explained the situation. Then I advised the borrowers to transfer their package, which I sent in its entirety. The borrowers got their loan and I received a very warm thank-you note—and several referrals, which more than made up for my lost time and costs.

If the problem is such that no lender can make you the loan, sit down with your lender and find out exactly what you need to do to correct it and how long after that before you can make application again. Few borrowers are completely hopeless.

What do you lose by being rejected? Normally, you will have paid the credit report and appraisal fee at application. These are not refundable. Some lenders will collect a fee for processing or underwriting (garbage fees). Others might collect an application fee that will include the cost of the appraisal and credit report, and some fee income to the lender itself. The application fee is usually nonrefundable. If any fees are required for loan application, find out if any or all of the fees are refundable if the lender denies the loan, and get it in writing.

Potentially the most expensive fee that you may have to pay arises if the lender charges you to transfer the loan package. The lender may try to hit you with 0.5% to the full 1% of the origination fee. If the lender approved the loan and you wanted to transfer it, then I agree that you should pay. But, if the lender cannot do the loan, the whole matter comes back to reputation and integrity. Any lender should be more than willing to help you if it cannot make the loan. If the lender wants to charge you for transferring the package, it may be cheaper to start over with another lender than to pay 1% in additional cost.

Will the loan denial affect your credit? No. Being turned down for a loan is not in itself bad credit, although it may very well be the result of having bad credit. Nothing on your credit report will ever show that you were turned down for a loan.

18

SUMMARY-Caveat Emptor

Buyer Beware. That is the best advice to anyone when purchasing a home and obtaining a mortgage. Nothing is simple, or free. The lending business changes so abruptly in relatively short periods that even those of us who are exposed to it daily are often caught not knowing the answer to a question. Because real estate financing is a dynamic, ever-changing industry, there will never be a source book that can completely and concisely cover financing and still remain 100% reliable for any extended length of time. Existing loan programs will change or no longer be offered, while other innovative loan products will be developed to meet the current demands of the market. There are also many regional programs for homebuyers, such as the revenue bond authorities, that I could not begin to cover in detail. The secondary market will also change its underwriting guidelines from time to time. When the market is down or stable, the secondary market will relax its rules, only to tighten them up again when things heat up or start to get beyond its ability to control the market. Never assume that any guideline is absolute. The 28%/36% qualifying ratios are not written in stone. And, not a month goes by without some story appearing about how FHA or VA is going to change its loan program.

This book has explained the basics of borrowing and the guidelines that direct them, so that you can understand the loan process. In this way, you can approach the financing of real estate with a degree of knowledge and, as a result, you will not feel overwhelmed and intimidated by the lender. If you do not agree with what the lender tells you, or you are not sure you have received the best advice, seek a second opinion from another lender. It doesn't cost you anything to ask questions. Remember, always ask further questions if you are unsure of the answer. It is better to *feel* stupid for asking than it is to *be* stupid for not having asked. Questions can save you valuable time and money.

APPENDIX
FORMS

APPLICATION CHECKLIST

EMPLOYMENT & INCOME(2 FULL YEARS):
[ ] *All Employers: Names and Addresses. Copies of past 2 years W-2 forms if available. Copies of most recent paystubs if available.
[ ] *Social Security & Retirement Income: Copies of most recent awards letter, statement, and evidence of receipt of income.
[ ] *Interest & Dividend Income: Copies of most recent statements, past two years 1099 forms(2 years tax returns may be required).
[ ] *Rental Income: Copies of current leases. Evidence of receipt of rent for most recent 6 - 12 month period. Possibly 2 yrs. returns.
[ ] *Alimony/Child Support: Copy of complete executed separation or divorce decree. Evidence of receipt of payments.

SELF-EMPLOYED and/or COMMISSIONED INCOME:
[ ] *Copies of past 2 years full federal **tax returns,** signed.
[ ] *Year-to-Date **Profit and Loss** Statement, by bookkeeper/accountant.
[ ] *Year-to-Date **Balance Sheet,** by bookkeeper/account.(if applicable).
[ ] *CORPORATIONS and/or PARTNERSHIPS: (25% or more ownership).
       *2 years federal **corporate tax returns,** signed.
       *Signed, **P & L and Balance Sheet,** most recent quarter.

CASH:
[ ] *Names, Addresses, Account Numbers of **Banks, Stock Brokers, etc.**
[ ] *Copies of most recent 2 - 6 months **statements** if applicable.
       *If there are any recent large increases in balances, please explain and be able to verify the source.
[ ] *SALE OF PROPERTY: Copy of Sales Contract & Closing Statement.
[ ] *GIFTS: Signed gift letter. The donor's ability to give & receipt of the funds must be verified prior to approval, in most cases.

DEBTS:
[ ] *Names, Addresses, Account Numbers of **all debts,** including lines of credit, credit cards, and student loans.
[ ] *Alimony, Child Support: Copy of complete, executed separation and/or divorce decree.

OTHER:
[ ] *Copy of executed **Sales Contract.**
[ ] *Copy of property listing if available.
[ ] *Earnest Money Deposit check number and account number.
[ ] *If Renting, name and address of **Landlord(s)** for 2 year period.
[ ] *Social Security Numbers of all borrowers.
[ ] *Amount of **Life Insurance** and any cash value.
[ ] *Year, Make, and Value of all **cars.** On cars newer than 4 years owned free and clear, please provide a copy of the **title.**
[ ] *Estimate of value of all **Personal Property.**

[ ]   **F.H.A. & V.A.::**
           *Copy of picture side of **Driver's License.**
           *Copy of Most Recent **Paystub** if borrower receives one.
           *Copy of Most Recent **Bank statement(s)** for all funds being used for the purchase.
[ ]   **V.A.:**
           *Original **Certificate of Eligibility.**
           *Copy of **DD 214**(Discharge Papers) if available.
           *Original or carbon of most recent paystub.
ON ALL ITEMS TO BE VERIFIED, PLEASE PROVIDE ANY TELEPHONE NUMBERS AND CONTACT PEOPLE, IF POSSIBLE. THIS WILL HELP SPEED THE LOAN PROCESS.

Uniform Residential Loan Application

This application is designed to be completed by the Borrower(s) with the Lender's assistance. The Co-Borrower Section and all other Co-Borrower questions must be completed and the appropriate box(es) checked if ☐ another person will be jointly obligated with the Borrower on the loan, or ☐ the Borrower is relying on income from alimony, child support or separate maintenance or on the income or assets of another person as a basis for repayment of the loan, or ☐ the Borrower is married and resides in, or the property is located in, a community property state.

I. TYPE OF MORTGAGE AND TERMS OF LOAN

Mortgage Applied for	☐ VA ☐ Conventional ☐ Other:		Agency Case Number		Lender Case Number
	☐ FHA ☐ FmHA				

Amount	Interest Rate	No. of Months	Amortization Type	☐ Fixed Rate ☐ Other (explain):
$	%			☐ GPM ☐ ARM (type):

II. PROPERTY INFORMATION AND PURPOSE OF LOAN

Subject Property Address (street, city, state & zip code)	No. of Units

Legal Description of Subject Property (attach description if necessary)	Year Built

Purpose of Loan	☐ Purchase ☐ Construction ☐ Other (explain):	Property will be:
	☐ Refinance ☐ Construction-Permanent	☐ Primary Residence ☐ Secondary Residence ☐ Investment

Complete this line if construction or construction-permanent loan.

Year Lot Acquired	Original Cost	Amount Existing Liens	(a) Present Value of Lot	(b) Cost of Improvements	Total (a + b)
	$	$	$	$	$

Complete this line if this is a refinance loan.

Year Acquired	Original Cost	Amount Existing Liens	Purpose of Refinance	Describe Improvements ☐ made ☐ to be made
	$	$		Cost: $

Title will be held in what Name(s)	Manner in which Title will be held	Estate will be held in: ☐ Fee Simple
Source of Down Payment, Settlement Charges and/or Subordinate Financing (explain)		☐ Leasehold (show expiration date)

III. BORROWER INFORMATION

Borrower	Co-Borrower
Borrower's Name (include Jr. or Sr. if applicable)	Co-Borrower's Name (include Jr. or Sr. if applicable)

Social Security Number	Home Phone (incl. area code)	Age	Yrs. School	Social Security Number	Home Phone (incl. area code)	Age	Yrs. School

☐ Married ☐ Unmarried (include single, divorced, widowed) ☐ Separated	Dependents (not listed by Co-Borrower) no. ages	☐ Married ☐ Unmarried (include single, divorced, widowed) ☐ Separated	Dependents (not listed by Borrower) no. ages

Present Address (street, city, state, zip code) ☐ Own ☐ Rent ___ No. Yrs.	Present Address (street, city, state, zip code) ☐ Own ☐ Rent ___ No. Yrs.

If residing at present address for less than seven years, complete the following:

Former Address (street, city, state, zip code) ☐ Own ☐ Rent ___ No. Yrs.	Former Address (street, city, state, zip code) ☐ Own ☐ Rent ___ No. Yrs.

Former Address (street, city, state, zip code) ☐ Own ☐ Rent ___ No. Yrs.	Former Address (street, city, state, zip code) ☐ Own ☐ Rent ___ No. Yrs.

IV. EMPLOYMENT INFORMATION

Borrower	Co-Borrower
Name & Address of Employer ☐ Self Employed	Yrs. on this job	Name & Address of Employer ☐ Self Employed	Yrs. on this job

	Yrs. employed in this line of work/profession		Yrs. employed in this line of work/profession

Position/Title/Type of Business	Business Phone (incl. area code)	Position/Title/Type of Business	Business Phone (incl. area code)

If employed in current position for less than two years or if currently employed in more than one position, complete the following:

Name & Address of Employer ☐ Self Employed	Dates (from - to)	Name & Address of Employer ☐ Self Employed	Dates (from - to)
	Monthly Income $		Monthly Income $
Position/Title/Type of Business	Business Phone (incl. area code)	Position/Title/Type of Business	Business Phone (incl. area code)

Name & Address of Employer ☐ Self Employed	Dates (from - to)	Name & Address of Employer ☐ Self Employed	Dates (from - to)
	Monthly Income $		Monthly Income $
Position/Title/Type of Business	Business Phone (incl. area code)	Position/Title/Type of Business	Business Phone (incl. area code)

Freddie Mac Form 65/Rev. 5/91 (Amended) ♻ Printed on Recycled Paper

Page 1 of 4

Fannie Mae Form 1003/Rev. 5/91 (Amended)

185

Gross Monthly Income	Borrower	Co-Borrower	Total	Combined Monthly Housing Expense	Present	Proposed
Base Empl. Income *	$	$	$	Rent	$	
Overtime				First Mortgage (P&I)		$
Bonuses				Other Financing (P&I)		
Commissions				Hazard Insurance		
Dividends/Interest				Real Estate Taxes		
Net Rental Income				Mortgage Insurance		
Other (before completing, see the notice in "describe other income." below)				Homeowner Assn. Dues		
				Other:		
Total	$	$	$	Total	$	$

* Self Employed Borrower(s) may be required to provide additional documentation such as tax returns and financial statements.

Describe Other Income *Notice:* Alimony, child support, or separate maintenance income need not be revealed if the Borrower (B) or Co-Borrower (C) does not choose to have it considered for repaying this loan.

B/C		Monthly Amount
		$

This Statement and any applicable supporting schedules may be completed jointly by both married and unmarried Co-Borrowers if their assets and liabilities are sufficiently joined so that the Statement can be meaningfully and fairly presented on a combined basis; otherwise separate Statements and Schedules are required. If the Co-Borrower section was completed about a spouse, this Statement and supporting schedules must be completed about that spouse also.

Completed ☐ Jointly ☐ Not Jointly

ASSETS	Cash or Market Value	Liabilities and Pledged Assets. List the creditor's name, address and account number for all outstanding debts, including automobile loans, revolving charge accounts, real estate loans, alimony, child support, stock pledges, etc. Use continuation sheet, if necessary. Indicate by (*) those liabilities which will be satisfied upon sale of real estate owned or upon refinancing of the subject property.		
Description			Monthly Pmt. & Mos. Left to Pay	Unpaid Balance
Cash deposit toward purchase held by:	$	LIABILITIES		
		Name and address of Company	$ Pmt./Mos.	$
List checking and savings accounts below				
Name and address of Bank, S&L, or Credit Union				
		Acct. no.		
		Name and address of Company	$ Pmt./Mos.	$
Acct. no.	$			
Name and address of Bank, S&L, or Credit Union				
		Acct. no.		
		Name and address of Company	$ Pmt./Mos.	$
Acct. no.	$			
Name and address of Bank, S&L, or Credit Union				
		Acct. no.		
		Name and address of Company	$ Pmt./Mos.	$
Acct. no.	$			
Name and address of Bank, S&L, or Credit Union				
		Acct. no.		
		Name and address of Company	$ Pmt./Mos.	$
Acct. no.	$			
Stocks & Bonds (Company name/number & description)	$			
		Acct. no.		
		Name and address of Company	$ Pmt./Mos.	$
Life insurance net cash value	$			
Face amount: $				
Subtotal Liquid Assets	$			
Real estate owned (enter market value from schedule of real estate owned)	$	Acct. no.		
Vested interest in retirement fund	$	Name and address of Company	$ Pmt./Mos.	$
Net worth of business(es) owned (attach financial statement)	$			
Automobiles owned (make and year)	$			
		Acct. no.		
		Alimony/Child Support/Separate Maintenance Payments Owed to:	$	
Other Assets (itemize)	$	Job Related Expense (child care, union dues, etc.)	$	
		Total Monthly Payments	$	
Total Assets a.	$	Net Worth (a minus b) ▶ $	Total Liabilities b.	$

VI. ASSETS AND LIABILITIES (cont.)

Schedule of Real Estate Owned (If additional properties are owned, use continuation sheet.)

Property Address (enter S if sold, PS if pending sale or R if rental being held for income)	Type of Property	Present Market Value	Amount of Mortgages & Liens	Gross Rental Income	Mortgage Payments	Insurance, Maintenance, Taxes & Misc.	Net Rental Income
		$	$	$	$	$	$
Totals		$	$	$	$	$	$

List any additional names under which credit has previously been received and indicate appropriate creditor name(s) and account number(s):

Alternate Name	Creditor Name	Account Number

VII. DETAILS OF TRANSACTION

a. Purchase price	$
b. Alterations, improvements, repairs	
c. Land (if acquired separately)	
d. Refinance (incl. debts to be paid off)	
e. Estimated prepaid items	
f. Estimated closing costs	
g. PMI, MIP, Funding Fee paid in cash	
h. Discount (if Borrower will pay)	
i. Total costs (add items a through h)	
j. Subordinate financing	
k. Borrower's closing costs paid by Seller	
l. Other Credits (explain)	
m. Loan amount (exclude PMI, MIP, Funding Fee financed)	
n. PMI, MIP, Funding Fee financed	
o. Loan amount (add m & n)	
p. Cash from/to Borrower (subtract j, k, l & o from i)	

VIII. DECLARATIONS

If you answer "yes" to any questions a through i, please use continuation sheet for explanation.

	Borrower Yes No	Co-Borrower Yes No
a. Are there any outstanding judgments against you?	☐ ☐	☐ ☐
b. Have you been declared bankrupt within the past 7 years?	☐ ☐	☐ ☐
c. Have you had property foreclosed upon or given title or deed in lieu thereof in the last 7 years?	☐ ☐	☐ ☐
d. Are you a party to a lawsuit?	☐ ☐	☐ ☐
e. Have you directly or indirectly been obligated on any loan which resulted in foreclosure, transfer of title in lieu of foreclosure, or judgment? (This would include such loans as home mortgage loans, SBA loans, home improvement loans, educational loans, manufactured (mobile) home loans, any mortgage, financial obligation, bond, or loan guarantee. If "Yes," provide details, including date, name and address of Lender, FHA or VA case number, if any, and reasons for the action.)	☐ ☐	☐ ☐
f. Are you presently delinquent or in default on any Federal debt or any other loan, mortgage, financial obligation, bond, or loan guarantee? If "Yes," give details as described in the preceding question.	☐ ☐	☐ ☐
g. Are you obligated to pay alimony, child support, or separate maintenance?	☐ ☐	☐ ☐
h. Is any part of the down payment borrowed?	☐ ☐	☐ ☐
i. Are you a co-maker or endorser on a note?	☐ ☐	☐ ☐
j. Are you a U.S. citizen?	☐ ☐	☐ ☐
k. Are you a permanent resident alien?	☐ ☐	☐ ☐
Do you intend to occupy the property as your primary residence?	☐ ☐	☐ ☐

IX. ACKNOWLEDGMENT AND AGREEMENT

The undersigned specifically acknowledge(s) and agree(s) that: (1) the loan requested by this application will be secured by a first mortgage or deed of trust on the property described herein; (2) the property will not be used for any illegal or prohibited purpose or use; (3) all statements made in this application are made for the purpose of obtaining the loan indicated herein; (4) occupation of the property will be as indicated above; (5) verification or reverification of any information contained in the application may be made at any time by the Lender, its agents, successors and assigns, either directly or through a credit reporting agency, from any source named in this application, and the original copy of this application will be retained by the Lender, even if the loan is not approved; (6) the Lender, its agents, successors and assigns will rely on the information contained in the application and I/we have a continuing obligation to amend and/or supplement the information provided in this application if any of the material facts which I/we have represented herein should change prior to closing; (7) in the event my/our payments on the loan indicated in this application become delinquent, the Lender, its agents, successors and assigns, may, in addition to all their other rights and remedies, report my/our name(s) and account information to a credit reporting agency; (8) ownership of the loan may be transferred to successor or assign of the Lender without notice to me and/or the administration of the loan account may be transferred to an agent, successor or assign of the Lender with prior notice to me; (9) the Lender, its agents, successors and assigns make no representations or warranties, express or implied, to the Borrower(s) regarding the property, the condition of the property, or the value of the property.

Certification: I/We certify that the information provided in this application is true and correct as of the date set forth opposite my/our signature(s) on this application and acknowledge my/our understanding that any intentional or negligent misrepresentation(s) of the information contained in this application may result in civil liability and/or criminal penalties including, but not limited to, fine or imprisonment or both under the provisions of Title 18, United States Code, Section 1001, et seq. and liability for monetary damages to the Lender, its agents, successors and assigns, insurers and any other person who may suffer any loss due to reliance upon any misrepresentation which I/we have made on this application.

Borrower's Signature	Date	Co-Borrower's Signature	Date
X		X	

X. INFORMATION FOR GOVERNMENT MONITORING PURPOSES

The following information is requested by the Federal Government for certain types of loans related to a dwelling, in order to monitor the Lender's compliance with equal credit opportunity, fair housing and home mortgage disclosure laws. You are not required to furnish this information, but are encouraged to do so. The law provides that a Lender may neither discriminate on the basis of this information, nor on whether you choose to furnish it. However, if you choose not to furnish it, under Federal regulations this Lender is required to note race and sex on the basis of visual observation or surname. If you do not wish to furnish the above information, please check the box below. (Lender must review the above material to assure that the disclosures satisfy all requirements to which the Lender is subject under applicable state law for the particular type of loan applied for.)

BORROWER ☐ I do not wish to furnish this information

Race/National Origin: ☐ American Indian or Alaskan Native ☐ Asian or Pacific Islander ☐ Black, not of Hispanic origin ☐ Hispanic ☐ White, not of Hispanic origin

Sex: ☐ Female ☐ Male

CO-BORROWER ☐ I do not wish to furnish this information

Race/National Origin ☐ American Indian or Alaskan Native ☐ Asian or Pacific Islander ☐ Black, not of Hispanic origin ☐ Hispanic ☐ White, not of Hispanic origin

Sex: ☐ Female ☐ Male

To be Completed by Interviewer	Interviewer's Name (print or type)	Name and Address of Interviewer's Employer
This application was taken by: ☐ face-to-face interview ☐ by mail ☐ by telephone	Interviewer's Signature ___ Date ___ Interviewer's Phone Number (incl. area code)	

Continuation Sheet/Residential Loan Application

Use this continuation sheet if you need more space to complete the Residential Loan Application. Mark **B** for Borrower or **C** for Co-Borrower.	Borrower:	Agency Case Number:
	Co-Borrower:	Lender Case Number:

I/We fully understand that it is a Federal crime punishable by fine or imprisonment, or both, to knowingly make any false statements concerning any of the above facts as applicable under the provisions of Title 18, United States Code, Section 1001, et seq.

Borrower's Signature:	Date	Co-Borrower's Signature:	Date
X		X	

LENDER NAME AND ADDRESS

MORTGAGE SERVICING TRANSFER DISCLOSURE

NOTICE TO MORTGAGE LOAN APPLICANTS: THE RIGHT TO COLLECT YOUR MORTGAGE LOAN PAYMENTS MAY BE TRANSFERRED. FEDERAL LAW GIVES YOU CERTAIN RIGHTS. READ THIS STATEMENT AND SIGN IT ONLY IF YOU UNDERSTAND ITS CONTENTS.

Because you are applying for a mortgage loan covered by the Real Estate Settlement Procedures Act (RESPA) (12 U.S.C. §2601 et seq.) you have certain rights under that Federal law. This statement tells you about those rights. It also tells you what the chances are that the servicing for this loan may be transferred to a different loan servicer. "Servicing" refers to collecting your principal, interest and escrow account payments. If your loan servicer changes, there are certain procedures that must be followed. This statement generally explains those procedures.

Transfer Practices and Requirements

If the servicing of your loan is assigned, sold, or transferred to a new servicer, you must be given written notice of that transfer. The present loan servicer must send you notice in writing of the assignment, sale or transfer of the servicing not less than 15 days before the date of the transfer. The new loan servicer must also send you notice within 15 days after the date of the transfer. Also, a notice of prospective transfer may be provided to you at settlement (when title to your new property is transferred to you) to satisfy these requirements. The law allows a delay in the time (not more than 30 days after a transfer) for servicers to notify you under certain limited circumstances, when your servicer is changed abruptly. This exception applies only if your servicer is fired for cause, is in bankruptcy proceedings, or is involved in a conservatorship or receivership initiated by a Federal agency.

Notices must contain certain information. They must contain the effective date of the transfer of the servicing of your loan to the new servicer, the name, address, and toll-free or collect call telephone number of the new servicer, and toll-free or collect call telephone numbers of a person or department for both your present servicer and your new servicer to answer your questions about the transfer of servicing. During the 60-day period following the effective date of the transfer of the loan servicing, a loan payment received by your old servicer before its due date may not be treated by the new loan servicer as late, and a late fee may not be imposed on you.

Complaint Resolution

Section 6 of RESPA (12 U.S.C. §2605) gives you certain consumer rights, whether or not your loan servicing is transferred. If you send a "qualified written request" to your loan servicer concerning the servicing of your loan, your servicer must provide you with a written acknowledgment within 20 business days of receipt of your request. A "qualified written request" is a written correspondence, other than notice on a payment coupon or other payment medium supplied by the servicer, which includes your name and account number, and your reasons for the request. Not later than 60 business days after receiving your request, your servicer must make any appropriate corrections to your account, and must provide you with a written clarification regarding any dispute. During this 60-day period, your servicer may not provide information to a consumer reporting agency concerning any overdue payment related to such period or qualified written request.

Damages and Costs

Section 6 of RESPA also provides for damages and costs for individuals or classes of individuals in circumstances where servicers are shown to have violated the requirements of that Section.

Servicing Transfer Estimates by Original Lender

The following is the best estimate of what will happen to the servicing of your mortgage loan:

1. ☐ We do not service mortgage loans. We intend to assign, sell, or transfer the servicing of your loan to another party. You will be notified at settlement regarding the servicer.

   OR

2. ☐ We are able to service this loan and presently intend to do so. However, that may change in the future. For all the loans that we make in the 12-month period after your loan is funded, we estimate that the chances that we will transfer the servicing of those loans is between:

   ☐ 0 to 25% ☐ 26 to 50% ☐ 51 to 75% ☐ 76 to 100%

   This is only our best estimate and it is not binding.
   Business conditions or other circumstances may affect our future transferring decisions.

3. This is our record of transferring the servicing of the loans we have made in the past:

YEAR	PERCENTAGE OF LOANS TRANSFERRED (Rounded to Nearest Quartile - 0%, 25%, 50%, 75% or 100%)
19	%
19	%
19	%

The estimates in 2. and 3. above do not include transfers to affiliates or subsidiaries. If the servicing of your loan is transferred to an affiliate or subsidiary in the future, you will be notified in accordance with RESPA.

_____   _____
LENDER (Signature not Mandatory)   DATE

ACKNOWLEDGMENT OF MORTGAGE LOAN APPLICANT

I/we have read this disclosure form, and understand its contents, as evidenced by my/our signature(s) below.

_____   _____
APPLICANT'S SIGNATURE   DATE

_____
CO-APPLICANT'S SIGNATURE

INSTRUCTIONS TO PREPARER: For applications received in calendar year 1991 after the effective date of this Notice, the information in 3. above will be for calendar year 1990 only; for applications received in 1992, this information will be for calendar years 1990 and 1991; and for applications received in 1993 and thereafter, this information will be for the previous three calendar years.

CONVENTIONAL/F.H.A. QUALIFYING SHEET

	BORROWER	CO-BORROWER
GROSS MONTHLY INCOME:		
BASE INCOME:	$_____	$_____
OTHER: Overtime:	$_____	$_____
Bonus:	$_____	$_____
Commission:	$_____	$_____
Interest/Div.	$_____	$_____
_____	$_____	$_____

[A] **TOTAL G.M.I.:** $_____   + $_____   = $_____

TOTAL HOUSE PAYMENT:

PRINCIPAL & INTEREST:	$_____
TAXES:	$_____
HAZARD INSURANCE:	$_____
* ASSOCIATION/CONDO FEES:	$_____
* MORTGAGE INSURE:	$_____
* OTHER:	$_____
(*If required)	

[B] **TOTAL HOUSING EXPENSE:** $_____ .... = $_____

[C] HOUSING EXPENSE RATIOS: CONVENTIONAL: **28% OF GMI**
                              F.H.A.:   **29% of GMI**

[B]$_____divided by [A]$_____ = HOUSE PAYMENT RATIO: %
                                    (Should not exceed [C]). ========

DEBTS:

Creditor:	Balance	Remaining Months/	Payment
_____	$_____	____ @	$_____
_____	_____	____ @	_____
_____	_____	____ @	_____
_____	_____	____ @	_____
_____	_____	____ @	_____
_____	_____	____ @	_____
TOTAL:	$_____		$_____ = $_____

Long-term Debt: Conventional = Over 10 months; 95%LTV = All Debt.
                 F.H.A.   = Over 6 months.

[D] **TOTAL HOUSING EXPENSE[B] AND LONG-TERM MONTHLY DEBTS:** $_____

[E] **TOTAL PAYMENTS RATIOS:**   CONVENTIONAL: **36% OF GMI**
                                  F.H.A.:   **41% OF GMI**

[D] $_____ divided by [A]_____= TOTAL PAYMENTS RATIO: %
                                     (Should not exceed [E])   ========

NOTE: On one year A.R.M.s use the maximum second year payment to qualify if it has yearly caps of 2% and the loan-to-value is over 80%. 95% LTV conventional loans use ratios of **25% and 33%**(never exceeds 28%/36%).

This guide is meant only to help pre-qualify the borrower. It should not be considered as the eqivalent of a lender's approval or denial. Lenders and loan products may vary considerably. Follow up with a competent lender.

GOOD FAITH ESTIMATE OF CLOSING COSTS

Sales Price:$_____Loan Amount:$_____W/MIP or Funding Fee$_____
****

801 ORIGINATION FEE(___%). (FHA: Use loan amt. w/o MIP).........$_____

802 DISCOUNT FEE   (___%). (FHA/VA: Use loan amt. with MIP/FF)..$_____

803 APPRAISAL FEE: Conventional: $250+. FHA/V.A.: $200+........$_____

804 CREDIT REPORT: Individuals/Couples: $35/$65 Business:$40/80.$_____

805 CONSTRUCTION INSPECTION FEE: $35 - $75......................$_____

808 VA FUNDING FEE or FHA MIP. Add only if not financed.(___%)..$_____

809 TAX SERVICE FEE: (FHA/VA will not allow borrower to pay)...$_____

1105 DOCUMENT PREPARATION FEE(FHA/VA-borrower cannot pay).........$_____

901 PREPAID INTEREST(Loan X int. rate divided by 360=$_____x 30)$_____

902 PRIVATE MORTGAGE INSURANCE, first yr. premium(not financed)..$_____

903 HOMEOWNER'S INSURANCE, first yr. premium($2.50/1000 of value)$_____

1001 HOMEOWNER'S INSURANCE ESCROW(____Months).....................$_____

1002 MORTGAGE INSURANCE ESCROW   (____Months).....................$_____

1003 PROPERTY TAX ESCROW   (____Months).....................$_____
     FLOOD INSURANCE..$_____

1107 ATTORNEY'S FEES..$_____

1108 TITLE INSURANCE:
     Mortgagee(lender) Coverage($3.50/1000 of loan amount)........$_____
     Mortgagor(borrower) Coverage($4.00/1000 of loan amount)......$_____

1201 RECORDING FEES:
     Deed: (Call local government where property is located......$_____
     D/T: to get recording fees)..............................$_____

1301 SURVEY(varies depending on size & distance of property)......$_____

1302 PEST INSPECTION(usually paid by the seller)..................$_____

1303 OTHER FEES(varies lender to lender).........................$_____

     _____$_____

TOTAL OF CLOSING COSTS AND PREPAIDS:...........................$_____

     SELLER PAID ITEMS (Subtract from total if previously added)..$_____

TOTAL OF CLOSING COSTS AND PREPAIDS TO BORROWER.................$_____

Request for Verification of Employment

U.S. Department of Housing and Urban Development

Department of Veterans Affairs

USDA, Farmers Home Administration

HUD OMB Approval No. 2502-0059 (exp. 7/31/89)
VA OMB Approval No. 2900-0460
FmHA OMB Approval No. 0575-0009

Privacy Act Notice: This information is to be used by the agency collecting it in determining whether you qualify as a prospective mortgagor under its program. It will not be disclosed outside the agency except to your employer(s) for verification of employment and as required and permitted by law. You do not have to give us this information, but if you do not, your application for approval as a prospective mortgagor or borrower may be delayed or rejected. The information requested in this form is authorized by Title 38, USC, Chapter 37 (if VA); by 12 USC, Section 1701 et. seq. (if HUD/FHA); and Title 42 USC, 1471 et. seq., or 7 USC., 1921 et. seq. (if USDA, FmHA).

Public reporting burden for this collection of information is estimated to average **10 to 30 minutes** per response, including the time for reviewing instructions, searching existing data sources, gathering and maintaining the data needed, and completing and reviewing the collection of information. Send comments regarding this burden estimate or any other aspect of this collection of information, including suggestions for reducing this burden, to the Reports Management Officer, Office of Information Policies and Systems, U.S. Department of Housing and Urban Development, Washington, D.C. 20410-3600 and to the Office of Management and Budget, Paperwork Reduction Project (2502-0059), Washington, D.C. 20503.

Lender or Local Processing Agency (LPA): Complete items 1 through 7. Have the applicant complete item 8. Forward the completed form directly to the employer named in item 1.

Employer: Complete either parts II and IV or parts III and IV. Return the form directly to the lender or local processing agency named in item 2 of part I.

Part I - Requested of:

Requested by:

1. Name & Address of Employer	2. Name & Address of Lender or Local Processing Agent (LPA)
3. Name & Address of Applicant	4. I certify that this verification has been sent directly to the employer and has not passed through the hands of the applicant or any other interested party. Signature of Lender, Official of LPA, or FmHA Loan Packager
I have applied for a mortgage loan or rehabilitation loan and stated that I am/was employed by you. My signature in the block below authorizes verification of my employment information.	X 5. Title
8. Applicant's Signature & Employer Identification	6. Date 7. HUD/FHA/CPD, VA or FmHA No.

X

Part II - Verification of Present Employment

10. Present Position	11. Date of Employment	12. Probability of Continued Employment	13a. Salaried [ ] Yes [ ] No Commission [ ] Yes [ ] No	13b. Is overtime/bonus likely to continue? Overtime: [ ] Yes [ ] No Bonus: [ ] Yes [ ] No

14. Current Base Pay [ ] Annual [ ] Monthly [ ] Weekly [ ] Hourly $ _____ Other (specify):	16a. Monthly Taxable Pay (for Military Personnel Only) Base Pay	Career C Pay	Pro Pay

15a. Base Earnings Year-to-Date Past Year $ _____ $ _____	Flight Pay	Other (specify)
b. Overtime Year-to-Date Past Year $ _____ $ _____	16b. Monthly Nontaxable Pay (for Military Personnel Only) Quarters	VHA	Clothing
c. Commissions Year-to-Date Past Year $ _____ $ _____			
d. Bonuses Year-to-Date Past Year $ _____ $ _____	Rations	Other (specify)

17. Remarks: If paid hourly, please indicate average hours worked each week during current and past year.

AVERAGE HOURS WORKED PER WEEK: _____ HOURS

	INDICATE FUTURE RAISES DUE:	IF THIS EMPLOYEE WAS OUT FOR ANY LENGTH OF TIME, PLEASE INDICATE DATES:
GROSS EARNINGS 19____ $ _____	DATE _____	
GROSS EARNINGS 19____ $ _____	AMOUNT _____	FROM _____
GROSS EARNINGS YTD 19____ $ _____	(Indicate per Year, Month Week, Hour ►) PER _____	TO _____

Part III - Verification of Previous Employment

18. Salary/Wage at Termination: [ ] Yearly [ ] Monthly [ ] Weekly	Base Pay $	Overtime $	Commissions $	Bonus $

19. Dates of Employment   20. Reasons for Leaving

from: _____ to: _____

21. Position Held

Part IV - Certification

Federal statutes provide severe penalties for any fraud, intentional misrepresentation, or criminal connivance or conspiracy purposed to influence the issuance of any guaranty or insurance by the VA or USDA, FmHA Administrators, or the FHA Commissioner.

22. Signature	23. Title of Employer	24. Date
X		

Previous editions may be used until supply is exhausted

FmHA form 410-5   VA form 26-8497

form HUD-92004-G (2/89)
ref. handbooks 4155.1, 4310.5

EMPLOYER-RETURN BOTH COMPLETED COPIES TO LENDER

Federal National Mortgage Association

REQUEST FOR VERIFICATION OF DEPOSIT

INSTRUCTIONS: LENDER - Complete Items 1 thru 8. Have applicant(s) complete Item 9. Forward directly to depository named in Item 1.
DEPOSITORY - Please complete Items 10 thru 15 and return DIRECTLY to lender named in Item 2.

PART I - REQUEST

1. TO (Name and address of depository)	2. FROM (Name and address of lender)

3. SIGNATURE OF LENDER	4. TITLE	5. DATE	6. LENDER'S NUMBER OPTIONAL

7. INFORMATION TO BE VERIFIED

TYPE OF ACCOUNT	ACCOUNT IN NAME OF	ACCOUNT NUMBER	BALANCE
			$
			$
			$
			$

TO DEPOSITORY: I have applied for a mortgage loan and stated in my financial statement that the balance on deposit with you is as shown above. You are authorized to verify this information and to supply the lender identified above with the information requested in Items 10 thru 12. Your response is solely a matter of courtesy for which no responsibility is attached to your institution or any of your officers.

8. NAME AND ADDRESS OF APPLICANT(s)	9. SIGNATURE OF APPLICANT(s)

TO BE COMPLETED BY DEPOSITORY

PART II - VERIFICATION OF DEPOSITORY

10. DEPOSIT ACCOUNTS OF APPLICANT(s)

TYPE OF ACCOUNT	ACCOUNT NUMBER	CURRENT BALANCE	AVERAGE BALANCE FOR PREVIOUS TWO MONTHS	DATE OPENED
		$	$	
		$	$	
		$	$	
		$	$	

11. LOANS OUTSTANDING TO APPLICANT(s)

LOAN NUMBER	DATE OF LOAN	ORIGINAL AMOUNT	CURRENT BALANCE	INSTALLMENTS (Monthly/Quarterly)	SECURED BY	NUMBER OF LATE PAYMENTS
		$	$	$ per		
		$	$	$ per		
		$	$	$ per		

12. ADDITIONAL INFORMATION WHICH MAY BE OF ASSISTANCE IN DETERMINATION OF CREDIT WORTHINESS: (Please include information on loans paid-in-full as in Item 11 above)

13. SIGNATURE OF DEPOSITORY	14. TITLE	15. DATE

The confidentiality of the information you have furnished will be preserved except where disclosure of this information is required by applicable law. The form is to be transmitted directly to the lender and is not to be transmitted through the applicant or any other party.

43506-5 (6/78)
FNMA Form 1006

PREVIOUS EDITION WILL BE USED UNTIL STOCK IS EXHAUSTED

GIFT LETTER

I,_____ , am the_____
             (name of donor)   (relationship to borrower)

of _____ , and am giving a gift in the amount
         (name of borrower)

of $_____ for the purchase of _____
        (amount of gift)   (address of property)

_____ .

This is an outright gift from me and does not have to be repaid.   There is no
repayment expected or implied.

The source of the funds for the gift is_____ ,
                                              (name of bank or institution)

_____ .
              (complete mailing address of institution)

The account number is _____ .

_____   _____
      (donor's signature)   (borrower's signature)

_____   _____

F.H.A. CERTIFICATION(FHA loans only):

WARNING: Section 1010 of Title 18, U.S.C."Department of Housing and Urban
           Development Transaction," provides "Whoever, for the purpose of...
           influencing in any way the action of such Department...makes,
passes, utters, or publishes any statement, knowing the same to be false...
shall be fined not more than $5,000 or imprisoned not more than two years, or
both."

_____   _____
   (donor's acknowledgement)   (borrower's acknowledgement)

_____   _____

_____
                        Donor's address

____ - _____
   (donor's telephone number)

```
                 MORTGAGE INSURANCE COMPARISON CHART
-----------------------------------------------------------------
LTV:      95%                90%                 85%

                    30 Year Fixed
          1.0%/.49        .40/.34            .30/.25
          1.0%/.39        .36/.29            .24/.24
          1.0%/.34        .50/.29            .30/.29
          1.0%/.44        .40/.34            .30/.29

             30 Year Single Premium Financed
                         2.95%              2.30%
                         2.20%              1.50%
                         2.45%              2.30%

                    15 Year Fixed
           .90/.25        .40/.20            .25/.20
           .84/.29        .36/.22            .24/.22
           .90/.34        .40/.29            .25/.24

             15 Year Single Premium Financed
                         1.20%              1.05%
                         1.10%               .90%
                         1.15%               .95%

                    30 Year A.R.M.
           .50/.44                           .35/.34
           .36/.375                          .28/.28
           .40/.39                           .30/.34

          30 Year A.R.M. Single Premium Financed
                         3.75%              2.65%
                         2.65%              1.75%
                         2.95%              1.95%

                    15 Year A.R.M.
           .40/.30                           .30/.25
           .36/.32                           .28/.28

          15 Year A.R.M. Single Premium Financed
                         1.45%              1.30%
                         1.35%              1.10%
                         1.65%              1.30%
```

These rates are only to show comparative costs & should not be
considered absolute. Get current rates from a lender.
The standard premiums are quoted as the "Up-front" and "Renewal"
premiums with the upfront paid at closing and the renewal is
escrowed(1/12th) into the monthly payment. Example: 30 year fixed
95% LTV = 1.0% up-front & .49 renewal. The renewal premium is per
100 of loan amount. The single premiums are financed into the loan.
The total cannot exceed the maximum allowable LTV.

F.H.A. MAXIMUM LOAN WORKSHEET

ALLOWABLE CLOSING COSTS FOR DETERMINING ACQUISITION COST. Indicate whether borrower, seller, or third party is paying.	CALCULATION 1

ALLOWABLE CLOSING COSTS FOR DETERMINING
ACQUISITION COST. Indicate whether
borrower, seller, or third party is paying.

Origination Fee $_____

Appraisal/Inspection Fee $_____

Credit Report Fee $_____

Attorneys Fee $_____

Title Insurance $_____

Recording Fees(Total combined $_____
city/county & state)

Survey Fee(not condos) $_____

Inspection Fee(up to $200). $_____

TOTAL $_____

**FHA Allowable Closing Costs $_____
(Total X 57%)

***Total Paid by Seller or $_____
   Third Party.

CALCULATION 1

Sales Price(or appraised $_____
value, whichever is less).

**FHA Allowable Closing
Costs(57% of Good Faith).   +$_____

***Closing costs paid by
Seller or Third Party.   -$_____

Acquisition Cost   =$_____

                      X $____95%*____

                            =$_____

                      +$____500.00____

Loan Amount   =$_____

(FHA Veterans: 100% of first $25,000 of
Acquisition Cost, 95% of the amount above
$25,000 of Acquisition Cost).

*Sales price of $50,000 or less: 97% x
Acquisition Cost = maximum loan amount(Do
not add $500.00).

CALCULATION 2

Sales Price or Appraised Value, Whichever is Less: $_____
(Do Not Include Closing Costs)

Closing Costs paid for purchaser by Seller or Third Party: - $_____
(Over the 6% maximum contribution limit).

                                                          = $_____

                                                    X ____*97.75%____

                                   LOAN AMOUNT   = $_____
*98.75% for properties with an appraised value of $50,000 or less.

MORTGAGE AMOUNT: LESSER OF CALCULATION 1 OR 2: $_____

```
                    NOTICE TO HOMEOWNER
        Assumption of HUD/FHA Insured Mortgages
              Release of Personal Liability
```

You are legally obligated to make the monthly payments required by your mortgage (deed of trust) and promissory note.

The Department of Housing and Urban Development (HUD) has acted to keep investors and non-creditworthy purchasers from acquiring one-to-four family residential properties covered by certain FHA-insured mortgages. There are minor exceptions to the restriction on investors: loans to public agencies and some non-profit organizations, Indian tribes or servicepersons; and loans under special mortgage insurance programs for property sold by HUD, rehabilitation loans or refinancing of insured mortgages. Your lender can advise you if you are included in one of these exceptions.

HUD will therefore direct the lender to accelerate this FHA-insured mortgage loan if all or part of the property is sold or transferred to a purchaser or recipient (1) who will not occupy the property as his or her principal or secondary residence, or (2) who does occupy the property but whose credit has not been approved in accordance with HUD requirements. This policy will apply except for certain sales or transfers where acceleration is prohibited by law.

When a loan is accelerated, the entire balance is declared "immediately due and payable." Since HUD will not approve the sale of the property covered by this mortgage to an investor or to a person whose credit has not been approved, you, the original homeowner, would remain liable for the mortgage debt even though the title to the property might have been transferred to the new buyer.

Even if you sell your home by letting an approved purchaser (that is, a creditworthy owner-occupant) assume your mortgage, you are still liable for the mortgage debt unless you obtain a release from liability from your mortgage lender. FHA-approved lenders have been instructed by HUD to prepare such a release when an original homeowner sells his or her property to a creditworthy purchaser who executes an agreement to assume and pay the mortgage debt and thereby agrees to become the substitute mortgagor. The release is contained in Form HUD-92210-1, ("Approval of Purchaser and Release of Seller"). You should ask for it if the mortgage lender does not provide it to you automatically when you sell your home to a creditworthy owner-occupant purchaser who executes an agreement to assume personal liability for the debt. When this form is executed, you are no longer liable for the mortgage debt.

_____   _____
Mortgagor   Date

_____
Co-Mortgagor

HOMEOWNER'S FACT SHEET
Mortgage Insurance Premium (MIP) Refunds
and Distributive Shares

REFUNDS OF UNEARNED ON-TIME MIP

When a mortgage insurance premium is paid in a one-time payment at the time of mortgage closing, the borrower will be eligible for a refund of any unearned premium if the insurance is terminated prior to maturity of the mortgage with no insurance claim involved. HUD began the one-time premium system September 1, 1983, for a limited number of insurance programs. If you are not sure that the MIP was paid in full at loan closing, ask your lender. You do not need to be the original borrower to be eligible for a refund.

HOW ARE MIP REFUND AMOUNTS DETERMINED?

HUD determines the amount of the premium refund by multiplying the insured mortgage amount at the time the mortgage was insured by the applicable premium refund factor for mortgages insured in the year the mortgage was endorsed for insurance. The applicable premium refund factor is determined each year, taking into account projected salaries and expenses, prospective losses generated by insurance claims and expected future payments of premium refunds. As an example, a borrower with a $50,000 30 year term mortgage at 12 percent interest paid off after five years would receive a refund of approximately $760 (50 x 15.20). At the end of ten years, the refund would be approximatedly $275 (50 x 5.50), and after 20 years, approximately $65 (50 x 1.30), would be refunded. Mortgages with different interest rates will get slightly different refund amounts.

DISTRIBUTIVE SHARES

A distributive share is a payment to a homeowner out of any existing participation reserves of the Mutual Mortgage Insurance (MMI) Fund. HUD analyzes the total reserves of the MMI Fund in terms of it's expected income and expenses. Reserves in excess of what is needed to cover expected expenses are participating reserves. You are eligible for a distributive share if:

1. Your mortgage is insured under any MMI Fund Section of the Act. Most Section 203 mortgages(including 245 Graduated Payment Mortgages) are in the MMI Fund.

2. Your mortgage insurance is terminated by payment in full, voluntarily terminated, or terminated by default that does not result in a claim to HUD.

3. Your mortgage(at time of termination of the FHA insurance) is part of a group of mortgages for which HUD has determined that a distributive share amount is payable(mortgages are grouped by mortgage characteristics such as year endorsed for insurance and term to maturity).

HOW ARE DISTRIBUTIVE SHARE AMOUNTS DETERMINED?

Each year in December, HUD determines the amount to be paid on eligible cases, from each group, terminating the following year. Groups with low loss experience are more likely to receive a distributive share than groups with higher losses. In no case will a distributive share be greater than the premiums paid on the mortgage. Currently, a distributive for a 30 year mortgage is authorized only when a mortgage has been insured for twelve years or more at the time of termination. An example, a $10,000, 30 year term mortgage, endorsed in 1970 and terminated in 1984 would pay a share of $250 (10 x 25.00). A similar mortgage endorsed in 1968 would pay a share of $563.80 (10 X 56.30).

PAYMENT OF MIP REFUND AND/OR DISTRIBUTIVE SHARES

1. When termination of the FHA Insurance is required before maturity of a mortgage, the lender submits a Form HUD-2344, Lenders Request For Termination of Home Mortgage Insurance, to HUD. For maturities the lender responds to HUD's request for confirmation that the mortgage is paid in full. In either instance, the lender provides HUD with the current name(s) and address of the borrower(mortgagor).

2. HUD determines if a refund of MIP and/or distributive share is due. If a payment is due, HUD sends a claim form to the borrower for signature and return to HUD. This form is normally sent within 90 days after termination.

3. After receipt of the signed form, HUD has the payment mailed to the borrower. Payment is normally made within 45 days after receipt of the claim form.

4. For those qualifying for payment, it is important that a forwarding address be provided to the lender at the time of mortgage insurance termination so that HUD can send the claim form to the proper location. The borrower should verify that the lender furnished a current mailing address to HUD.

ASSUMPTIONS

When an FHA-insured mortgage is assumed, the insurance continues in force and there will be no refund or unearned premiums or distributive shares. In the case where the original borrowers financed the one-time MIP, the assumptors assume the payments of the remaining MIP as a part of the total mortgage payment. On the other hand, when the original borrowers paid the one-time MIP in cash, they would not be able to recover from HUD that portion which might be considered unearned premiums unless they negotiate with the assumptors in a side agreement. HUD will not become involved in these negotiations.

BORROWER INQUIRIES

Requests for information should be forwarded to:

U.S. Department of Housing and Urban Development
Director, Mortgage Insurance Accounting and Servicing, OFA
Attn: Insurance Operations Division
P.O. Box 23699
Washington, D.C. 20026-3699

Include the FHA Case Number for the mortgage, date the HUD Insurance was terminated, and whether your inquiry pertains to REfund or One-Time MIP or Distributive Share. Please wait 90 days after termination of FHA Insurance before submitting an eligibility inquiry.

Borrower

Co-borrower

F.H.A. ASSUMPTION CHART

	INVESTOR ASSUMING FROM INVESTOR	INVESTOR ASSUMING FROM OWNER-OCCUPANT	OWNER-OCCUPANT ASSUMING FROM INVESTOR	OWNER-OCCUPANT ASSUMING FROM OWNER-OCCUPANT
MORTGAGE ORIGINATED* PRIOR TO 12/01/86				
PAYDOWN TO 75% LTV?	NO	NO	NO	NO
CREDITWORTHINESS REVIEW NECESSARY?**	NO	NO	NO	NO
MORTGAGE ORIGINATED* ON OR AFTER 12/01/86 BUT PRIOR TO 02/05/88				
PAY DOWN TO 75% LTV?	NO	NO	NO	NO
CREDIT WORTHINESS REVIEW NECESSARY?**	THE FIRST 24 MONTHS AFTER SETTLEMENT.	THE FIRST 12 MONTHS AFTER SETTLEMENT.	THE FIRST 24 MONTHS AFTER SETTLEMENT.	THE FIRST 12 MONTHS AFTER SETTLEMENT.
MORTGAGE ORIGINATED* ON OR AFTER 02/05/88 BUT PRIOR TO 12/15/89				
PAY DOWN TO 75% LTV?	YES, IF ORIGINAL BORROWER IS RELEASED.	YES, IF ORIGINAL BORROWER IS RELEASED.	N/A	NO
CREDIT WORTHINESS REVIEW NECESSARY?**	THE FIRST 24 MONTHS AFTER SETTLEMENT.	THE FIRST 12 MONTHS AFTER SETTLEMENT.	THE FIRST 24 MONTHS AFTER SETTLEMENT.	THE FIRST 12 MONTHS AFTER SETTLEMENT.
MORTGAGE ORIGINATED* ON OR AFTER 12/15/89				
PAY DOWN TO 75% LTV?	NOT ELIGIBLE	NOT ELIGIBLE	N/A	NO
CREDIT WORTHINESS REVIEW NECESSARY?	NOT ELIGIBLE	NOT ELIGIBLE	N/A	FOR THE LIFE OF THE MORTGAGE.

*ORIGINATION DATE REFERS TO THE FOLLOWING:
    12/01/86: DATE APPLICATION WAS SIGNED.
    02/05/88 and 12/15/89: DATE APPRAISED VALUE WAS APPROVED BY THE D.E. UNDERWRITER OR THE
                            CONDITIONAL COMMITMENT WAS ISSUED.

**PLEASE NOTE THAT THE CREDITWORTHINESS REVIEW IS ALWAYS REQUIRED IF THERE IS A REQUEST BY THE SELLER TO BE
RELEASED FROM LIABILITY.

```
                 V.A. NET INCOME RESIDUAL QUALIFYING
-----------------------------------------------------------------------------
INCOME:
     Borrower's Base Monthly Income:.......................+$_____

     Other:................................................+$_____

     Co-Borrower's Base Monthly Income:....................+$_____

     Other:................................................+$_____

     Real Estate Income:...................................+$_____
        (VA=80% of Gross rent, 90% on subject property)
     Total Monthly Effective Income:.......................+$_____

     Minus Federal Taxes(monthly withholding)..............-$_____
     (Do not count rental income, child support or tax free
     income in taxable income).
     NET EFFECTIVE INCOME:.............................(A)=$_____
HOUSING EXPENSE:                                            --------------
     Principal and Interest:...............................+$_____

     Hazard(Homeowner's) Insurance(1/12th):................+$_____

     Property Taxes(1/12th):...............................+$_____

     TOTAL MORTGAGE PAYMENT(PITI):.........................=$_____

     Maintenance and common Expense(get from lender or VA).+$_____

     Utilities(get from lender or VA):.....................+$_____

     TOTAL HOUSING EXPENSE:............................(B)=$_____
DEBTS:                                                      --------------
     State and Local Income Tax(monthly withholding):......+$_____

     Social Security(monthly withholding):................+$_____

     Total Recurring Installment Payments(6 months+).......+$_____

     Child Support and/or Child Care(monthly):.............+$_____

     TOTAL RECURRING DEBTS:................................=$_____

     Add Total Housing Expense(B):.........................+$_____

     TOTAL FIXED PAYMENTS:.............................(C)=$_____
RESIDUAL INCOME:                                            --------------
     Net Effective Income(A):..............................+$_____

     Minus Total Fixed Payments(C):........................-$_____
     RESIDUAL INCOME:(see Chart in section on VA):.....(D)=$_____
-----------------------------------------------------------------------------
     PROPOSED HOUSE PAYMENT(PITI):.........................+$_____

     LONG TERM MONTHLY DEBT PAYMENTS:......................+$_____

     TOTAL MONTHLY HOUSE AND DEBT PAYMENTS:................=$_____

     DIVIDED BY GROSS MONTHLY INCOME........................./$_____
     SHOULD NOT EXCEED 41%.................................=$_____
     (This can be exceeded with compensating factors.)      --------------
```

Worksheet for Computing Guaranty
Under Public Law 100-198

HOME LOANS

1. Proposed Loan Amount: $_____
    If loan is $45,000 or less, complete item 2.
    If loan is over $45,000, complete item 3.

2. If item 1 is $45,000 or less, multiply item 1
    by 0.50 and show product here and in item 4: $_____
    (Skip to item 4).

3. If item 1 is over $45,000, multiply item 1
    by 0.40 and show product: $_____

    (a) If product is less than $22,500,
         enter $22,500 in item 4.

    (b) If product is greater than $22,500,
         but does not exceed $36,000, enter
         the amount in item 4.

    (c) If product is over $36,000, enter
         $36,000 in item 4.

4. Preliminary guaranty amount: $_____

5. Show the amount of guaranty used by the
    veteran that has not been restored: $_____

6. Final guaranty amount: $_____
    (Subtract item 5 from item 4).

7. Percentage of loan to be guaranteed: _____%
    (Divide the amount in item 6 by the amount in
    item 1).

U.S. DEPARTMENT OF HOUSING AND URBAN DEVELOPMENT

WATCH OUT FOR LEAD-BASED PAINT POISONING

NOTIFICATION

TO: PURCHASERS OF HOUSING CONSTRUCTED BEFORE 1978

If the building was constructed before 1978, there is a possibility that it may contain lead-based paint.

PLEASE READ THE FOLLOWING INFORMATION CONCERNING LEAD PAINT POISONING

The interiors of older homes and apartments often have layers of lead-based paint on the walls, ceilings, window sills and door frames. Lead-based paint and primers may also have been used on outside porches, railings, garages, fire escapes and lamp posts. When the paint chips, flakes or peels off, there may be a real danger for babies and young children.

Children may eat paint chips or chew on painted railings, window sills or other items when parents are not around. Children can also ingest lead even if they do not specifically eat paint chips. For example, when children play in an area where there are loose paint or dust particles containing lead, they may get these particles on their hands, put their hands into their mouths, and ingest a dangerous amount of lead.

Has your child been especially cranky or irritable? Is he or she eating normally? Does your child have stomachaches and vomiting? Does he or she complain about headaches? Is your child unwilling to play? These may be signs of lead poisoning, although many times there are no symptoms at all. Lead poisoning can eventually cause mental retardation, blindness and even death.

If you suspect that your child has eaten chips of paint or someone told you this, you should take your child to the doctor or clinic for testing. If the test shows that your child has an elevated blood lead level, treatment is available. Contact your doctor or local health department for help or more information. Lead screening and treatment are available through the Medicaid Program for those who are eligible.

Inform other family members and baby-sitters of the dangers of lead-poisoning. You can safeguard your child from lead poisoning by preventing him or her from eating paint that may contain lead.

Look at your walls, ceilings, door frames, window sills. Are there places where the paint is peeling, flaking or chipping? If so, there are some things you can do immediately to protect your child:

    (1) Cover all furniture and appliances;

    (2) Get a broom or stiff brush and remove all loose pieces of paint from walls, woodwork and ceilings;

    (3) Sweep up all pieces of paint and plaster and put them in a paper bag or wrap them in newspaper. Put these packages in the trash can. DO NOT BURN THEM;

    (4) Do not leave paint chips on the floor. Damp mop floors in and around the work area to remove all dust and paint particles. Keeping the floor clear of paint chips, dust and dirt is easy and very important; and

    (5) Do not allow loose paint to remain within your children's reach since children may pick loose paint off the lower part of the walls.

AS A HOMEOWNER:

You should keep your home in good shape. Water leaks from faulty plumbing, defective roofs or exterior holes and breaks may admit rain or dampness into the interior of your home, damaging walls or ceilings, causing paint to peel, crack or flake. These conditions should be corrected immediately. Before repainting, all surfaces that are peeling, chipping or loose should be thoroughly cleaned by washing, sanding, or brushing the loose paint from the surface; then repaint with two (2) coats of non-leaded paint; or cover the surface with other material such as wallpaper or paneling. SIMPLY PAINTING OVER DETERIORATED PAINTED SURFACES DOES NOT REMOVE THE HAZARD.

When lead-based paint is removed by scraping or sanding, a dust is created, which may be hazardous. The dust can enter the body either by breathing or swallowing it. The use of heat or paint removers could create a vapor or fume which may cause poisoning if inhaled over a long period of time. The removal of lead-based paint should not be undertaken by amateurs and every precaution should be taken to safeguard workers and occupants during the removal process. Whenever possible, the removal of lead based paint should take place when there are no children and pregnant women on the premises.

_____

I have received a copy of the Notice entitled ''Watch Out for Lead Paint Poisoning''.

| _____ | _____ |
| DATE | SIGNATURE |

Form 4720 (8711)

FannieMae

Self-Employed Income Analysis

Borrower Name _____

Property Address _____

General Instructions: This form is to be used as a guide in Underwriting the Self-employed borrower. The underwriter has a choice in analyzing the Individual Tax return by either the Schedule Analysis Method or the Adjusted Gross Income (AGI) Method.

The Schedule Analysis Method derives total income by analyzing Schedule C, D, E, and F for stable continuing self-employed income.

Schedule Analysis Method

A. Individual Tax Return (Form 1040)

	19__	19__	19__
1. Schedule C:			
a. Net Profit or Loss			
b. Depletion .... (+)			
c. Depreciation .... (+)			
d. Less: 20% Exclusion for Meals and Entertainment .... (−)			
2. Schedule D			
Recurring Capital Gains .... (+)			
3. Schedule E			
Part II: Partnership/S Corporation Income (Loss)**			
4. Schedule F			
a. Net Profit or Loss			
b. Depreciation .... (+)			
5. Schedule 2106			
Total Expenses .... (−)			
6. W-2 income from Corporation .... (+)			
7. Total			

**Partnership Income (Loss) = [From IRS Schedule K-1 (Form 1065)]
Ordinary Income (Loss) (+) Guaranteed Payments
S Corporation Income (Loss) = [From IRS Schedule K-1 (Form 1120-s)]
Ordinary Income (Loss) + Other Income (Loss)

B. Corporate Tax Return Form (1120) - Corporate Income to qualify the borrower will be considered only if the borrower can provide evidence of access to the funds.

	19__	19__	19__
1. Taxable Income (Tax and Payments Section) .... (+)			
2. Total Tax (Tax and Payments Section) .... (−)			
3. Depreciation (Deductions Section) .... (+)			
4. Depletion (Deductions Section) .... (+)			
5. Mortgages, notes, bonds payable in less than one year (Balance Sheets Section) .... (−)			
6. Subtotal			
7. Times individual percentage of ownership .... X ___%	X ___%	X ___%
8. Subtotal			
9. Dividend Income reflected on borrower's individual income tax returns .... (−)			
10. Total Income available to borrower			

C. S Corporation Tax Returns (Form 1120s) or Partnership Tax Returns (Form 1065) - Partnership or S Corporation income to qualify the borrower will be considered only if the borrower can provide evidence of access to the funds.

	19__	19__	19__
1. Depreciation (Deductions Section) .... (+)			
2. Depletion (Deductions Section) .... (+)			
3. Mortgages, notes, bonds payable in less than one year (Balance Sheets Section) .... (−)			
4. Subtotal			
5. Times individual percentage of ownership .... X ___%	X ___%	X ___%
6. Total income available to borrower			
Total Income Available (add A, B, C) .... I _____	II _____	III _____

D. Year-to-Date Profit and Loss

Year-to-date income to qualify the borrower will be considered only if that income is in line with the previous year's earnings or if audited financial statements are provided.

1. Salary/Draws to Individual .... $ _____
2. Total Allowable add back $ _____ X _____% of individual ownership = $ _____
3. Total net profit $ _____ X _____% of individual ownership = $ _____
4. Total .... $ _____

Combined Total I, II, III, YTD = $ _____ divided by _____ months = $ _____ Monthly Average

This form is only a reference to help organize information from the tax returns. You must refer to the selling guide for our complete underwriting requirements on the self-employed.

Fannie Mae
Form 1084A Nov. 89

A.	U.S. DEPARTMENT OF HOUSING AND URBAN DEVELOPMENT SETTLEMENT STATEMENT

B.	T Y P E O F L O A N
1. ☐ FHA 2. ☐ FMHA 3. ☐ CONV. UNINS.
4. ☐ VA 5. ☐ CONV. INS.
6. FILE NUMBER: 7. LOAN NUMBER:
8. MORTGAGE INS. CASE NO.:

C. NOTE: *This form is furnished to give you a statement of actual settlement costs. Amounts paid to and by the settlement agent are shown. Items marked "(p.o.c.)" were paid outside the closing; they are shown here for informational purposes and are not included in the totals.*

D. NAME OF BORROWER:
   ADDRESS OF BORROWER:

E. NAME OF SELLER:
   ADDRESS OF SELLER:

F. NAME OF LENDER:
   ADDRESS OF LENDER:

G. PROPERTY
   LOCATION:

H. SETTLEMENT AGENT:
   PLACE OF SETTLEMENT:

I. SETTLEMENT DATE:

J. SUMMARY OF BORROWER'S TRANSACTION		K. SUMMARY OF SELLER'S TRANSACTION	
100. GROSS AMOUNT DUE FROM BORROWER:		400. GROSS AMOUNT DUE TO SELLER:	
101. Contract sales price		401. Contract sales price	
102. Personal property		402. Personal property	
103. Settlement charges to borrower (from line 1400)		403.	
104.		404.	
105.		405.	
ADJUSTMENTS FOR ITEMS PAID BY SELLER IN ADVANCE:		ADJUSTMENTS FOR ITEMS PAID BY SELLER IN ADVANCE:	
106. City/town taxes to		406. City/town taxes to	
107. County taxes to		407. County taxes to	
108. Assessments to		408. Assessments to	
109.		409.	
110.		410.	
111.		411.	
112.		412.	
120. GROSS AMOUNT DUE FROM BORROWER: ▶		420. GROSS AMOUNT DUE TO SELLER: ▶	
200. AMOUNTS PAID BY OR IN BEHALF OF BORROWER		500. REDUCTIONS IN AMOUNT DUE TO SELLER	
201. Deposit or earnest money		501. Excess deposit (see instructions)	
202. Principal amount of new loan(s)		502. Settlement charges to seller (line 1400)	
203. Existing loan(s) taken subject to		503. Existing loan(s) taken subject to	
204.		504. Payoff of first mortgage loan	
205.		505. Payoff of second mortgage loan	
206.		506.	
207.		507.	
208.		508.	
209.		509.	
ADJUSTMENTS FOR ITEMS UNPAID BY SELLER:		ADJUSTMENTS FOR ITEMS UNPAID BY SELLER:	
210. City/town taxes to		510. City/town taxes to	
211. County taxes to		511. County taxes to	
212. Assessments to		512. Assessments to	
213.		513.	
214.		514.	
215.		515.	
216.		516.	
217.		517.	
218.		518.	
219.		519.	
220. TOTAL PAID BY/FOR BORROWER: ▶		520. TOTAL REDUCTIONS IN AMOUNT DUE SELLER: ▶	
300. CASH AT SETTLEMENT FROM/TO BORROWER		600. CASH AT SETTLEMENT TO/FROM SELLER	
301. Gross amount due from borrower (line 120)		601. Gross amount due to seller (line 420)	
302. Less amount paid by/for borrower (line 220)	( )	602. Less total reductions in amount due seller (line 520)	( )
303. CASH (☐ FROM) (☐ TO) BORROWER: ▶		603. CASH (☐ TO) (☐ FROM) SELLER: ▶	

Previous Edition Is Obsolete
Form No. 1581
5/87

SB-4-3538-000-1
HUD-1 (3-86)
RESPA, HB 4305.2

To Reorder Call: Great Lakes Business Forms, Inc.
Nationally 1-800-253-0209 Michigan 1-800-358-2643

COPY

205

L. SETTLEMENT CHARGES

700. TOTAL SALES/BROKER'S COMMISSION:					PAID FROM BORROWER'S FUNDS AT SETTLEMENT	PAID FROM SELLER'S FUNDS AT SETTLEMENT
BASED ON PRICE $		@	% =			
DIVISION OF COMMISSION (LINE 700) AS FOLLOWS:						
701. $	to					
702. $	to					
703. Commission paid at settlement						
704.						
800. ITEMS PAYABLE IN CONNECTION WITH LOAN:						
801. Loan Origination fee	%					
802. Loan Discount	%					
803. Appraisal Fee to:						
804. Credit Report to:						
805. Lender's Inspection fee						
806. Mortgage Insurance application fee to						
807. Assumption fee						
808.						
809.						
810.						
811.						
900. ITEMS REQUIRED BY LENDER TO BE PAID IN ADVANCE						
901. Interest from	to	@ $	/day			
902. Mortgage insurance premium for	mo. to					
903. Hazard insurance premium for	yrs. to					
904. Flood Insurance Premium for	yrs. to					
905.						
1000. RESERVES DEPOSITED WITH LENDER:						
1001. Hazard insurance	months @ $	per month				
1002. Mortgage insurance	months @ $	per month				
1003. City property taxes	months @ $	per month				
1004. County property taxes	months @ $	per month				
1005. Annual assessments	months @ $	per month				
1006. Flood Insurance	months @ $	per month				
1007.	months @ $	per month				
1008.	months @ $	per month				
1100. TITLE CHARGES						
1101. Settlement or closing fee to						
1102. Abstract or title search to						
1103. Title examination to						
1104. Title insurance binder to						
1105. Document preparation to						
1106. Notary fees to						
1107. Attorney's fees to						
(includes above items Numbers:				)		
1108. Title insurance to						
(includes above items Numbers:				)		
1109. Lender's coverage $						
1110. Owner's coverage $						
1111.						
1112.						
1113.						
1200. GOVERNMENT RECORDING AND TRANSFER CHARGES:						
1201. Recording fees: Deed $	; Mortgage $	; Releases $				
1202. City/county tax/stamps: Deed $	; Mortgage $					
1203. State tax/stamps: Deed $	; Mortgage $					
1204.						
1205.						
1300. ADDITIONAL SETTLEMENT CHARGES:						
1301. Survey to						
1302. Pest inspection to						
1303.						
1304.						
1305.						
1306.						
1307.						
1400. TOTAL SETTLEMENT CHARGES (Enter on line 103, Section J – and – line 502, Section K) ▶						

I have carefully reviewed the HUD-1 Settlement Statement and to the best of my knowledge and belief, it is a true and accurate statement of all receipts and disbursements made on my account or by me in this transaction. I further certify that I have recieved a copy of HUD-1 Settlement Statement.

Borrowers _____ Sellers _____

The HUD-1 Settlement Statement which I have prepared is a true and accurate account of this transaction. I have caused or will cause the funds to be disbursed in accordance with this statement.

Settlement Agent _____ Date _____

WARNING: It is a crime to knowingly make false statements to the United States on this or any other similar form. Penalties upon conviction can include a fine or imprisonment. For details see: Title 18 U.S. Code Section 1001 and Section 1010.

Form No. 1582   SB-4-3538-000-1   **PAGE 2**

COPY

Example: $100,000 Loan, 80% LTV, at 10% for 30 Years, 1% Origination & 1% Discount
TRUTH-IN-LENDING STATEMENT
ALL NUMBERICAL DISCLOSURES EXCEPT THE LATE PAYMENT DISCLOSURE ARE ESTIMATES.
NOTICE TO BORROWER(S) REQUIRED BY FEDERAL LAW AND FEDERAL RESERVE REGULATION Z.
REAL PROPERTY TRANSACTION SECURED BY A FIRST LIEN ON DWELLING.

```
LENDER:                              DATE: 01/01/92
                                     TYPE: CONVENTIONAL
                                 BORROWER: JOE BORROWER
                              CO-BORROEWR: MARY BORROWER
                                  ADDRESS: 123 HAPPY STREET
                          CITY, STATE, ZIP: DEBT TOWN, USA
                                 PROPERTY: 456 HAPPIER ST.
                          CITY, STATE, ZIP: MOREDEBT TOWN, USA
```

ANNUAL PERCENTAGE RATE	FINANCE CHARGE	AMOUNT FINANCED	TOTAL OF PAYMENTS
The cost of your credit as a yearly rate.	The dollar amount the credit will cost you.	The amount of credit provided to you or on your behalf.	The amount you will have paid after you have made all payments as scheduled.
10.242% e	$218,770.86 e	$97,138.89 e	$315,909.75 e

ITEMIZATION: You have a right at this time to an ITEMIZATION of AMOUNT FINANCED.
( ) I do not want an itemization _____(Initials)
( ) I do want an itemization _____(Initials)
PAYMENT SCHEDULE:

NUMBER OF PAYMENTS	AMOUNTS OF PAYMENTS	WHEN PAYMENTS ARE DUE	NUMBER OF PAYMENTS	AMOUNTS OF PAYMENTS	WHEN PAYMENTS ARE DUE
359	$877.58	03/01/92			
1	$858.53	02/01/22			

VARIABLE RATE FEATURE: This loan does not have a Variable Rate Feature.
SECURITY: (X) You are giving a security interest in the real property located at
456 HAPPIER ST., MOREDEBT TOWN, USA.
(X) cannot assume the remaining balance due under original mortgage terms.
( ) may assume subject to lender's conditions the remaining balance due under
original mortgage terms.
FILING/RECORDING FEES: $
PROPERTY INSURANCE: (X) Property hazard insurance in the amount of $100,000 with a loss payable
clause to the lender is a required condition of this loan. The borrower can purchase this insurance
from any insurance company acceptable to the lender.
LATE CHARGES: If your payment is not received within 15 days, a late charge of 5.00% of the overdue
amount will be added.
PREPAYMENT PENALTY: You will not be charged a penalty to prepay this loan in full or in part. You
may not be entitled to a refund of part of the finance charge.
SEE CONTRACT DOCUMENTS.
See your contract documents for any additional information about non-payment, default, any required
repayment in full before the scheduled date, and prepayment refunds and penalties.
COPY RECEIVED:
I/We hereby acknoledge reading and receiving a complete copy of this disclosure along with copies of
documents referred to in this disclosure.

```
-------------------------------------        ------------------------------------   --------
Signature                            date        Signature                          date
ITEMIZATION:
Date of Closing   1/01/92            Date of First Payment:  3/01/92
Principal:        $100,000           Insurance Type:         NONE
Term:                360 months      Period/year:            12
Note Rate:        10.00%
-------------------------------------------------------------------------------------------
Origination Fees $1,000.00   Principal:     $100,000.00   Principal:         $100,000.00
Discount Fees     1,000.00   -Total Prepaids   2,861.11   Total Interest:    215,909.75
Other Fees            0.00   --------------------------   Rem. Insurance:          0.00
Odd Days interest   861.11                                --------------------------
Escrow                0.00   AMOUNT FINANCED: 97,138.89    TOTAL PAYMENTS:    315,909.75
Initial Premium       0.00
--------------------------   Interest         215,909.75
Total Prepaids:  $2,861.11   Rem. Insurance         0.00
                             Total Prepaids     2,861.11
                             --------------------------
                 TOTAL FINANCE CHARGE $218,770.86  A.P.R.              10.242%
```

NOTICE OF RIGHT TO CANCEL

YOUR RIGHT TO CANCEL:

You are entering into a transaction that will result in a security interest in your home. You have a legal right under federal law to cancel this transaction, without cost, within three business days from whichever of the following three events occurs last:

    (1) the date of the transaction which is _____ ; or

    (2) the date you received your Truth in Lending disclosures; or

    (3) the date you received this notice of your right to cancel.

The box indicated below, if checked, applies only to you if your loan is to increase the amount of credit already provided to you.

□ If this is a new transaction to increase the amount of credit provided to you, your cancellation will apply only to the increase in the amount of credit. It will not affect the amount you presently owe or the security interest we already have in your home.

HOW TO CANCEL:

If you decide to cancel this transaction, you may do so by notifying us, in writing, at ·

_____.

You may use any written statement that is signed, dated and states your intention to cancel this transaction, or you may use this notice by dating and signing below. If you use this notice, you may want to make a copy since it contains important information about your rights and it is proof of when you cancelled.

If you cancel by mail or telegram, the notice must be sent no later than midnight of _____ or midnight of the third business day after the latest of the three events listed above. If you use any other means to cancel, it must be delivered to the above address no later than that time.

I HEREBY CANCEL THIS TRANSACTION _____

                              (Customer's Signature)   (Date)

If you cancel the transaction, the security interest is also cancelled. Within 20 days of receiving of your notice, we must take the steps necessary to reflect the fact that the security interest in your home has been cancelled and we must return to you any money or property you have given to us or to anyone else in connection with this transaction. If we have given you any money or property, you may keep it until we have performed our obligations. You must then offer to return the money or property; if the return of the property itself is impractical or unfair, you must offer its reasonable value. You may offer to return the property at your home or at the location of the property. Money must be returned to the address indicated above. If we do not take possession of the money or property within 20 days of your offer, you may keep it without further obligation.

CUSTOMER'S CERTIFICATION

I HEREBY CERTIFY THAT I HAVE RECEIVED TWO COPIES OF THE ABOVE NOTICE

UNIFORM RESIDENTIAL APPRAISAL REPORT

File No _____

SUBJECT

Property Address	
City	County	State	Zip Code
Legal Description	
Owner Occupant	Map Reference
Sale Price $	Date of Sale
Loan charges concessions to be paid by seller $	
R E Taxes $	Tax Year	HOA $/Mo
Lender/Client	

Census Tract _____

LENDER DISCRETIONARY USE

Sale Price	$
Date	
Mortgage Amount	$
Mortgage Type	
Discount Points and Other Concessions	
Paid by Seller	$
Source	

PROPERTY RIGHTS APPRAISED
- [ ] Fee Simple
- [ ] Leasehold
- [ ] Condominium (HUD/VA)
- [ ] De Minimis PUD

NEIGHBORHOOD

LOCATION	[ ] Urban	[ ] Suburban	[ ] Rural
BUILT UP	[ ] Over 75%	[ ] 25-75%	[ ] Under 25%
GROWTH RATE	[ ] Rapid	[ ] Stable	[ ] Slow
PROPERTY VALUES	[ ] Increasing	[ ] Stable	[ ] Declining
DEMAND/SUPPLY	[ ] Shortage	[ ] In Balance	[ ] Over Supply
MARKETING TIME	[ ] Under 3 Mos	[ ] 3-6 Mos	[ ] Over 6 Mos

PRESENT LAND USE	%	LAND USE CHANGE	PREDOMINANT OCCUPANCY	SINGLE FAMILY HOUSING
Single Family		Not Likely	Owner	PRICE $ (000) / AGE (yrs)
2-4 Family		Likely	Tenant	
Multi-Family		In process	Vacant (0-5%)	Low
Commercial		To ___	Vacant (over 5%)	High
Industrial				Predominant
Vacant				—

NEIGHBORHOOD ANALYSIS — Good / Avg / Fair / Poor
- Employment Stability
- Convenience to Employment
- Convenience to Shopping
- Convenience to Schools
- Adequacy of Public Transportation
- Recreation Facilities
- Adequacy of Utilities
- Property Compatibility
- Protection from Detrimental Cond
- Police & Fire Protection
- General Appearance of Properties
- Appeal to Market

Note: Race or the racial composition of the neighborhood are not considered reliable appraisal factors.

COMMENTS _____

SITE

Dimensions	
Site Area	Corner Lot
Zoning Classification	Zoning Compliance
HIGHEST & BEST USE: Present Use	Other Use

Topography	
Size	
Shape	
Drainage	
View	
Landscaping	
Driveway	
Apparent Easements	
FEMA Flood Hazard	Yes* ___ No ___
FEMA* Map/Zone	

UTILITIES	Public	Other	SITE IMPROVEMENTS	Type	Public	Private
Electricity			Street			
Gas			Curb/Gutter			
Water			Sidewalk			
Sanitary Sewer			Street Lights			
Storm Sewer			Alley			

COMMENTS (Apparent adverse easements, encroachments, special assessments, slide areas, etc.): _____

IMPROVEMENTS

GENERAL DESCRIPTION	EXTERIOR DESCRIPTION	FOUNDATION	BASEMENT	INSULATION
Units	Foundation	Slab	Area Sq. Ft.	Roof [ ]
Stories	Exterior Walls	Crawl Space	% Finished	Ceiling [ ]
Type (Det./Att.)	Roof Surface	Basement	Ceiling	Walls [ ]
Design (Style)	Gutters & Dwnspts.	Sump Pump	Walls	Floor [ ]
Existing	Window Type	Dampness	Floor	None [ ]
Proposed	Storm Sash	Settlement	Outside Entry	Adequacy [ ]
Under Construction	Screens	Infestation		Energy Efficient Items
Age (Yrs.)	Manufactured House			
Effective Age (Yrs.)				

ROOM LIST

ROOMS	Foyer	Living	Dining	Kitchen	Den	Family Rm.	Rec. Rm.	Bedrooms	# Baths	Laundry	Other	Area Sq. Ft
Basement												
Level 1												
Level 2												

Finished area above grade contains ___ Rooms ___ Bedroom(s) ___ Bath(s) ___ Square Feet of Gross Living Area

INTERIOR

SURFACES	Materials/Condition
Floors	
Walls	
Trim/Finish	
Bath Floor	
Bath Wainscot	
Doors	

HEATING	
Type	
Fuel	
Condition	
Adequacy	
COOLING	
Central	
Other	
Condition	
Adequacy	

KITCHEN EQUIP.	
Refrigerator	
Range/Oven	
Disposal	
Dishwasher	
Fan/Hood	
Compactor	
Washer/Dryer	
Microwave	
Intercom	

ATTIC	
None [ ]	
Stairs [ ]	
Drop Stair [ ]	
Scuttle [ ]	
Floor [ ]	
Heated [ ]	
Finished [ ]	

Fireplace(s) #____

IMPROVEMENT ANALYSIS — Good / Avg / Fair / Poor
- Quality of Construction
- Condition of Improvements
- Room Sizes/Layout
- Closets and Storage
- Energy Efficiency
- Plumbing-Adequacy & Condition
- Electrical-Adequacy & Condition
- Kitchen Cabinets-Adequacy & Cond
- Compatibility to Neighborhood
- Appeal & Marketability
- Estimated Remaining Economic Life ___ Yrs
- Estimated Remaining Physical Life ___ Yrs

AUTOS

CAR STORAGE	Garage	[ ] Attached	[ ] Adequate	[ ] House Entry
No Cars ___	Carport	[ ] Detached	[ ] Inadequate	[ ] Outside Entry
Condition	None	[ ] Built-in	[ ] Electric Door	[ ] Basement Entry

Additional Features _____

COMMENTS

Depreciation (Physical, functional and external inadequacies, repairs needed, modernization, etc.): _____

General market conditions and prevalence and impact in subject/market area regarding loan discounts, interest buydowns and concessions: _____

Fannie Mae Form 1004 10/86

UNIFORM RESIDENTIAL APPRAISAL REPORT

File No.

Purpose of Appraisal is to estimate Market Value as defined in the Certification & Statement of Limiting Conditions

COST APPROACH

BUILDING SKETCH (SHOW GROSS LIVING AREA ABOVE GRADE)

If for Freddie Mac or Fannie Mae show only square foot calculations and cost approach comments in this space

ESTIMATED REPRODUCTION COST-NEW-OF IMPROVEMENTS:

Dwelling	Sq. Ft. @ $	= $	
	Sq. Ft. @ $	=	
Extras		=	
		=	
Special Energy Efficient Items		=	
Porches, Patios, etc.		=	
Garage/Carport	Sq. Ft. @ $	=	
Total Estimated Cost New		= $	

	Physical	Functional	External
Less			
Depreciation			= $
Depreciated Value of Improvements			= $
Site Imp. "as is" (driveway, landscaping, etc.)			= $
ESTIMATED SITE VALUE			= $

(If leasehold, show only leasehold value.)

INDICATED VALUE BY COST APPROACH .... = $

(Not Required by Freddie Mac and Fannie Mae)

Does property conform to applicable HUD/VA property standards? ☐ Yes ☐ No

If No, explain:

Construction Warranty ☐ Yes ☐ No

Name of Warranty Program

Warranty Coverage Expires

The undersigned has recited three recent sales of properties most similar and proximate to subject and has considered these in the market analysis. The description includes a dollar adjustment, reflecting market reaction to those items of significant variation between the subject and comparable properties. If a significant item in the comparable property is superior to, or more favorable than, the subject property, a minus (−) adjustment is made, thus reducing the indicated value of subject; if a significant item in the comparable is inferior to, or less favorable than, the subject property, a plus (+) adjustment is made, thus increasing the indicated value of the subject.

SALES COMPARISON ANALYSIS

ITEM	SUBJECT	COMPARABLE NO. 1		COMPARABLE NO. 2		COMPARABLE NO. 3	
Address							
Proximity to Subject							
Sales Price	$		$		$		$
Price/Gross Liv. Area	$	$		$		$	
Data Source							
VALUE ADJUSTMENTS	DESCRIPTION	DESCRIPTION	+ (−) $ Adjustment	DESCRIPTION	+ (−) $ Adjustment	DESCRIPTION	+ (−) $ Adjustment
Sales or Financing							
Concessions							
Date of Sale/Time							
Location							
Site/View							
Design and Appeal							
Quality of Construction							
Age							
Condition							
Above Grade	Total Bdrms Baths	Total Bdrms Baths		Total Bdrms Baths		Total Bdrms Baths	
Room Count							
Gross Living Area	Sq. Ft.	Sq. Ft.		Sq. Ft.		Sq. Ft.	
Basement & Finished							
Rooms Below Grade							
Functional Utility							
Heating/Cooling							
Garage/Carport							
Porches, Patio,							
Pools, etc.							
Special Energy Efficient Items							
Fireplace(s)							
Other (e.g. kitchen)							
equip., remodeling)							
Net Adj. (total)		+ − $		+ − $		+ − $	
Indicated Value of Subject		$		$		$	

Comments on Sales Comparison:

INDICATED VALUE BY SALES COMPARISON APPROACH .... $

INDICATED VALUE BY INCOME APPROACH (If Applicable) Estimated Market Rent $ _____ /Mo. x Gross Rent Multiplier _____ = $

This appraisal is made ☐ "as is" ☐ subject to the repairs, alterations, inspections or conditions listed below ☐ completion per plans and specifications.

Comments and Conditions of Appraisal:

Final Reconciliation:

RECONCILIATION

This appraisal is based upon the above requirements, the certification, contingent and limiting conditions, and Market Value definition that are stated in

☐ FmHA, HUD &/or VA instructions.

☐ Freddie Mac Form 439 (Rev. 7/86)/Fannie Mae Form 1004B (Rev. 7/86) filed with client _____ 19 _____ ☐ attached

I (WE) ESTIMATE THE MARKET VALUE, AS DEFINED, OF THE SUBJECT PROPERTY AS OF _____ 19 _____ to be $

I (We) certify that to the best of my (our) knowledge and belief the facts and data used herein are true and correct, that I (we) personally inspected the subject property, both inside and out, and have made an exterior inspection of all comparable sales cited in this report, and that I (we) have no undisclosed interest, present or prospective therein

Appraiser(s) SIGNATURE _____

NAME _____

Review Appraiser SIGNATURE _____

(If applicable) NAME _____

☐ Did ☐ Did Not Inspect Property

Freddie Mac Form 70 10/86

Fannie Mae Form 1004 10/86

DEFINITION OF MARKET VALUE: The most probable price which a property should bring in a competitive and open market under all conditions requisite to a fair sale, the buyer and seller, each acting prudently, knowledgeably and assuming the price is not affected by undue stimulus. Implicit in this definition is the consummation of a sale as of a specified date and the passing of title from seller to buyer under conditions whereby: (1) buyer and seller are typically motivated; (2) both parties are well informed or well advised, and each acting in what he considers his own best interest; (3) a reasonable time is allowed for exposure in the open market; (4) payment is made in terms of cash in U.S. dollars or in terms of financial arrangements comparable thereto; and (5) the price represents the normal consideration for the property sold unaffected by special or creative financing or sales concessions* granted by anyone associated with the sale.

*Adjustments to the comparables must be made for special or creative financing or sales concessions. No adjustments are necessary for those costs which are normally paid by sellers as a result of tradition or law in a market area; these costs are readily identifiable since the seller pays these costs in virtually all sales transactions. Special or creative financing adjustments can be made to the comparable property by comparisons to financing terms offered by a third party institutional lender that is not already involved in the property or transaction. Any adjustment should not be calculated on a mechanical dollar for dollar cost of the financing or concession but the dollar amount of any adjustment should approximate the market's reaction to the financing or concessions based on the appraiser's judgment.

CERTIFICATION AND STATEMENT OF LIMITING CONDITIONS

CERTIFICATION: The Appraiser certifies and agrees that:

1. The Appraiser has no present or contemplated future interest in the property appraised; and neither the employment to make the appraisal, nor the compensation for it, is contingent upon the appraised value of the property.

2. The Appraiser has no personal interest in or bias with respect to the subject matter of the appraisal report or the participants to the sale. The "Estimate of Market Value" in the appraisal report is not based in whole or in part upon the race, color, or national origin of the prospective owners or occupants of the property appraised, or upon the race, color or national origin of the present owners or occupants of the properties in the vicinity of the property appraised.

3. The Appraiser has personally inspected the property, both inside and out, and has made an exterior inspection of all comparable sales listed in the report. To the best of the Appraiser's knowledge and belief, all statements and information in this report are true and correct, and the Appraiser has not knowingly withheld any significant information.

4. All contingent and limiting conditions are contained herein (imposed by the terms of the assignment or by the undersigned affecting the analyses, opinions, and conclusions contained in the report).

5. This appraisal report has been made in conformity with and is subject to the requirements of the Code of Professional Ethics and Standards of Professional Conduct of the appraisal organizations with which the Appraiser is affiliated.

6. All conclusions and opinions concerning the real estate that are set forth in the appraisal report were prepared by the Appraiser whose signature appears on the appraisal report, unless indicated as "Review Appraiser". No change of any item in the appraisal report shall be made by anyone other than the Appraiser, and the Appraiser shall have no responsibility for any such unauthorized change.

CONTINGENT AND LIMITING CONDITIONS: The certification of the Appraiser appearing in the appraisal report is subject to the following conditions and to such other specific and limiting conditions as are set forth by the Appraiser in the report.

1. The Appraiser assumes no responsibility for matters of a legal nature affecting the property appraised or the title thereto, nor does the Appraiser render any opinion as to the title, which is assumed to be good and marketable. The property is appraised as though under responsible ownership.

2. Any sketch in the report may show approximate dimensions and is included to assist the reader in visualizing the property. The Appraiser has made no survey of the property.

3. The Appraiser is not required to give testimony or appear in court because of having made the appraisal with reference to the property in question, unless arrangements have been previously made therefor.

4. Any distribution of the valuation in the report between land and improvements applies only under the existing program of utilization. The separate valuations for land and building must not be used in conjunction with any other appraisal and are invalid if so used.

5. The Appraiser assumes that there are no hidden or unapparent conditions of the property, subsoil, or structures, which would render it more or less valuable. The Appraiser assumes no responsibility for such conditions, or for engineering which might be required to discover such factors.

6. Information, estimates, and opinions furnished to the Appraiser, and contained in the report, were obtained from sources considered reliable and believed to be true and correct. However, no responsibility for accuracy of such items furnished the Appraiser can be assumed by the Appraiser.

7. Disclosure of the contents of the appraisal report is governed by the Bylaws and Regulations of the professional appraisal organizations with which the Appraiser is affiliated.

8. Neither all, nor any part of the content of the report, or copy thereof (including conclusions as to the property value, the identity of the Appraiser, professional designations, reference to any professional appraisal organizations, or the firm with which the Appraiser is connected), shall be used for any purposes by anyone but the client specified in the report, the borrower if appraisal fee paid by same, the mortgagee or its successors and assigns, mortgage insurers, consultants, professional appraisal organizations, any state or federally approved financial institution, any department, agency, or instrumentality of the United States or any state or the District of Columbia, without the previous written consent of the Appraiser; nor shall it be conveyed by anyone to the public through advertising, public relations, news, sales, or other media, without the written consent and approval of the Appraiser.

9. On all appraisals, subject to satisfactory completion, repairs, or alterations, the appraisal report and value conclusion are contingent upon completion of the improvements in a workmanlike manner.

Date: .... Appraiser(s) ....

Freddie Mac Form 439 JUL 86   HYG 89   Forms and Worms • Incorporated 315 Whitney Ave New Haven CT 06511 1 (800) 243-4545   Item # 115800   Fannie Mae Form 1004B JUL 86

211

Comparison of 30- and 15-year $100,000 loans at 10% interest

30 Yr	360.00			
Pay #	Payment	Principal	Interest	Balance
1	877.57	44.24	833.33	99955.76
2	877.57	44.61	832.96	99911.15
3	877.57	44.98	832.59	99866.18
4	877.57	45.35	832.22	99820.82
5	877.57	45.73	831.84	99775.09
6	877.57	46.11	831.46	99728.98
7	877.57	46.50	831.07	99682.48
8	877.57	46.88	830.69	99635.60
9	877.57	47.27	830.30	99588.32
10	877.57	47.67	829.90	99540.65
11	877.57	48.07	829.51	99492.59
12	877.57	48.47	829.10	99444.12
13	877.57	48.87	828.70	99395.25
14	877.57	49.28	828.29	99345.97
15	877.57	49.69	827.88	99296.28
16	877.57	50.10	827.47	99246.18
17	877.57	50.52	827.05	99195.66
18	877.57	50.94	826.63	99144.72
19	877.57	51.37	826.21	99093.36
20	877.57	51.79	825.78	99041.56
21	877.57	52.23	825.35	98989.34
22	877.57	52.66	824.91	98936.68
23	877.57	53.10	824.47	98883.58
24	877.57	53.54	824.03	98830.04
25	877.57	53.99	823.58	98776.05
26	877.57	54.44	823.13	98721.61
27	877.57	54.89	822.68	98666.72
28	877.57	55.35	822.22	98611.37
29	877.57	55.81	821.76	98555.56
30	877.57	56.28	821.30	98499.28
31	877.57	56.74	820.83	98442.54
32	877.57	57.22	820.35	98385.32
33	877.57	57.69	819.88	98327.63
34	877.57	58.17	819.40	98269.45
35	877.57	58.66	818.91	98210.79
36	877.57	59.15	818.42	98151.65
37	877.57	59.64	817.93	98092.00
38	877.57	60.14	817.43	98031.87
39	877.57	60.64	816.93	97971.23
40	877.57	61.14	816.43	97910.08
41	877.57	61.65	815.92	97848.43
42	877.57	62.17	815.40	97786.26
43	877.57	62.69	814.89	97723.57
44	877.57	63.21	814.36	97660.37
45	877.57	63.74	813.84	97596.63
46	877.57	64.27	813.31	97532.36
47	877.57	64.80	812.77	97467.56
48	877.57	65.34	812.23	97402.22
49	877.57	65.89	811.69	97336.33
50	877.57	66.44	811.14	97269.90
51	877.57	66.99	810.58	97202.91
52	877.57	67.55	810.02	97135.36
53	877.57	68.11	809.46	97067.25
54	877.57	68.68	808.89	96998.57
55	877.57	69.25	808.32	96929.32
56	877.57	69.83	807.74	96859.50
57	877.57	70.41	807.16	96789.09
58	877.57	71.00	806.58	96718.09
59	877.57	71.59	805.98	96646.50
60	877.57	72.18	805.39	96574.32
61	877.57	72.79	804.79	96501.53
62	877.57	73.39	804.18	96428.14
63	877.57	74.00	803.57	96354.14
64	877.57	74.62	802.95	96279.52
65	877.57	75.24	802.33	96204.28
66	877.57	75.87	801.70	96128.41
67	877.57	76.50	801.07	96051.91
68	877.57	77.14	800.43	95974.77
69	877.57	77.78	799.79	95896.98

15 Yr	180.00			
Pay #	Payment	Principal	Interest	Balance
1	1074.61	241.27	833.33	99758.73
2	1074.61	243.28	831.32	99515.45
3	1074.61	245.31	829.30	99270.14
4	1074.61	247.35	827.25	99022.78
5	1074.61	249.42	825.19	98773.37
6	1074.61	251.49	823.11	98521.87
7	1074.61	253.59	821.02	98268.28
8	1074.61	255.70	818.90	98012.58
9	1074.61	257.83	816.77	97754.75
10	1074.61	259.98	814.62	97494.77
11	1074.61	262.15	812.46	97232.62
12	1074.61	264.33	810.27	96968.28
13	1074.61	266.54	808.07	96701.75
14	1074.61	268.76	805.85	96432.99
15	1074.61	271.00	803.61	96161.99
16	1074.61	273.26	801.35	95888.74
17	1074.61	275.53	799.07	95613.21
18	1074.61	277.83	796.78	95335.38
19	1074.61	280.14	794.46	95055.23
20	1074.61	282.48	792.13	94772.76
21	1074.61	284.83	789.77	94487.92
22	1074.61	287.21	787.40	94200.72
23	1074.61	289.60	785.01	93911.12
24	1074.61	292.01	782.59	93619.11
25	1074.61	294.45	780.16	93324.66
26	1074.61	296.90	777.71	93027.76
27	1074.61	299.37	775.23	92728.39
28	1074.61	301.87	772.74	92426.52
29	1074.61	304.38	770.22	92122.13
30	1074.61	306.92	767.68	91815.21
31	1074.61	309.48	765.13	91505.73
32	1074.61	312.06	762.55	91193.68
33	1074.61	314.66	759.95	90879.02
34	1074.61	317.28	757.33	90561.74
35	1074.61	319.92	754.68	90241.82
36	1074.61	322.59	752.02	89919.23
37	1074.61	325.28	749.33	89593.95
38	1074.61	327.99	746.62	89265.96
39	1074.61	330.72	743.88	88935.24
40	1074.61	333.48	741.13	88601.76
41	1074.61	336.26	738.35	88265.50
42	1074.61	339.06	735.55	87926.44
43	1074.61	341.88	732.72	87584.56
44	1074.61	344.73	729.87	87239.82
45	1074.61	347.61	727.00	86892.22
46	1074.61	350.50	724.10	86541.71
47	1074.61	353.42	721.18	86188.29
48	1074.61	356.37	718.24	85831.92
49	1074.61	359.34	715.27	85472.58
50	1074.61	362.33	712.27	85110.25
51	1074.61	365.35	709.25	84744.89
52	1074.61	368.40	706.21	84376.50
53	1074.61	371.47	703.14	84005.03
54	1074.61	374.56	700.04	83630.47
55	1074.61	377.68	696.92	83252.78
56	1074.61	380.83	693.77	82871.95
57	1074.61	384.01	690.60	82487.94
58	1074.61	387.21	687.40	82100.74
59	1074.61	390.43	684.17	81710.31
60	1074.61	393.69	680.92	81316.62
61	1074.61	396.97	677.64	80919.65
62	1074.61	400.27	674.33	80519.38
63	1074.61	403.61	670.99	80115.77
64	1074.61	406.97	667.63	79708.79
65	1074.61	410.37	664.24	79298.43
66	1074.61	413.78	660.82	78884.64
67	1074.61	417.23	657.37	78467.41
68	1074.61	420.71	653.90	78046.70
69	1074.61	424.22	650.39	77622.49

Comparison of 30- and 15-year $100,000 loans at 10% interest (continued)

70	877.57	78.43	799.14	95818.55	70	1074.61	427.75	646.85 77194.73
71	877.57	79.08	798.49	95739.47	71	1074.61	431.32	643.29 76763.42
72	877.57	79.74	797.83	95659.73	72	1074.61	434.91	639.70 76328.51
73	877.57	80.41	797.16	95579.32	73	1074.61	438.53	636.07 75889.97
74	877.57	81.08	796.49	95498.24	74	1074.61	442.19	632.42 75447.79
75	877.57	81.75	795.82	95416.49	75	1074.61	445.87	628.73 75001.91
76	877.57	82.43	795.14	95334.06	76	1074.61	449.59	625.02 74552.32
77	877.57	83.12	794.45	95250.94	77	1074.61	453.34	621.27 74098.99
78	877.57	83.81	793.76	95167.12	78	1074.61	457.11	617.49 73641.87
79	877.57	84.51	793.06	95082.61	79	1074.61	460.92	613.68 73180.95
80	877.57	85.22	792.36	94997.39	80	1074.61	464.76	609.84 72716.19
81	877.57	85.93	791.64	94911.47	81	1074.61	468.64	605.97 72247.55
82	877.57	86.64	790.93	94824.82	82	1074.61	472.54	602.06 71775.01
83	877.57	87.36	790.21	94737.46	83	1074.61	476.48	598.13 71298.53
84	877.57	88.09	789.48	94649.37	84	1074.61	480.45	594.15 70818.08
85	877.57	88.83	788.74	94560.54	85	1074.61	484.45	590.15 70333.62
86	877.57	89.57	788.00	94470.97	86	1074.61	488.49	586.11 69845.13
87	877.57	90.31	787.26	94380.66	87	1074.61	492.56	582.04 69352.57
88	877.57	91.07	786.51	94289.59	88	1074.61	496.67	577.94 68855.90
89	877.57	91.82	785.75	94197.77	89	1074.61	500.81	573.80 68355.10
90	877.57	92.59	784.98	94105.18	90	1074.61	504.98	569.63 67850.12
91	877.57	93.36	784.21	94011.82	91	1074.61	509.19	565.42 67340.93
92	877.57	94.14	783.43	93917.68	92	1074.61	513.43	561.17 66827.50
93	877.57	94.92	782.65	93822.75	93	1074.61	517.71	556.90 66309.79
94	877.57	95.72	781.86	93727.04	94	1074.61	522.02	552.58 65787.76
95	877.57	96.51	781.06	93630.52	95	1074.61	526.37	548.23 65261.39
96	877.57	97.32	780.25	93533.21	96	1074.61	530.76	543.84 64730.63
97	877.57	98.13	779.44	93435.08	97	1074.61	535.18	539.42 64195.45
98	877.57	98.95	778.63	93336.13	98	1074.61	539.64	534.96 63655.80
99	877.57	99.77	777.80	93236.36	99	1074.61	544.14	530.47 63111.66
100	877.57	100.60	776.97	93135.76	100	1074.61	548.67	525.93 62562.99
101	877.57	101.44	776.13	93034.32	101	1074.61	553.25	521.36 62009.74
102	877.57	102.29	775.29	92932.03	102	1074.61	557.86	516.75 61451.89
103	877.57	103.14	774.43	92828.90	103	1074.61	562.51	512.10 60889.38
104	877.57	104.00	773.57	92724.90	104	1074.61	567.19	507.41 60322.19
105	877.57	104.86	772.71	92620.04	105	1074.61	571.92	502.68 59750.27
106	877.57	105.74	771.83	92514.30	106	1074.61	576.69	497.92 59173.58
107	877.57	106.62	770.95	92407.68	107	1074.61	581.49	493.11 58592.09
108	877.57	107.51	770.06	92300.17	108	1074.61	586.34	488.27 58005.75
109	877.57	108.40	769.17	92191.77	109	1074.61	591.22	483.38 57414.53
110	877.57	109.31	768.26	92082.46	110	1074.61	596.15	478.45 56818.38
111	877.57	110.22	767.35	91972.24	111	1074.61	601.12	473.49 56217.26
112	877.57	111.14	766.44	91861.11	112	1074.61	606.13	468.48 55611.13
113	877.57	112.06	765.51	91749.04	113	1074.61	611.18	463.43 54999.95
114	877.57	113.00	764.58	91636.05	114	1074.61	616.27	458.33 54383.68
115	877.57	113.94	763.63	91522.11	115	1074.61	621.41	453.20 53762.27
116	877.57	114.89	762.68	91407.22	116	1074.61	626.59	448.02 53135.68
117	877.57	115.84	761.73	91291.38	117	1074.61	631.81	442.80 52503.88
118	877.57	116.81	760.76	91174.57	118	1074.61	637.07	437.53 51866.80
119	877.57	117.78	759.79	91056.78	119	1074.61	642.38	432.22 51224.42
120	877.57	118.77	758.81	90938.02	120	1074.61	647.73	426.87 50576.69
121	877.57	119.75	757.82	90818.26	121	1074.61	653.13	421.47 49923.55
122	877.57	120.75	756.82	90697.51	122	1074.61	658.58	416.03 49264.98
123	877.57	121.76	755.81	90575.75	123	1074.61	664.06	410.54 48600.91
124	877.57	122.77	754.80	90452.98	124	1074.61	669.60	405.01 47931.32
125	877.57	123.80	753.77	90329.18	125	1074.61	675.18	399.43 47256.14
126	877.57	124.83	752.74	90204.35	126	1074.61	680.80	393.80 46575.34
127	877.57	125.87	751.70	90078.49	127	1074.61	686.48	388.13 45888.86
128	877.57	126.92	750.65	89951.57	128	1074.61	692.20	382.41 45196.66
129	877.57	127.98	749.60	89823.59	129	1074.61	697.97	376.64 44498.69
130	877.57	129.04	748.53	89694.55	130	1074.61	703.78	370.82 43794.91
131	877.57	130.12	747.45	89564.43	131	1074.61	709.65	364.96 43085.26
132	877.57	131.20	746.37	89433.23	132	1074.61	715.56	359.04 42369.70
133	877.57	132.29	745.28	89300.94	133	1074.61	721.52	353.08 41648.18
134	877.57	133.40	744.17	89167.54	134	1074.61	727.54	347.07 40920.64
135	877.57	134.51	743.06	89033.03	135	1074.61	733.60	341.01 40187.04
136	877.57	135.63	741.94	88897.40	136	1074.61	739.71	334.89 39447.33
137	877.57	136.76	740.81	88760.64	137	1074.61	745.88	328.73 38701.45
138	877.57	137.90	739.67	88622.74	138	1074.61	752.09	322.51 37949.36
139	877.57	139.05	738.52	88483.69	139	1074.61	758.36	316.24 37191.00
140	877.57	140.21	737.36	88343.49	140	1074.61	764.68	309.92 36426.32
141	877.57	141.38	736.20	88202.11	141	1074.61	771.05	303.55 35655.27

142	877.57	142.55	735.02	88059.56	142	1074.61	777.48	297.13	34877.79
143	877.57	143.74	733.83	87915.82	143	1074.61	783.96	290.65	34093.83
144	877.57	144.94	732.63	87770.88	144	1074.61	790.49	284.12	33303.34
145	877.57	146.15	731.42	87624.73	145	1074.61	797.08	277.53	32506.26
146	877.57	147.37	730.21	87477.36	146	1074.61	803.72	270.89	31702.54
147	877.57	148.59	728.98	87328.77	147	1074.61	810.42	264.19	30892.13
148	877.57	149.83	727.74	87178.94	148	1074.61	817.17	257.43	30074.96
149	877.57	151.08	726.49	87027.86	149	1074.61	823.98	250.62	29250.98
150	877.57	152.34	725.23	86875.52	150	1074.61	830.85	243.76	28420.13
151	877.57	153.61	723.96	86721.91	151	1074.61	837.77	236.83	27582.36
152	877.57	154.89	722.68	86567.02	152	1074.61	844.75	229.85	26737.61
153	877.57	156.18	721.39	86410.84	153	1074.61	851.79	222.81	25885.81
154	877.57	157.48	720.09	86253.36	154	1074.61	858.89	215.72	25026.92
155	877.57	158.79	718.78	86094.56	155	1074.61	866.05	208.56	24160.88
156	877.57	160.12	717.45	85934.45	156	1074.61	873.26	201.34	23287.61
157	877.57	161.45	716.12	85773.00	157	1074.61	880.54	194.06	22407.07
158	877.57	162.80	714.77	85610.20	158	1074.61	887.88	186.73	21519.19
159	877.57	164.15	713.42	85446.05	159	1074.61	895.28	179.33	20623.91
160	877.57	165.52	712.05	85280.53	160	1074.61	902.74	171.87	19721.17
161	877.57	166.90	710.67	85113.63	161	1074.61	910.26	164.34	18810.91
162	877.57	168.29	709.28	84945.33	162	1074.61	917.85	156.76	17893.06
163	877.57	169.69	707.88	84775.64	163	1074.61	925.50	149.11	16967.57
164	877.57	171.11	706.46	84604.53	164	1074.61	933.21	141.40	16034.36
165	877.57	172.53	705.04	84432.00	165	1074.61	940.99	133.62	15093.37
166	877.57	173.97	703.60	84258.03	166	1074.61	948.83	125.78	14144.55
167	877.57	175.42	702.15	84082.61	167	1074.61	956.73	117.87	13187.81
168	877.57	176.88	700.69	83905.72	168	1074.61	964.71	109.90	12223.10
169	877.57	178.36	699.21	83727.37	169	1074.61	972.75	101.86	11250.36
170	877.57	179.84	697.73	83547.52	170	1074.61	980.85	93.75	10269.51
171	877.57	181.34	696.23	83366.18	171	1074.61	989.03	85.58	9280.48
172	877.57	182.85	694.72	83183.33	172	1074.61	997.27	77.34	8283.21
173	877.57	184.38	693.19	82998.95	173	1074.61	1005.58	69.03	7277.63
174	877.57	185.91	691.66	82813.04	174	1074.61	1013.96	60.65	6263.68
175	877.57	187.46	690.11	82625.57	175	1074.61	1022.41	52.20	5241.27
176	877.57	189.03	688.55	82436.55	176	1074.61	1030.93	43.68	4210.34
177	877.57	190.60	686.97	82245.95	177	1074.61	1039.52	35.09	3170.82
178	877.57	192.19	685.38	82053.76	178	1074.61	1048.18	26.42	2122.64
179	877.57	193.79	683.78	81859.97	179	1074.61	1056.92	17.69	1065.72
180	877.57	195.41	682.17	81664.56	180	1074.61	1065.72	8.88	0.00
181	877.57	197.03	680.54	81467.53				
182	877.57	198.68	678.90	81268.85				
183	877.57	200.33	677.24	81068.52				
184	877.57	202.00	675.57	80866.52				
185	877.57	203.68	673.89	80662.84				
186	877.57	205.38	672.19	80457.46				
187	877.57	207.09	670.48	80250.36				
188	877.57	208.82	668.75	80041.55				
189	877.57	210.56	667.01	79830.99				
190	877.57	212.31	665.26	79618.67				
191	877.57	214.08	663.49	79404.59				
192	877.57	215.87	661.70	79188.72				
193	877.57	217.67	659.91	78971.06				
194	877.57	219.48	658.09	78751.58				
195	877.57	221.31	656.26	78530.27				
196	877.57	223.15	654.42	78307.12				
197	877.57	225.01	652.56	78082.11				
198	877.57	226.89	650.68	77855.22				
199	877.57	228.78	648.79	77626.44				
200	877.57	230.68	646.89	77395.76				
201	877.57	232.61	644.96	77163.15				
202	877.57	234.55	643.03	76928.60				
203	877.57	236.50	641.07	76692.10				
204	877.57	238.47	639.10	76453.63				
205	877.57	240.46	637.11	76213.18				
206	877.57	242.46	635.11	75970.71				
207	877.57	244.48	633.09	75726.23				
208	877.57	246.52	631.05	75479.71				
209	877.57	248.57	629.00	75231.14				
210	877.57	250.65	626.93	74980.49				
211	877.57	252.73	624.84	74727.76				
212	877.57	254.84	622.73	74472.92				
213	877.57	256.96	620.61	74215.95				

214

214	877.57	259.11	618.47	73956.85
215	877.57	261.26	616.31	73695.58
216	877.57	263.44	614.13	73432.14
217	877.57	265.64	611.93	73166.51
218	877.57	267.85	609.72	72898.65
219	877.57	270.08	607.49	72628.57
220	877.57	272.33	605.24	72356.24
221	877.57	274.60	602.97	72081.64
222	877.57	276.89	600.68	71804.74
223	877.57	279.20	598.37	71525.55
224	877.57	281.53	596.05	71244.02
225	877.57	283.87	593.70	70960.15
226	877.57	286.24	591.33	70673.91
227	877.57	288.62	588.95	70385.29
228	877.57	291.03	586.54	70094.26
229	877.57	293.45	584.12	69800.81
230	877.57	295.90	581.67	69504.91
231	877.57	298.36	579.21	69206.55
232	877.57	300.85	576.72	68905.70
233	877.57	303.36	574.21	68602.34
234	877.57	305.89	571.69	68296.45
235	877.57	308.43	569.14	67988.02
236	877.57	311.00	566.57	67677.01
237	877.57	313.60	563.98	67363.42
238	877.57	316.21	561.36	67047.21
239	877.57	318.84	558.73	66728.36
240	877.57	321.50	556.07	66406.86
241	877.57	324.18	553.39	66082.68
242	877.57	326.88	550.69	65755.80
243	877.57	329.61	547.96	65426.19
244	877.57	332.35	545.22	65093.84
245	877.57	335.12	542.45	64758.72
246	877.57	337.92	539.66	64420.80
247	877.57	340.73	536.84	64080.07
248	877.57	343.57	534.00	63736.50
249	877.57	346.43	531.14	63390.06
250	877.57	349.32	528.25	63040.74
251	877.57	352.23	525.34	62688.51
252	877.57	355.17	522.40	62333.34
253	877.57	358.13	519.44	61975.22
254	877.57	361.11	516.46	61614.10
255	877.57	364.12	513.45	61249.98
256	877.57	367.16	510.42	60882.83
257	877.57	370.21	507.36	60512.61
258	877.57	373.30	504.27	60139.31
259	877.57	376.41	501.16	59762.90
260	877.57	379.55	498.02	59383.36
261	877.57	382.71	494.86	59000.65
262	877.57	385.90	491.67	58614.75
263	877.57	389.12	488.46	58225.63
264	877.57	392.36	485.21	57833.27
265	877.57	395.63	481.94	57437.65
266	877.57	398.92	478.65	57038.72
267	877.57	402.25	475.32	56636.47
268	877.57	405.60	471.97	56230.87
269	877.57	408.98	468.59	55821.89
270	877.57	412.39	465.18	55409.50
271	877.57	415.83	461.75	54993.67
272	877.57	419.29	458.28	54574.38
273	877.57	422.79	454.79	54151.60
274	877.57	426.31	451.26	53725.29
275	877.57	429.86	447.71	53295.43
276	877.57	433.44	444.13	52861.99
277	877.57	437.06	440.52	52424.93
278	877.57	440.70	436.87	51984.23
279	877.57	444.37	433.20	51539.86
280	877.57	448.07	429.50	51091.79
281	877.57	451.81	425.76	50639.99
282	877.57	455.57	422.00	50184.41
283	877.57	459.37	418.20	49725.05
284	877.57	463.20	414.38	49261.85
285	877.57	467.06	410.52	48794.79

286	877.57	470.95	406.62	48323.85
287	877.57	474.87	402.70	47848.97
288	877.57	478.83	398.74	47370.14
289	877.57	482.82	394.75	46887.32
290	877.57	486.84	390.73	46400.48
291	877.57	490.90	386.67	45909.58
292	877.57	494.99	382.58	45414.59
293	877.57	499.12	378.45	44915.47
294	877.57	503.28	374.30	44412.19
295	877.57	507.47	370.10	43904.72
296	877.57	511.70	365.87	43393.02
297	877.57	515.96	361.61	42877.06
298	877.57	520.26	357.31	42356.80
299	877.57	524.60	352.97	41832.20
300	877.57	528.97	348.60	41303.23
301	877.57	533.38	344.19	40769.85
302	877.57	537.82	339.75	40232.03
303	877.57	542.30	335.27	39689.72
304	877.57	546.82	330.75	39142.90
305	877.57	551.38	326.19	38591.52
306	877.57	555.98	321.60	38035.54
307	877.57	560.61	316.96	37474.94
308	877.57	565.28	312.29	36909.66
309	877.57	569.99	307.58	36339.66
310	877.57	574.74	302.83	35764.92
311	877.57	579.53	298.04	35185.39
312	877.57	584.36	293.21	34601.03
313	877.57	589.23	288.34	34011.80
314	877.57	594.14	283.43	33417.66
315	877.57	599.09	278.48	32818.57
316	877.57	604.08	273.49	32214.49
317	877.57	609.12	268.45	31605.37
318	877.57	614.19	263.38	30991.18
319	877.57	619.31	258.26	30371.87
320	877.57	624.47	253.10	29747.39
321	877.57	629.68	247.89	29117.72
322	877.57	634.92	242.65	28482.79
323	877.57	640.21	237.36	27842.58
324	877.57	645.55	232.02	27197.03
325	877.57	650.93	226.64	26546.10
326	877.57	656.35	221.22	25889.74
327	877.57	661.82	215.75	25227.92
328	877.57	667.34	210.23	24560.58
329	877.57	672.90	204.67	23887.68
330	877.57	678.51	199.06	23209.17
331	877.57	684.16	193.41	22525.01
332	877.57	689.86	187.71	21835.15
333	877.57	695.61	181.96	21139.54
334	877.57	701.41	176.16	20438.13
335	877.57	707.25	170.32	19730.87
336	877.57	713.15	164.42	19017.73
337	877.57	719.09	158.48	18298.64
338	877.57	725.08	152.49	17573.55
339	877.57	731.13	146.45	16842.43
340	877.57	737.22	140.35	16105.21
341	877.57	743.36	134.21	15361.85
342	877.57	749.56	128.02	14612.29
343	877.57	755.80	121.77	13856.49
344	877.57	762.10	115.47	13094.39
345	877.57	768.45	109.12	12325.94
346	877.57	774.86	102.72	11551.08
347	877.57	781.31	96.26	10769.77
348	877.57	787.82	89.75	9981.95
349	877.57	794.39	83.18	9187.56
350	877.57	801.01	76.56	8386.55
351	877.57	807.68	69.89	7578.86
352	877.57	814.41	63.16	6764.45
353	877.57	821.20	56.37	5943.25
354	877.57	828.04	49.53	5115.20
355	877.57	834.94	42.63	4280.26
356	877.57	841.90	35.67	3438.36
357	877.57	848.92	28.65	2589.44

216

30-year $100,000 at 10% interest (continued)

358	877.57	855.99	21.58	1733.45
359	877.57	863.13	14.45	870.32
360	877.57	870.32	7.25	0.00

FACTORS FOR MONTHLY PRINCIPAL & INTEREST PAYMENTS
The factors are per thousand of the loan amount and are rounded.
The resulting payment may be a few cents off of the actual payment.

RATE	15 YEARS	20 YEARS	30 YEARS
5.000%	7.9079	6.5995	5.3682
5.125%	7.9732	6.6688	5.4449
5.250%	8.0388	6.7384	5.5220
5.375%	8.1047	6.8085	5.5997
5.500%	8.1708	6.8789	5.6779
5.625%	8.2373	6.9497	5.7566
5.750%	8.3041	7.0208	5.8357
5.875%	8.3712	7.0924	5.9154
6.000%	8.4386	7.1643	5.9955
6.125%	8.5062	7.2366	6.0761
6.250%	8.5742	7.3093	6.1572
6.375%	8.6425	7.3823	6.2387
6.500%	8.7111	7.4557	6.3207
6.625%	8.7799	7.5295	6.4038
6.750%	8.8491	7.6036	6.4860
6.875%	8.9185	7.6781	6.5693
7.000%	8.9883	7.7530	6.6530
7.125%	9.0583	7.8282	6.7372
7.250%	9.1286	7.9038	6.8218
7.375%	9.1992	7.9797	6.9068
7.500%	9.2701	8.0559	6.9922
7.625%	9.3413	8.1325	7.0779
7.750%	9.4128	8.2095	7.1641
7.875%	9.4845	8.2868	7.2507
8.000%	9.5565	8.3644	7.3377
8.125%	9.6288	8.4424	7.4250
8.250%	9.7014	8.5207	7.5127
8.375%	9.7743	8.5993	7.6001
8.500%	9.8474	8.6782	7.6891
8.625%	9.9208	8.7575	7.7779
8.750%	9.9945	8.8371	7.8670
8.875%	10.0684	8.9170	7.9565
9.000%	10.1427	8.9973	8.0462
9.125%	10.2172	9.0778	8.1363
9.250%	10.2919	9.1587	8.2268
9.375%	10.3669	9.2400	8.3175
9.500%	10.4423	9.3213	8.4085
9.625%	10.5178	9.4031	8.5000
9.750%	10.5936	9.4852	8.5915
9.875%	10.6700	9.5676	8.6835
10.000%	10.7461	9.6502	8.7757
10.125%	10.8227	9.7332	8.8682
10.250%	10.9000	9.8164	8.9610
10.375%	10.9766	9.9000	9.0541
10.500%	11.0540	9.9838	9.1474
10.625%	11.1316	10.0679	9.2410
10.750%	11.2095	10.1523	9.3348
10.875%	11.2876	10.2370	9.4289
11.000%	11.3660	10.3219	9.5232
11.125%	11.4446	10.4071	9.6178
11.250%	11.5235	10.4926	9.7126
11.375%	11.6026	10.5783	9.8077
11.500%	11.6819	10.6643	9.9029
11.625%	11.7615	10.7510	9.9984
11.750%	11.8413	10.8371	10.0941
11.875%	11.9214	10.9238	10.1900
12.000%	12.0017	11.0109	10.2861
12.125%	12.0822	11.0981	10.3825
12.250%	12.1630	11.1857	10.4790
12.375%	12.2399	11.2734	10.5757
12.500%	12.3252	11.3614	10.6726
12.625%	12.4067	11.4496	10.7697
12.750%	12.4484	11.5381	10.8669
12.875%	12.5703	11.6268	10.9644
13.000%	12.6524	11.7158	11.0620
13.125%	12.7348	11.8049	11.1598
13.250%	12.8174	11.8943	11.2577
13.375%	12.9002	11.9839	11.3559
13.500%	12.9832	12.0738	11.4541
13.625%	13.0664	12.1638	11.5526
13.750%	13.1499	12.2541	11.6511
13.875%	13.2335	12.3445	11.7499
14.000%	13.3174	12.4352	11.8487
14.250%	13.4858	12.6172	12.0469
14.500%	13.6550	12.8000	12.2456
14.750%	13.8250	12.9836	12.4448
15.000%	14.9959	13.1679	12.6444

BORROWER'S NOTIFICATION
and INTEREST RATE
DISCLOSURE STATEMENT

U.S. Department of Housing
and Urban Development
Office of Housing
Federal Housing Commissioner

Condition of Property

The property you are buying is not HUD/FHA approved and HUD/FHA does not warrant the condition or the value of the property. An appraisal will be performed to estimate the value of the property, but this appraisal does not guarantee that the house is free of defects. You should inspect the property yourself very carefully or hire a professional home inspection service to inspect the property for you. If you have a professional home inspection service perform an inspection of the property, you may include some of the cost of the inspection in your mortgage.

Interest Rate and Discount Points

*HUD does not regulate the interest rate or the discount points that may be paid by you or the seller or other third party. You should shop around to be sure you are satisfied with the loan terms offered and with the service reputation of the lender you have chosen.

*The interest rate, any discount points and the length of time the lender will honor the loan terms are all negotiated between you and the lender.

*The seller can pay the discount points, or a portion thereof, if you and the seller agree to such an arrangement.

*Lenders may agree to guarantee or "lock-in" the loan terms for a definite period of time(i.e. 30, 60, or 90 days) or may permit your loan to be

determined by future market conditions, also known as "floating". Lenders may require a fee to lock in the interest rate or the terms of the loan. Your agreement with the lender will determine the degree, if any, that the interest rate and discount points may rise before closing.

*After your loan is approved at a given interest rate and discount points, any increase in the discount points which you are going to pay or an increase of more than one percent in the interest rate requires reunderwriting of the loan.

*If the lender determines you are eligible for the mortgage, your agreement with the seller may require you to complete the transaction or lose your deposit on the property.

Don't Commit Loan Fraud

It is important for you to understand that you are required to provide complete and accurate information when applying for a mortgage loan.

*Do not overstate your income or your assets.

*Disclose all loans and debts(including money that may have been borrowed to make the down-payment).

*Do not provide false letters-of-credit, cash-on-hand statements, gift letters or sweat equity letters.

*Do not accept funds to be used for your down-payment from any other party(seller, real estate salesperson, builder, etc.) involved in the transaction.

*Do not falsely certify that a property will be used for your primary residence when you are actually going to use it as a rental property.

*Do not act as a "stawbuyer"(somebody who purchases a property for another person and then transfers title of the property to that person), nor should you give that person personal or credit information for them to use in any such scheme.

*Do not apply for a loan by assuming the indentity of another person.

Penalties for Loan Fraud: Federal laws provide severe penalties for fraud, misrepresentation, or conspiracy to influence wrongly the issuance of mortgage insurance by HUD. You can be subject to a possible prison term and fine of up to $10,000 for providing false information. Additionally, you could be prohibited from obtaining a HUD-insured loan for an indefinate period.

Report Loan Fraud: If you are aware of any fraud in HUD programs or if an individual tries to persuade you to make false statements on a loan application, you should report the matter by calling your nearest HUD office or the HUD Regional Inspector General, or call the HUD Hotline on 1(800)347-3735.

Lead Based Paint: If the property you are buying was built before 1978, there is a possibility that it may contain lead based paint. Be sure you receive a copy of the consumer pamphlet "Watch Out for Lead Paint Poisioning" and read it to learn about lead paint poisioning.

If you believe you have been subject to discrimination because of your race, color, religion, sex, handicap, familial status, or national origin, you should call the HUD Fair Housing and Equal Opportunity Complaint Hotline: 1(800)669-9777.

This statement must be delivered to you at the time of initial loan application. Return one copy to your lender as proof of notification and keep one copy for your records.

You, the borrower(s), must be certain that you understand the transaction. Sign here only after you have read this entire document. Seek professional advice if you are uncertain.

GLOSSARY

adjustable rate mortgage (ARM) A loan that allows the interest rate, and usually the payment, to adjust periodically during the life of the loan. Most ARMs start at a lower-than-market interest rate and then adjust based on a prevailing index plus margin.

amortization The continuous regular payment of a set amount on a loan, which will reduce and pay it off in a given period of time.

annual percentage rate (A.P.R.) The interest rate on credit as expressed by a combination of the loan interest rate and certain loan costs. The Truth-in-Lending statement of Regulation Z of the Federal Reserve requires the A.P.R. to be quoted.

balloon payment When a debt is paid off in less than the set amortization period by paying the remaining principal balance, a balloon payment of the loan has been made. A loan with a 30 year amortization payment with the remaining principal to be paid off in five years is a balloon loan.

basis points One basis point equals 0.01%, one hundred basis points equal 1.0%.

bond A security for payment of an obligation. In mortgage lending, bonds are backed by mortgage loans that are pooled together and the resultant bond can be sold in the secondary market.

broker In mortgage lending, a broker is someone who acts as an intermediary between the borrower and the actual lender. A broker is typically an independent agent representing several lending sources.

buy-down A loan that is *bought down* below its original interest rate and/or payment. A permanent buy-down will reduce the interest rate and payment for the life of the loan, while a temporary buy-down will reduce the payments on the loan only in the beginning years.

certificate of reasonable value (C.R.V.) The name given to a Veteran's Administration (VA) appraisal.

C.H.A.R.M. booklet   Consumer Handbook on Adjustable Rate Mortgages, which must be given to any borrower who applies for an ARM. This is a federally required disclosure.

chattel   Personal property that is not a part of the real estate and can be moved.

closing costs   The sum of all costs in relation to the purchase and/or loan closing, excluding the down payment.

cloud   A defect on the title of the property that would prevent the purchaser from obtaining a clear title.

collateral   The security for a loan. Something of value against which the loan is secured. A mortgage is secured by real estate.

commitment   A promise to do something. In mortgage lending, the lender will commit to make the loan, or commit to make the loan at a specific rate and points. Some lenders will require a commitment fee to guarantee the commitment.

common area   Part of a property owned by all of the owners. In a condominium or planned unit development there are common areas owned by the property owners jointly.

compensating factor   A positive factor that can help to influence the loan approval. Long-term good credit, a large amount of assets, or increasing income are some examples.

condominium   A property where the unit is owned individually and the land and all other improvements are owned jointly with all the owners, or the condominium association.

conforming   In mortgage lending, a loan that conforms to the guidelines set forth by Fannie Mae or Freddie Mac is said to be conforming.

construction loan   A short-term, temporary loan, made by a lender to pay the cost of constructing a building, which is paid off upon completion by cash or a permanent mortgage. The construction loan is secured by the real estate.

conventional loan   A loan that is not insured, guaranteed, or funded by the government.

covenants and restrictions   The rules and regulations governing the maintenance and use of an area. Condominiums and Planned Unit (P.U.D.) Developments will have covenants and restrictions.

creditor   A lender, or someone who lends money to a borrower (debtor).

D.E. underwriter   A direct endorsement underwriter who is approved by the FHA to underwrite (approve/reject) FHA-insured loans. The underwriter will normally be employed by the lender making the loan.

deed   The document that shows ownership in real property.

deed of trust   A mortgage that secures the note by the real property, and appoints a third party trustee to act in the lender's behalf, without having to go to court to proceed with foreclosure when the borrower defaults on the loan.

default   A condition of the mortgage that occurs any time the borrower is not in compliance with the terms of the loan. A late payment is a default. A default that is not corrected will result in the loan being called for payment in full.

depreciation   When the value of property goes down. Some depreciation is taken as a tax write-off and is considered to be a paper loss because the actual value has not diminished.

discount points   Points, expressed as a percent of the loan, that are used to buy the interest rate down. Sometimes discount points are used as fee income by the lender. If 10% is the rate with no discount points, or the rate is at par, a rate of 9.75% would have points added to buy it down from 10%. The borrower gets a discounted rate by paying additional points, or interest, up-front.

disintermediation   The movement of funds from one place to another to seek a higher yield. If money is moving out of bank accounts and into higher-paying instruments, such as government bonds, this movement can create a shortage of funds, or higher interest rates.

due-on-sale clause   A clause in a mortgage that requires the loan to be paid off if the property is sold or conveyed to another person.

earnest money   The deposit on a contract. It is part of the consideration on a binding contract. It can be in the form of cash or a note.

encroachment   When some part of a property is on an adjoining property. If a fence or roof overhang from one property is on the other property, it is encroaching on the latter. A lender will not make a loan on the property until either the encroachment is corrected or title insurance insures against it.

equity   The value of property beyond any lien against it. That portion that is owned without liability.

escrow   Money held by the lender to pay future claims. Taxes and insurance are normally added into the monthly payment and held in escrow until they are due to be paid.

fair-market value   The value a purchaser will pay for a property; on an appraisal it is value as determined by comparing the property to similar properties that have sold in the community.

Federal Home Loan Mortgage Corporation (FHLMC or Freddie Mac)   A quasi-governmental agency that acts as a secondary market investor to buy and sell mortgage loans. It sets many of the underwriting guidelines on conventional loans, along with Fannie Mae (FNMA).

Federal Housing Administration (FHA)   A section of the U.S. Department of Housing and Urban Development that insures loans by the full faith and credit of the U. S. government. It sets the guidelines for the approval and insurance of these FHA loans.

Federal National Mortgage Association (FNMA)   A secondary market investor that was originally a government agency and is now a private corporation whose stock is traded on the N.Y. Stock Exchange. It buys and sells mortgages that meet its guidelines. Also known as Fannie Mae.

fee simple   The highest form of ownership that someone can hold in a property. This is the most common form of ownership.

first mortgage   A first lien on real estate, or a loan that has priority over other mortgages on the same property.

fixed rate mortgage (FRM)   A mortgage with an interest rate that does not change or adjust.

fixture   A part of the property that is attached and conveys with it. The opposite of chattel.

foreclosure   Legal action by the lender upon default to have the property sold to pay the securing mortgage.

front end zero   In mortgage insurance, the up-front or first year's premium is allowed to be financed into the loan so that it does not have to be paid at closing.

funding fee   The VA funding fee is a closing cost that may be paid by anyone, or financed into the mortgage as long as the total does not exceed the maximum 100% loan currently allowed by Ginnie Mae (GNMA). The fee is 1.25% on LTVs over 95% to 100% loans, 0.75% on loans over 90% LTV up to 95%, 0.50% on loans with at least 10% down, and 0.50% on assumptions.

Government National Mortgage Association (GNMA or Ginnie Mae)   A government agency that participates in the secondary market and is involved in buying, selling, and guaranteeing government loans such as FHA and VA.

grace period   The time between the due date and the past-due date of a loan during which there is no late charge.

graduated payment mortgage (GPM)   A loan that starts out with a substantially lower payment and then increases the payments each year until a level payment is reached that will pay off the loan over the remaining amortization period. There is usually negative amortization.

gross income   Total income before withholding is subtracted. Gross monthly income (GMI) is used to qualify borrowers.

growing equity mortgage (GEM)   A loan in which the normal payment is increased each year so that the amortization is accelerated, paying off the mortgage in a shorter period of time.

hazard insurance   That portion of the homeowner's insurance that protects the property against fire and other forms of destruction.

HUD (Department of Housing and Urban Development)   The government agency that governs FHA and other housing programs.

index   A figure, normally compiled from other indicators, that is used to establish rates on ARMs.

judgment   An unsecured lien filed against a borrower for non-payment of a debt.

jumbo loans   Nonconforming loans that are higher than the loan amounts acceptable to FNMA and FHLMC.

late charge   The penalty imposed when a late payment is made or received after the grace period of a loan.

lien   A debt that is secured by something of value. A mortgage is a lien on real estate.

loan-to-value (LTV)   The amount of the total value of the property that is secured by the mortgage. An $80,000 mortgage on a $100,000 property has 80% LTV. Total loan-to-value (TLTV) is the sum of all liens on a property.

lock-in   The ability to have an interest rate and/or points locked in, or guaranteed, for a specific period of time.

long-term debt (LTD)   Any debt that exceeds the maximum pay-off period as set by the guidelines for individual loans.

margin   The interest added onto the index of an ARM to determine the adjustment of the interest rate.

mortgage   A legal instrument that makes real estate security for a loan.

mortgagee   The holder of a mortgage loan.

mortgagor   The borrower of a mortgage loan.

mortgage banker   A lender who deals regularly with the secondary market. A mortgage banker originates, closes, services, and sells the loans.

mortgage broker   A lender who deals with other lenders as an intermediary, or broker, of the other lender's loans.

mortgage insurance   Insurance on a mortgage that protects the lender against losses due to default and/or foreclosure. It is required on all conventional loans with less than 20% down payment. It is not life insurance. It is sometimes called Private Mortgage Insurance, or P.M.I.

mortgage insurance premium (MIP)   Mortgage insurance on FHA loans that is backed by the full faith and credit of the U.S. government.

negative amortization   This situation occurs when the borrowers are charged more interest than they are paying. The unpaid interest is added back into the principal amount of the loan.

nonconforming   Loans that do not conform to standard conventional loan guidelines set by Fannie Mae or Freddie Mac. Jumbo loans are nonconforming.

note   The legal instrument that shows the borrower is obligated to pay the loan.

origination fee   The fee the lender gets for originating and closing the loan, usually 1% of the loan amount.

PITI The basic house payment. P = principal, I = interest, T = taxes, I = hazard insurance. Additional parts of the payment might be the following: MI = mortgage insurance, HOA = homeowner's association fees or road maintenance fees.

planned unit development (P.U.D.) A comprehensive development that encompasses several different sections and amenities.

points Points are a percentage of the loan amount. Discount points are charged to make up the difference between a lower loan amount and the actual required rate, which is higher. Some lenders will charge extra points as fee income. The origination fee is often included as part of the total points.

principal The amount of the loan.

private mortgage insurance The same as mortgage insurance.

Realtor A registered name for any real estate agent who belongs to the National Association of Realtors.

second mortgage Secondary financing behind or after the primary or first mortgage.

secondary market Investors who buy and sell large numbers of mortgage loans from the primary lenders. Fannie Mae, or the Federal National Mortgage Association (FNMA); and Freddie Mac, or the Federal Home Loan Mortgage Corporation (FHLMC) are two of the largest.

servicing The job of collecting the monthly house payments from a loan and making sure that they are properly credited. The loan servicer must make sure that the loans stay current, that the taxes and insurance are paid, and that the borrower is notified of the loan status and any changes.

subordination A second mortgage is subordinate to a first mortgage.

survey Most lenders will require a physical survey of the property. This is done by a registered surveyor who will measure the lot lines and show the footprint of the house and all outbuildings, roads, rights of way, easements, and water located on the property.

title To hold title to property is to show ownership. A deed is evidence of holding title to property.

title insurance Insurance that insures against any defects in the title that would give less than clear title to the property.

Normal exceptions are mortgages, easements, and rights of way. The borrower normally pays for this as a normal closing cost. However, the seller or other third party can pay the insurance premium.

total loan-to-value (TLTV)   The total of all mortgages on the property expressed as a percentage of the value. Such as, a $100,000 house with an $80,000 first mortgage and a $10,000 second mortgage = 90% TLTV.

underwriter   A person who underwrites a mortgage loan is the one who either approves or rejects it based on certain guidelines pertaining to that loan. Some lenders approve loans by loan committees.

Veteran's Administration (VA)   This federal agency oversees the VA loan guarantee program.

value   the worth of a property, being the lesser of the sales price or appraised value.

INDEX